HF
5549.5
E45
W525
1987

# ■ CONTENTS ■

ROCK

O9-BTI-662

134317

# INTRODUCTION

International career can mean different things to different people. To me it has meant travel, variety, a life-long learning experience and a lot more money than I could have made in many stateside jobs. My own international career didn't just happen, of course. It was—and is—based on a very definite career philosophy, one that I've lived by, counseled others in, and seen practiced by a high percentage of winners in the international career marketplace.

Put quite simply, those international careers that are really worth having don't come ready-made. Instead, they're built and crafted piece by piece. Sure, there are lots of international *jobs* that you can get hired into or even seek out, and some of these will put you on some sort of upward path. If you stick with them long enough, you'll slowly ratchet your way up from one set of tasks to another, until whoever is pumping the ratchet handle wants to take a break or decides that you've gone far enough. This kind of existence, one step away from running on a treadmill, doesn't qualify as a career, at least not to me.

OK, so what is involved in an international career, as opposed to a series of international jobs? Plenty. First, there are all the good things that distinguish any career from a job: steadily increasing responsibility and authority, an ever-widening understanding of the field you're in, a constantly expanding circle of possibilities. To this,

# INTERNATIONAL CAREERS

WHERE TO FIND THEM

AN INSIDER'S GUIDE

HOW TO BUILD THEM

WILLIAMSON PUBLISHING
CHARLOTTE, VERMONT 05445

DAVID WIN

Copyright © 1987 by David Win

All rights reserved.
No portion of this book may be reproduced —
mechanically, electronically or by any other
means, including photocopying — without
written permission of the publisher.

Library of Congress Cataloging-in-Publication Data

Win, David.
    International careers, an insider's guide.

    Bibliography: p.
    Includes index.
    1. Americans — Employment — Foreign countries —
Handbooks, manuals, etc.    2. Vocational guidance —
Handbooks, manuals, etc.    I. Title.
HF5549.5.E45W525   1987        650.1'4        86-32547
ISBN 0-913589-28-4

Cover and interior design: Trezzo-Braren Studio
Typography: Villanti & Sons, Printers, Inc.
Printing: Capital City Press

Williamson Publishing Co.
Charlotte, Vermont 05445

Manufactured in the United States of America

10 9 8 7 6 5

Notice: The information contained in this book is true,
complete and accurate to the best of our knowledge.
All recommendations and suggestions are made
without any guarantees on the part of the author or
Williamson Publishing. The author and publisher
disclaim all liability incurred in connection with the
use of this information.

ROCKHURST COLLEGE LIBRARY

0 0006 0092340 3

Date Due

A Gift of
ROCKHURST COLLEGE
Library
Guild

an international career adds expertise in new countries or regions, the possibility of using the same experience in very different sectors to orient your career in entirely new directions, and an almost un-believable potential to leap from one type of career position to an-other. To compare with a game of chess, a job — even a good job — is like the moves you make with a pawn: one step at a time, and al-ways in the same general direction. Even the best of domestic careers gives you no more mobility than the king: any direction, but still just one step at a time. And are you ever vulnerable! But move into the international career arena, and presto! you're a bishop, a rook, or a knight, or all three put together, moving as far as you like in any direction, sweeping beyond other players' pieces, leaping over obstacles to strike opportunities that are several squares away.

This tremendous freedom and range of action doesn't just hap-pen. It comes from having an aggressive career philosophy, creating and constantly updating your own personal Big Picture, and main-taining a judicious mix of planning, adaptability, and willingness to change. In this sense, an international career is like sailing a boat through a series of islands, reefs and shoals: you know the direction you want to go, but to get there you have to take tacks that make sense in terms of the wind, currents and rocks.

Of course, it doesn't have to be a nonstop trip, nor do you need to have a precise final destination in mind. One of the most fasci-nating couples I've met has built careers around what you might metaphorically call professional island hopping. Every five years, they embark on a totally new type of international career and life-style, always in a different country, with first one, then the other person setting the new compass heading. Over the last fifteen years, they've accumulated an incredible variety of international career components, from director of a major zoo to running a top-notch international prep school. Try doing this on location in one country!

Although this sounds interesting and exotic, for most of us, a more sensible strategy is to keep moving toward a definite career goal, not zig-zag around the world just for fun. Yet, the mentality, tactics and techniques are the same. To take advantage of new possi-bilities and keep your career moving at the best possible pace, you have to know how to discover or create international opportunities and make them part of your career. Flexibility and an almost intui-tive sense of possibilities become important attributes.

All the while, you've got to keep your goals in sight and main-tain your orientation, even in shifting seas. You know where you are, and with a little thought and analysis, you can decide generally where you want to go, but don't expect your progress to be smooth or even. Sometimes, as you move toward your goal, you'll make a great surge forward as you catch the crest of a wave of opportunity. At other times, you may drift to the side, or even feel as though you've slipped back into a trough. The thing to remember, especially when you think you've gone down a blind channel or lost ground, is that every move has the potential to put you ahead of the game at some future date. Even as late as the mid-1970s, coming to Japan to work and study the language didn't look like a very productive career move to a lot of people. To those of us who did it, it has turned out to be one of the most valuable projects we could have undertaken. Because the international career environment is constantly generating new opportunities and improving old ones, everything you do has long-term potential value. You just have to be innovative in finding new applications for your acquired experiences.

# 1

# THE INTERNATIONAL CAREER ENVIRONMENT

ust how big is the international career environment? Let's take a quick look at the overall picture from the U.S. point of view.

■ **International trade is big, big business.** U.S. two-way trade (imports plus exports) now totals over 550 *billion* U.S. dollars, and there are billions more in international manufacturing, investment, and other transactions. Every one of those dollars contributes to the creation of new international career opportunities in manufacturing, marketing, distribution, franchising, licensing, services, and a hundred other fields.

■ **There's almost unbelievable potential for growth.** The United States exports only about 6 percent of gross national product (GNP) compared to over 25 percent for West Germany and over 35 percent for South Korea. As the United States pushes to increase exports, our dollar volume is going to reach phenomenal amounts, and as more American and foreign companies set up operations on each other's turf, the international business network is going to grow proportionately. *To you, this means increasing career opportunity, with more and more room at the top.*

■ **Our international trade is spread across the entire U.S. economy.** Twenty-two percent of our manufactured goods, 25 percent of our agricultural output, and over 41 *billion* dollars worth of services are exported each year. Imports, which are even larger in terms of dollars, also are spread throughout the economy. *Opportunities are everywhere, if you know where and how to look.*

■ **International opportunities extend far beyond business and trade.** A quick glance at the headlines any morning is a reminder that other international issues including politics, diplomacy, economics, technology transfer, agriculture assistance, media, and many, many others are just as important as international business and trade. This means that international career opportunities in almost any field are waiting to be discovered or created by ambitious individuals.

# THE RIGHT STUFF

**A**t first glance you might think that building an international career in these heady surroundings would be the same as playing the domestic career game. True, and skimming over the waves in a jet-powered hydrofoil is about the same as creaking along in a leaky rowboat, in that you start someplace and end up someplace else. It doesn't take long to figure out that there are big differences of kind, as well as degree. Furthermore, you'll find that some of the basic moves (for example, the use of personal contacts) must be executed in very different ways, and with very different style and timing, even though they may appear to be the same.

In fact, tactics that may get almost instant results in the United States can backfire in an international setting, as Americans from job-seekers to U.S. senators find, for example, when they put on a show of aggressive, go-get'em behavior in one of the many cultures that frowns on this sort of direct, open approach. And back in the United States, trying to work international trade conventions and international organizations for opportunities in typical domestic fashion can put you behind the eight ball instead of in an international corporate office. In short, the similiarities are there, but the minute you lose sight of the differences, you're putting yourself and your career-building efforts at risk.

To get started in the international marketplace, and to move up, you have to rely on the quality of your own efforts and have something to offer. This is a point worth repeating over and over to yourself as you build your international career.

The development of an international career is a lot like a South Seas Island treasure hunt. You may have a map of the archipelago where the treasure is located (in fact, that's what I've tried to provide with this book), but there's no "X" marking the spot—or even the island—where you'll find it. Instead, there are clues and signs that you have to analyze and put together to figure out where the Xs—the big, key breaks in your international career—are for you. It's essential to keep in mind that the Xs are going to be a little different on everybody's map, so you can only follow someone else's lead to a certain extent. In the main, your success depends on your originality and on your efforts. Your international career is out there, but it's up to you to go out and get it—no one's going to dig it up and hand it over to you.

$F$or a concrete example of what I mean, take a quick look at the case of two real-life college professors of about the same age, both, by coincidence, trained in economics. One of them, a second-generation Japanese-American, is totally fluent in Japanese, and has the additional advantage of living near a major West Coast center of U.S.-Japan trade

and business. The other, who speaks no foreign language, has the additional handicap of living in the eastern part of the United States, relatively far from a business center of any description. Looking at circumstances alone, you'd think that the bilingual Japanese-American would be a shoo-in to create a high-powered international career, yes? No.

For the bilingual prof, the name of the game has been "get a job." After all, with his qualifications, someone should want to give him one, or so he thinks. But why should they? He has the tools (language, understanding of economics, knowledge of the region, in-country contacts) but no track record outside of the ivory tower. Worse, his approach when stripped of high-flown rhetoric is simply "Hire me." This tells potential international employers that he lacks the qualities (including the initiative to create his own opportunities) that would help them meet their own goals. As far as I know, this prof is still waiting for someone to make him an offer.

The other prof took a different tack. He *used* his background to study international trade and business trends and create his own personal goals or Big Picture. Then, he targeted the country that his research indicated was the most promising. During two successive summer vacation periods, instead of pounding the pavement looking for a job handout, he went to his target country, attended meetings of the local American Chamber of Commerce, met with local businessmen and U.S. Embassy officials, and *refined his knowledge*. On the third vacation period, to no one's great surprise, he announced his affiliation with a new international consulting firm launched by local interests. His first clients, *impressed with the groundwork he'd done* to amass knowledge of both general trends and specific trade and business issues, were signed up before the ink on his contract had dried. This is one example of what I mean by relying on your own efforts and having something to offer. If you're willing to create your own opportunities, you can build almost any international career you want.

The tale of two profs illustrates another important characteristic of the international career market: *there are no "magic buttons" to push*, unless you happen to have a cousin who owns a trading company or a rich uncle who contributed heavily to some winning senator's campaign. Everyone wants to believe that the relatively small size of the U.S. international business community means that it's easier to break in, but unfortunately, it "ain't necessarily so." In fact, if you approach the problem with traditional domestic job search methods, the opposite may be true.

## SUBSTANCE OVER STYLE

In the first place, the international business and commercial community can be pretty clubby. Whether in the United States or overseas, the people in the international community tend to know each other, and to have a strong sense of uniqueness. They have specialized knowledge, they're up against specialized challenges, and they feel that in many ways they're a breed apart. You might say they're elitists, but only in a very positive sense. Savvy international managers and VP's — the people that are out there making things happen in the international environment — have had their baptism under fire. They have a thousand war stories to tell, each of which represents a valuable and hard-earned lesson. They want to work with equals, with others who know the score. The usual attempts to impress, such as the old cocktail party buzz-word routine, doesn't turn them on.

Unless you're taking what I call the "silver spoon" route (in which case you probably don't need this book), the people that you'll be dealing with are mostly international managers and VP's. Many of them haven't gone to Harvard or Stanford or gotten MBA's. (The CEO's of their companies might have, but normally the CEO's are only marginally involved in the international side of their companies.) In many cases, the international managers have come up the hard way; when they were building their international careers, the whole field was underdeveloped and undervalued. They're hard-eyed realists who are far more impressed by substance than by style.

There's no point in going to world trade association meetings and trying to hustle your way into a job. Nothing turns the members off more quickly. And if you're dealing with experienced international types, the aggressive, come-on-strong, "young Turk" routine that plays so well with many U.S. corporate recruiters leaves 'em cold partly because they know that it's precisely this kind of typically American behavior that causes many international deals to fall through by alienating the foreign buyer, seller, or partner. In addition, experienced international managers are usually "from Missouri." You've got to show them that you've got what it takes. There's no other way.

In domestic business circles, it often seems to be enough for the job candidate (or the newly employed MBA) to drop a few trendy cliches ("matrix management", "intrapreneurship" or what have you) to create the desired impression of knowledgeable competence. Not in the international business environment. These guys have been around. They don't want to hear your clever theories about supply-side macroeconomic trends and the J-curve effect on imports due to the revaluation of the yen, the yuan, or the won. They know where the beef is — or where it should be. What's it take to get a product into country X? How can I repatriate profits from country Y? What kind of reverse investment can we attract from country Z? Can you read this letter written in a foreign language, right here, right now? Can you help me write a reply? Who do I contact for more information? It doesn't take long to see who knows his/her way around the international business world and who doesn't. Put yourself in the former category, and you're a sure winner.

Many of these people are on very tight schedules, much more so than the average domestic manager or executive. They may spend as much as 60 percent of their time out of whatever country they're based in. A typical year may consist of six or eight weeks at home, followed by four to six weeks on an overseas trip involving stops in a half-dozen countries. The time at home is always hectic; the first two weeks are devoted to debriefing, reports and followup on the last overseas marketing or troubleshooting trip, and trying to get to the bottom of a bulging inbox; the last two weeks are spent getting ready for the next trip. There's precious little time for idle socializing or meeting with job seekers (no matter how clever the pretext). Therefore, these people tend to react very coolly to the "let me have five minutes to talk about international business" gambit.

So who can you talk to? Put your faith in multiplier organizations (the business support groups these hard-working people belong to), and be nice to the staff people, who can give you more tips than an insider trader. International types are different; they lead different lives, and they want to see if you possess the special qualities needed to help their business. The best way to do this is to be actively involved in the international agencies, organizations and multipliers where international managers and VP's — the people who will do your career the most good — spend some of their scarce time at home.

## GETTING SHIPSHAPE

**Y**ou want to build an international career, and you're anxious to get under way but there's no sense in shoving off in a boat with no sails, no engine, and no oars. To be sure your career voyage leads to international success instead of a struggle to stay afloat, you've got to be prepared.

First, know the organizations, agencies and multipliers that deal with international matters. I'm still amazed at the number of educated Americans with international aspirations — including high-powered stateside attorneys and businesspeople — who don't know the first thing about the way international business life is organized. Some of them spend thousands of dollars to go overseas to drum up business opportunities without even knowing what the Commerce Department does, or how to use the resources of an embassy. Predictably, the result is some very expensive wheel-spinning. Just being knowledgeable about key organizations puts you way ahead of 95 percent of the population.

Second, show what you can do by getting involved. You can't "use" international multipliers and organizations to get ahead, because (as I've pointed out) they're way ahead of you in terms of spotting any such game. So what do you do? You put yourself at their service. Then, believe me, the offers will come. Your assistance may range from taking tickets at the door during the monthly trade association dinner meeting to starting a new committee or doing research on an international topic and presenting the results at a committee meeting or full membership meeting. *Remember that your purpose is not to be impressive, but to be valuable.* Keep this very important distinction crystal clear at all times. In the international arena, where the emphasis is on substance rather than on style, the kind of flashy dog-and-pony show that a lot of would-be employees put on is more likely to be a put-off. Your approach has to be different: to develop and communicate useful information.

The international business environment is characterized by growth, change and flow. Since all three of these related characteristics create new career opportunities each and every day, you should start looking for them and thinking of how they can advance your international career.

Growth comes from a variety of factors: economic development, expansion of existing markets, the emergence of new industries, the reduction of trade barriers, changes in internal and external policy. To put this growth to work for you, you have to do some growing yourself, by acquiring new skills and expertise that translate into value and opportunities.

Change always accompanies growth, but also occurs without it. Shifting trade balances, new trading partners and trading patterns, the modification of national and international priorities, all mean changes that can help you get the international career you want. Of course, as with growth, you have to keep pace with the environment and the international career market. You've got to be adaptable enough to modify your outlook, your tactics, even your goals, in order to succeed.

Finally, there's flow. More than ever before, the international environment is characterized by flows of technology, capital, goods, services (including labor and management), organizational and administrative techniques, and a multitude of other things. Each of these flows creates currents of opportunity for you, provided you're willing to move across industrial lines and international boundaries to create your career.

The international career environment is big, it's growing, and it's in a constant state of flux. As a result, compared to the domestic scene, the international career market is a lot more flexible, more pragmatic, and consequently less hung up on matching people with formal job description requirements which — although they look good on paper, and satisfy the need to catalog, classify and pigeonhole that personnel departments seem to have — don't really indicate how well you're qualified for a given job.

## THE ENTREPRENEURIAL SPIRIT

In this respect, much of *the process of starting and building an international career is closer to entrepreneurship than to ordinary job-hunting*. I'm reminded of the true story of a man who, because he lacked formal training in computers, was turned down for a job at a small computer company. Within a few years, he'd made enough money in an international business he'd founded to buy the computer company! (I've always wondered what happened to the personnel director afterward.) Clearly, the ordinary criteria commonly applied by domestic businesses don't always spot real competence, and may often screen it out.

In contrast, the whole selection process in the international career market tends to be much less bureaucratic and more down to earth. In most of the offers I've gotten (including setting up an international operation for a top U.S. transportation conglomerate, playing a key role in organizing a joint venture to manufacture steel in South America, VP in charge of marketing for an electronics company, and in-country manager for an international construction company), the people making the offers realized full well that I knew relatively little about their specific businesses. But, as one of them put it, "I can see that you know what to do overseas, and I can teach you the rest." Or, as another one told me, "I know I can teach you all you need to know about my business. On the other hand, there's no guarantee that I can teach any of my people how to get along overseas." This practical attitude is one of the big advantages of the international career market.

Of course, in this imperfect world not every international company you come in contact with will have this objective approach, but the percentages are high enough to vastly increase your chances of success. If you have high-quality international components in your skills inventory, you can use them to double the odds in your favor, and you can always revert to conventional domestic tactics if that's what a given company or individual seems to want.

The international business world seems tailor-made for active career builders because of the opportunities it offers. If you're involved in international multiplier organizations (and you should be), you'll be talking to the members about their businesses. This activity helps to spot demand and career market niches. If you're active on a committee, you have a chance to participate in formulating or executing policies that help the members, giving them a chance to see your abilities. Throughout, you'll be able to get to know people, find out what's going on in the international business community, and become a potential factor in everyone's business planning. The result can be the offer of a lifetime, direct from a key international manager or executive in a member company. In the domestic career market, this kind of situation is almost impossible to create, because there simply isn't any way to get comparable experience and exposure through a single umbrella organization.

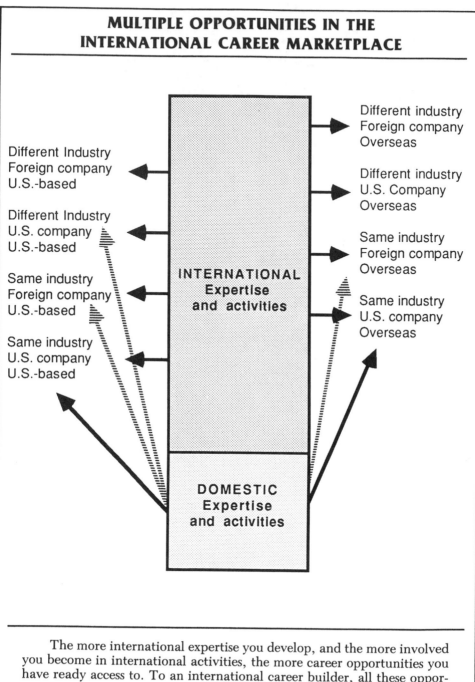

# MULTIPLE OPPORTUNITIES IN THE INTERNATIONAL CAREER MARKETPLACE

Different Industry
Foreign company
U.S.-based

Different Industry
U.S. company
U.S.-based

Same industry
Foreign company
U.S.-based

Same industry
U.S. company
U.S.-based

**INTERNATIONAL
Expertise
and activities**

**DOMESTIC
Expertise
and activities**

Different industry
Foreign company
Overseas

Different industry
U.S. Company
Overseas

Same industry
Foreign company
Overseas

Same industry
U.S. company
Overseas

The more international expertise you develop, and the more involved you become in international activities, the more career opportunities you have ready access to. To an international career builder, all these opportunities are close at hand. A domestic orientation, however, means stretching farther and farther to try to reach the same opportunities.

## JUMPING OFF THE CAREER LADDER

**O**nce you get started on your international career, the differences become even more apparent. For domestic careers, the commonly used expression "career ladder" is a good description. Not only do you have to climb up one rung at a time, you usually spend a good deal of time waiting for those above you, who often are stepping on your fingers—or on your head—and who may take you down with them if they fall. Passing (as you know, if you've ever tried it on a ladder) is both difficult and risky. Finally, your progress is hindered by the people behind and below you, who are grabbing at your ankles to pull themselves up at your expense. Fun.

To make matters worse, the career ladders in domestic careers aren't propped securely against a nice, solid wall. Far from it. Instead, they're leaning precariously against the slippery sides of the well-known corporate pyramid. At each new level, there's less room, so somebody (you?) has to fall off every time somebody else moves up. From time to time, a whole ladder full of career-builders gets toppled over by circumstances or by a competing group. More fun.

**W**ith international careers, however, there's a separate, flexible career structure standing well apart from the domestic pyramid. This structure, which has its own independent network of contacts, is distinguished by the fact that it offers many interchangeable routes to the top. And *because international business requires such a broad range of skills, there's a lot more room for generalists*, the very people best equipped to exploit the full range of international career possibilities.

## MANY ROUTES TO THE TOP

Furthermore, as you move up you can get exposure and opportunities that normally are available only to top executives in the domestic career scene. Why? For one thing, the existence of more routes to the top makes a lot of potential competitors into potential allies, partners, or employers. Secondly, in almost any international position your worth is more evident because your knowledge and expertise are in short supply. As a result, you can make quantum career leaps that would qualify you for the Liar's Club championship in domestic circles.

By building his international career around expertise in a specific geographic area, for example, one fellow I know made a diagonal tack that transformed him from an unusually competent but low-level manager in a dime-a-dozen job with no significant organizational responsibilities directly into the president and CEO of a $15 million medical equipment trading corporation overseas. Sure, he has loads of talent, but if he'd poured that talent into a domestic career he could have spent the rest of his life as a faceless middle manager.

Finally, you're one of a smaller and more select group, whose members will be more widely aware and appreciative of your abilities because you can develop more extensive direct contact with them.

At one point in my own career, I joined an international trade association and put in a lot of work on tasks that ranged from deciding on conference seating arrangements to planning overseas missions and giving a report on a proposed Foreign Trade Zone. I never once hit anyone up for a job or tried to make an impression but in the space of about eighteen months, I was approached by five different international businesspeople with career offers that included managing a liaison office in the People's Republic of China, marketing machine tools in Latin America and Asia, marketing oceanographic equipment worldwide, and positions in two different trading companies. This is what direct contact through multipliers (those business people's support groups) can do when you offer to help, and essentially show, rather then tell.

In contrast, several years later, with a much stronger international business and marketing background (including more languages and more extensive experience in both Asia and Latin America), I was totally ignored on at least two occasions when I had to rely on a typical domestic-type paper presentation of my background and credentials, rather than living proof of my ability, to go after existing openings with international outfits. I looked good, maybe too good, on paper, and with no chance to show that I actually could deliver more of the same, I may have been dismissed as just another overinflated self-promoter.

I hope the message is getting through: *international career building opens up a whole new dimension for you, but it is a different game, played on a different field, with different rules*, and you've got to make some changes to be successful at it. In many ways, it's more wide open, which means you have the freedom and the obligation to be more aware, more innovative, and more resourceful than in the domestic career market. In this sense, it's like football after the invention of the forward pass: suddenly, the pay-off is a much higher score, and the thrill of being part of (maybe even starring in) plays that don't even exist in the domestic career world. And for the foreseeable future, at least through the end of this century, there's a lot of rapid expansion going on, so there's plenty of room for you on any number of teams.

## A WOMAN'S PLACE

The unique possibilities inherent in the international career environment are especially important for women career builders. Although the United States has made strides in opening up the business world to women, the unfortunate fact is that women are seriously underrepresented at higher levels in most industrial and service sectors. The high profile you can acquire and maintain on an international career path can make the difference between the big time and the ho-hum of 9 to 5 camou-flaged by an empty title. For the same reason, women re-entering the job market after a prolonged absence can break in at much higher levels and reach far greater heights by putting themselves on an international course.

Since the international marketplace tends to judge people on substance rather than style (or membership in a bio-social group), a woman needn't waste time and energy trying to penetrate the musty bastions of male supremacy or struggling to find an opening in an old-boy network.

A woman in an international career is dealing with four main sets of attitude environments, each corresponding to a career market. First, there's the traditional domestic career market, which in many areas has yet to accord women the professional respect they deserve. Women

### CAREER MARKETS AND WOMEN

are underrepresented in middle and upper management positions.

Unfortunately, this is still where most jobs are, and many women find it necessary to start here in order to pick up, or brush up, general background and basic career components and skills.

The second environment in size, what I call the stateside-international career market, is in many ways the most favorable one for women to make the biggest career advances. In the first place, many of the skills required to do well in this area can be carried over from the domestic market with little or no modification. Management, law, bookkeeping and accounting, billing, shipping and receiving, purchasing, lending, property management, conference organizing, brokering, educational programs, and contract and grant supervision are all fields in which I've seen women move from strictly domestic to stateside-international responsibilities with a minimum of adaptation. And of course, there are countless others.

The atmosphere in the stateside-international market is more impartial than that of the domestic market. A far greater percentage of the time, you'll be judged on your performance and abilities, not your gender. In addition, since many men tend to shy away from group leadership, a high percentage of women assume top positions in the multipliers (international trade associations, international committees and so on) that serve the stateside-international business community. This, of course, means further exposure and contacts.

The third career and attitude environment is the overseas U.S. business community. Many of today's overseas managers and executives were hired into the domestic side of their companies years ago when virtually any woman in business was a secretary. These male executives were sent overseas as international operations expanded, so American career women are still a rarity in this overseas environment. However, those who are in it — and their numbers are increasing because of a new emphasis on hiring policies that are both rational and international — report that it's very favorable indeed. In fact, the scarcity of women in overseas business circles earns a greater respect for the few who have made it up to now, since their very presence indicates exceptional competence, persistence and resourcefulness. In addition, even businessmen who cling to stereotypes of women tend to ignore those same stereotypes and deal with reality overseas, because the situations they find themselves in demand it.

In overseas multiplier organizations, the hesitancy of many men to take charge of a peer group gives women excellent opportunities for leadership. Paradoxically, this is partly because these organizations are still predominantly composed of males, who are much more likely to view other males as competitors. This allows a well-prepared woman to make suggestions and observations, and to take charge of situations, where the same moves by a man might be met with resistance from the group.

F inally, there's the host-country's business, professional and official community. The most important thing for U.S. women dealing with this group is to avoid generalizations, reject stereotypes (including those that abound in otherwise sensible articles and books about women in

## ETHNOCENTRIC ATTITUDES

international business), and make all evaluations and assessments on a carefully thought out, case-by-case basis. Because it trips a lot of women up, this aspect of the international environment deserves some discussion.

According to conventional American wisdom, for example, women in the male-dominated societies of the Orient are viewed as inferior and relegated to second-class status. This sweeping generality, while fairly accurate as far as it goes, is lacking one key word that changes the whole picture for American women careerists. For it's not *all* women, but *Oriental* women who are most often so regarded. Does this change the picture? You bet it does.

Many Caucasian business women in male-dominated Asian societies find that they get absolutely first-class, professional treatment from host-country males in all business situations. In fact, because foreign women don't fit neatly into the host-country male's mental hierarchy, he may respond more favorably to them than to other males, whether local or foreign. Of course, there are variations between Asian countries and between business sectors within any given Asian country, which means that all foreign women doing business in the Orient need to be alert to the varied receptions they may get according to the country they deal with, and the type of business they do there. These differences aren't limited to Caucasian women, either. A Japanese businessman, for example, will have a different attitude toward a Chinese-American woman than toward a Nisei woman.

*All international careerists need to be aware of ethnocentric thinking, but women need to be even more careful.* Variations in the operating environment, such as those I've just discussed, can create a special set of problems for women who fail to open their minds to international reality as it is, instead of how they expect it to be. Let's see how narrow stereotyping can put a career at risk.

In the United States, many political and social issues, including the status of women, have a very different significance than they do elsewhere in the world. This is all too often disregarded, as it was when a major U.S. women's association decided to send a Women's Business Mission

## CROSSING CULTURAL LINES

(emphatically upper-case!) to Asia. In the context of American thinking, this probably seemed like a great idea, but in Asia, it created nothing but confusion. Most Asians don't make many connections between business, sociology, and politics. They expect a business mission (or any other business activity) to be oriented along product or service lines and specific business interests, not according to gender, and if they're going to meet with widget makers, their interest is the widgets, not the makers.

The Women's Mission organizers could have solved this perception gap by simply billing the mission as promoting specific products or services. In fact, this very Asian solution, which would have allowed the women to have a Women's Mission and the Asians to see it as a product-oriented mission, is exactly what one Asian multiplier proposed. The organizers, however, would have none of this. It was conceived as a Women's Mission in the United States, and it was going to be promoted as a Women's Mission in Asia.

Needless to say, this approach almost ended the mission before it got under way. When the advance woman, an international novice on a make-or-break career assignment, came to the Far East to make the rounds of host-country multipliers and other contacts, she was met with puzzlement at every stop. To the Asians, the whole concept made about as much sense as a mission for left-handed redheads, or members of the McTavish clan, or graduates of Slippery Rock University. They simply couldn't understand how the central theme related to doing business or what the business of the mission was. Some of them retreated behind the nervous smiles that are a sign of embarrassment and confusion all over the Orient.

Now the advance woman's ethnocentric assumptions made the situation even worse. She was sure that they were laughing at her, and making fun of the notion that women could be successful in business. Luckily, it was possible to convince her that the real problem was the imposition of American socio-political attitudes on a foreign business context. Henceforth, she discussed the mission in business terms, got completely different responses, and ended up with a highly satisfactory program. Since failure would have had negative repercussions not only for her company but also for every mission member, she saved herself from a major career setback.

With a little international sensitivity and savvy, this kind of situation can not only be avoided, but turned to a woman's advantage. The international career environment often allows properly prepared women to pull off moves that would be difficult or impossible for men. Since most cultures have been dominated by males, they tend to reflect male values, and males tend to be far more tightly locked into them. This may be one of the reasons that women are more adaptable and suffer less culture shock in a foreign environment. Rather than blindly accept or identify with a given way of doing things, they can judge each culture — including its business practices — on its merits, and in the process discover and create new career opportunities. This broader human perspective, which enables women to spot human needs and motivations that transcend culture, allows them to excel in international advertising, sales and marketing, and many other people-oriented careers.

F inally, women's holistic thought and perception enable them to spot important trends long before any rigorous, systematic analysis can. Call it intuition, if you will; by any name, it's a tremendous asset. Of course, to take advantage of it you need the courage to act on what you see, and the self-confidence to navigate uncharted waters ahead of the fleet.

## WOMEN EXCELLING

One young woman careerist recently used her human orientation and holistic thinking to turn the professional handicap of being a foreigner in Japan — one of the world's most difficult and demanding career markets — into an advantage. As a foreigner, she was constantly frustrated when she needed certain consumer products. Because of Japan's different marketing practices, and especially because of the language barrier, it often took foreigners days or weeks to track down a common item. As in so many international situations, the problem wasn't one of supply, but of knowledge.

By applying empathy, intuition, and initiative she turned her problem into an international job with excellent career potential. Knowing that Japanese are very customer-oriented, she reasoned that local retailers would want to solve the problem if possible. She also figured that not only Americans, but other foreigners must be having the same trouble she was, and that a creative, practical solution would be right in line with Japan's current "internationalization" campaign. So she went to one of Japan's largest retail chains with an idea.

Today, she heads up a new, special foreign consumer assistance section, staffed with five assistants of different nationalities, in one of Tokyo's largest department stores. Essentially her own boss, she'll be able to expand the concept to other branches later on and use the experience and retailing contacts she's making to create new opportunities and career directions.

The international career environment gave her two important advantages that let her show her stuff in spite of lacking formal credentials in consumer retailing. By domestic career standards (either U.S. or Japanese), she was operating under a double handicap — being a non-bilingual foreigner, and a female. But in the special situation she created, she had credibility through identification with the international customer population whose needs she intended to meet. She identified a problem and proposed a career-enhancing solution that a local national wouldn't be able to internalize, and therefore couldn't deal with as effectively. Secondly, in the local social and business context, the concept she created and sold might not have been accepted if proposed by a man, because it would have been outside the normal range of male business roles. As a foreigner and as a woman, she was able to get her proposal considered and accepted.

# SETTING SAIL TO SUCCESS

or most Americans, virtually every aspect of the international career environment represents uncharted waters. You may have heard that there are great opportunities out there, but you have no idea how to find them and turn them into an international career.

When I embarked on my own international career, I was in that same boat: I had very little idea what would be involved, or how to proceed. Over time, however, thanks to my own efforts, some good luck, and the nature of the international career market itself, my career developed in what I've come to recognize as a fairly typical success pattern. I've seen this pattern repeatedly in many international careers whether with people starting from scratch or those about to become CEO's themselves. Put in the simplest terms, international career success involves two main ingredients: a Big Picture of career goals and their relation to the international career environment, and constant changes in course — tacking — to reach those goals.

## YOUR BIG PICTURE

**F**irst, let's define our terms. Since your international career is yours, and yours alone, your Big Picture is anything you want it to be. *One of the biggest mistakes is to follow the crowd into a particular sector because it's trendy or hot.* In the first place, it's too easy to lose sight of your own goals in the stampede. More importantly, by the time the crowd discovers it, the best opportunities are taken, and there are too many people fighting over leftovers. Most people — especially if they rely on a traditional, domestic strategy — don't catch onto major business, trade and industrial shifts until after they've peaked. *Wall Street knows that when Harvard MBA's start flocking to any industry, smart money goes elsewhere.* The same is true of jobs and careers.

A good, personalized Big Picture incorporates everything from macroeconomic trends to your definition of "quality of life". First and foremost, it starts with you, and goes on to define the international career world in terms of where and how you can best fit in to get the most professional and personal value out of each experience. It takes into account your individual capabilities (fluency or flair for foreign languages, difficulty with math), your dreams and aspirations, and your personal motivations, inclinations, likes and dislikes. It gives great weight to your personal value system, and to your mental and emotional adaptability. It should definitely include the goals that you think will bring you the biggest measure of happiness and overall personal satisfaction.

The more clearly defined your Big Picture is, the less likely you are to compromise your goals or settle for second best somewhere along the line, as happens when you let yourself stay in a position that seems acceptable, but somehow doesn't seem to be quite right for you. At the same time, of course, you should be ready to change your Big Picture along the way; in fact, you'd be foolish not to change it as often as necessary to keep pace with the times and with your own personal and professional evolution. The more detail you've been able to give it, however, the easier it is to keep the changes on the level of fine tuning. Otherwise, you may find yourself backtracking, rather than tacking.

If a high-powered VP position was in your original Big Picture plan, then keep that level of responsibility, financial security, prestige and perks in place whenever you alter your course. If you've also always wanted to have a big house and servants, however, you should be aware that they're far more obtainable in some countries—even at relatively low managerial levels—than in others. If being an apartment-bound VP in Paris or Tokyo would make you envy the mansion of a middle manager in Macao, *keep an eye on both company life and quality of life*, and be sure you're managing both of them in the way that's best for you. If you lose sight of either one of them, you may end up frustrated or burned-out, or be forced to buck the tide to get back on course.

Once you've sketched out a Big Picture you feel comfortable with, put it up someplace where it will catch your eye, both figuratively and literally. (Actually writing it down on paper as an outline, a narrative, a list of possibilities, or a chart will take you a long way toward realizing it.) You don't have to meditate on it, but you should refer to it and modify it, if necessary, at some point before every career decision, to be sure that what you're doing now is connected to what you want to do later.

*One of the biggest mistakes you can make is to believe that the connection between now and later has to be direct.* In building your international career, you'll find that the shortest distance between two points is *not* always a straight line, and to get to that VP spot (or the Macao mansion) you may opt for a position that offers less material compensation—perhaps even less than you're making now—because it will give you the international expertise you need to break into your target sector. That's one reason I keep talking about tacking.

## A ZIG FOR EVERY ZAG

The Big Picture, as we've seen, combines the career goals that you've set for yourself with the tools and situations that you'll use to attain them. Tacking, as in sailing, is the method that will get you from one career position to another, until you reach your final destination. Just as in sailing, much of the course that you follow will be determined by the changing currents and shifting winds of circumstance, and the reefs and islands you encounter along the way.

As any good sailor can tell you, the race isn't won by skill alone, and definitely not by simply following the book. You have to size up the conditions, and adapt to them, without getting hung up on what's *traditionally* supposed to get results. You pick your own course, and you sail it the way you think is best. Use sonar when you can, and go by feel when you have to, but don't let inertia or indecision keep you stuck on a fixed course. My own experience provides a good illustration of how this works.

At some point in high school or shortly thereafter, I developed an interest in the Orient. By my second year in college, this interest had evolved into a plan of action; I was going to the Orient to learn more about it. So I located a Japanese language school in Tokyo, made arrangements for transfer of credits with the foreign studies department where I was a language major, and headed into the unknown.

When I returned to the United States a year later, I'd learned a lot of Japanese, and a lot more about the realities of a career in that geographic area. I still wanted to be involved with Asia, but the opportunities just weren't there — at least, not yet. So I continued in my previous Latin American area specialty, but kept up my study of Japanese language and business trends on the side. Several years later, I got another shot at Japan. By then, the world economy had changed. Japan had become a leader, and there were incredible opportunities for any American with business experience, international expertise and Japanese language ability.

Half the secret of breaking into the Orient at the level I wanted was Japanese, which I'd maintained on the side. Lesson one: never throw anything overboard or let it get too rusty; you might need it on some future tack. The other half, of course, was my international background. Even though I'd developed most of it in Latin America, it had enough depth and general value to qualify me for an excellent management position. Lesson two: international seamanship can help you in many different waters.

You probably won't have to tack from Latin America to the Orient to reach your goals, but I think you get the idea. With your Big Picture, intelligent planning, and the willingness to change course as necessary, you can reach virtually any point you aim at.

As you can see from the chart of my international career, when I started out, there was no way I could have foreseen the exact route that I would follow to reach my goal. In addition, I didn't have the benefit of the knowledge that I'm sharing with you in this book; if I had, I could have saved myself quite a bit of floundering at the start and invested my personal resources (including time, which is the most valuable of all) more precisely to get the greatest possible return. Nevertheless, I *gained perspective* with every move, and I never lost sight of my goals and dreams. Because of this, nothing I did was wasted, and in fact, the broad background I acquired has given me access to opportunities that a specialist might have missed.

Working out your own course is just as important as tacking. I'll guide you and give you information and tools of the trade that will save you time, energy and possible reverses, but no one can plot your course — nor should you let them. The experience of plotting it yourself is too valuable to entrust to anyone. It gives you the

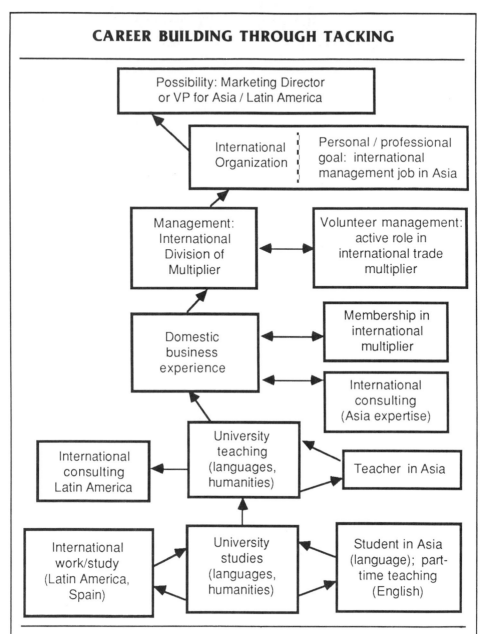

# CAREER BUILDING THROUGH TACKING

Possibility: Marketing Director
or VP for Asia / Latin America

International Organization | Personal / professional goal: international management job in Asia

Management: International Division of Multiplier

Volunteer management: active role in international trade multiplier

Domestic business experience

Membership in international multiplier

International consulting (Asia expertise)

University teaching (languages, humanities)

International consulting Latin America

Teacher in Asia

International work/study (Latin America, Spain)

University studies (languages, humanities)

Student in Asia (language); part-time teaching (English)

Latin America was prominent early in career because (1) opportunities there were good at that time (better than Asia); (2) it was impossible to study languages and related subjects in my area at that time. Later I shifted my course as the Asian area became more promising. In the future, I can combine my unique dual expertise to take a position involving both areas, Asia and Latin America. (These positions are becoming more common because of increasing Pacific basin trade and business relations connecting Asia with Latin America.)

perspective and substance of which international careers are made, and it adds immeasurably to the quality of your life. I'll be glad to teach you how to sail, but I can't tell you where to go, or exactly how to get there. *Following someone else's course is about as interesting — and as valuable — as painting by the numbers.* What you want is to give at least as much attention and energy to the process as you do to the result. You'll find that getting there really is half the fun.

O f course, no one can predict anything in life, and often tacking can yield serendipitous results far better than those originally intended. When early Portuguese navigators took an extreme tack (several thousand miles out into the Atlantic) because they'd learned that it would get them to

## REMAIN OPEN TO OPPORTUNITY

southern Africa faster than simply sailing down the coast, they stumbled upon Brazil, later the jewel of the Portugese Empire, and a far richer prize than the African territories they'd been aiming at. Like them — and like many others who've used tacking to create international careers — you may discover unexpected bonanzas on your way to your goal.

A former president of the Chamber of Commerce once told me that he'd essentially "fallen into" every major career event in his life, in the sense that none of the outstanding jobs that made up his career had been part of his original planning. He'd had to spot them on the run, and be ready to tack quickly to get himself headed in the new directions that they represented.

My own career development, even during phases when I was doing my best to consider all aspects of my Big Picture and follow a carefully plotted course, has borne this out. When I entered the Foreign Commercial Service, for example, I knew that this excellent career move would be greatly enhanced if I went to China or Japan, the two hottest areas in the booming Pacific basin. With my knowledge of both languages (which would get even better with daily use) and some in-country experience, I could write my own ticket.

So what happened? They assigned me to Korea, which at the time was virtually under martial law (a nightly curfew was just being lifted), and where I knew nothing of the language, the customs, or business practices. This accident (which I found out later was based on a mistaken entry of "fluent Korean" in my personnel file) was the best thing that could have happened for I hit the country just before a major economic and social transition. *Taking advantage of events as they occurred*, I was able to play a key role in a number of business developments, and in so doing acquire expertise and contacts that would never have been accessible to me in the more developed and competitive career environment of Japan or China.

This is why I won't try to show you any magic buttons to push. You can't get your career chart ready-made, as though it were a map from a vending machine. And your best career ideas — the ones that get results — won't come from someone else's crystal ball, nor from someone else's computer data base. You have to create your Big Picture, keep abreast of changing currents (no time like the present to start reading business publications on a daily basis), and be ready to change course when conditions require.

## WHY TACK?

**E**arlier, I discussed the concept of the career ladder (with all its drawbacks) and the fact that in most domestic career situations, the ladder is leaning unsteadily on a corporate pyramid. I've also pointed out that the international career market, because of its more varied structure, offers more and better routes to success. You've got to keep in mind that these routes not only aren't straight lines, they don't follow any set pattern. To take full advantage of the new opportunities this environment offers, you've got to change your thinking, your tactics, and maybe even your equipment.

In northern Brazil and on the Nile, local fishermen have used the same sailing technology for centuries. Their boats are rigged to sail in one direction only — with the wind. On the Nile, they sail up river driven by a reliable prevailing wind, and return with the current. If the wind fails, they simply sit at home; it's a waste, but at least there's nothing lost but time. In Brazil, there's a lot more faith and needless risk involved. In the morning, the fishing fleet lets the prevailing offshore breeze carry them out to sea; each afternoon, thanks to a daily reversal of wind direction, they let it drive them home. If the wind doesn't change? No one seems to want to think about it. Going with the wind like this seems easy, but there is actually a potential for disaster. Being able to tack could save you if the wind fails.

*If you use one-way, straight-course domestic career tactics and technology in the international market, you're not only limiting yourself, you're putting your career at risk.* Even though your methods seem to be working, you may be living in a fool's paradise.

Imagine, if you will, that you're a bright young business major, perhaps even an MBA. You've just landed a job with a major U.S. corporation, one with significant international operations. What's your next move?

If you have a typical "career ladder" mentality, you'll apply the general strategy that's evolved over the years in response to the nature of the domestic career environment. You'll work hard to learn all you can about your colleagues and higher-ups—who's who, who's in, who's out, who's hot and who's not. You'll apply the conventional wisdom about mentors and in-house networking. You'll spend your lunch hour building your image, happy hour probing for scuttlebutt, and weekends working your way into the good graces of the person who best fits your plans for self-promotion. At work, you'll be careful not to let your light shine too brightly, for fear it will draw attention away from your superiors or dim the image they're trying to project. For, as you'll soon learn, *career-ladder success means making your boss look good.*

If you're one of the chosen few who gets onto a so-called "fast track," you'll conclude that your strategy has worked. And indeed it might have—for a while. Remember, though, that the farther you go up the corporate pyramid, the less room there is, and the nastier the competition becomes. In addition, if the person whose coattails you're riding decides to change coats, you've come to the end of the line. If your mentor goes down or out, you may well go along too, and if your mentor's competitors, opponents or enemies can't get to him/her directly, they may try to get some satisfaction by knocking you off, or at least making your professional life miserable.

And if you don't make the fast track? Your career will gradually lose momentum. You'll find yourself making longer stops at each career station, and you'll end up shunted onto a siding where you and your career will gather dust and rust while you watch the fast-trackers roar by on their way to their own rendezvous with oblivion.

Now, if the typical domestic career ladder, leaning precariously as it is against a slippery pyramid, is such a cutthroat, risky place—and believe me, it is—why on earth do so many people try to climb it? Ignorance, for one thing: they don't realize that there's a better, more enjoyable, far more humane way to reach their goals. In the second place, international careers are still a relatively new phenomenon in the U.S. marketplace. The traditional (i.e., domestic) career-ladder system evolved at a time when there wasn't much in the way of a viable alternative, before the possibilities opened up by the international career environment had come into being.

At this point, you may be saying to yourself, "Hold it, hot shot! This whole argument assumes that no lateral tacking moves exist in the domestic job market—but they do!"

Well, yes, Virginia, there are lateral domestic moves, and of course you can make them. But unless the company you've targeted is in one heck of a growth phase (and not about to be swallowed up in a merger that will put three-fourths of its managers and executives out on the street), the "pyramid factor" still rules. In order to welcome you aboard (as they like to say), they have to pitch someone else into the drink — and the next time around, it just might be you. Besides, as I've pointed out, in the domestic career market there simply isn't any way to generate the number and quality of lateral tacking opportunities that you can in the international sector.

O f course, as I'll stress again and again, merely being in an international *job* doesn't mean that you're automatically going to create the best possible international *career*. If you merely transfer the domestic career-ladder process to the international arena, you're back in what you might

## A BASIC CHANGE IN APPROACH

call the "Light Brigade" deployment: competition to the left of you, competition to the right of you, competition in front of you. Your colleagues are trying to trip you up or elbow you aside (smiling all the while, of course), your subordinates are scheming on how to pass you, and higher-ups — fearful for their own security — are ready to squelch any displays of real ability.

For some reason, the absurdity of this situation, and the way to get out of it, seem to elude an awful lot of people. One fellow I used to work with, for example, still hasn't figured it out, even though he's put himself in an international job that could lead to an outstanding international career, if only he'd start following a truly international career strategy. Oh, his career plans have always seemed logical enough. First, he got an MBA, with a strong international specialty that included a foreign language. Then, through campus recruiting by major international companies, he landed a great-sounding position overseas. The world was his oyster! But unfortunately, instead of containing pearls, it was full of sand. Although he'd mastered an Asian language, had lived in Asia, and would have been happiest and most productive there, he was assigned to a series of stints in garden spots like Bombay, Borneo, and Bangladesh. Since he was so far out of sight, and out of mind at the home office, there was little he could do in terms of traditional networking, using old-boy connections, or picking up a corporate mentor, although he certainly tried.

After several years, during which he got blown further and further off course, our hero finally figured out that a lateral move was in order. Unfortunately, he'd spent his time trying to move up the traditional career ladder by playing traditional corporate politics, so clients and contacts in other companies were largely unaware of whatever abilities he might have had. In fact, he'd gotten in such a habit of trying to impress, that he came across as being a bit frantic. However, he did succeed in latching onto a like-minded individual in another major international outfit.

After jumping through the requisite hoops to prove his desire and loyalty to his new-found mentor, our man was hired. True, he's finally gotten to the geographical spot he wants, but in every other sense he's merely recreated the same narrow career ladder that blocked his progress in the past. His continued success (such as it is) depends totally on the agenda of his mentor who in turn relies on his own ties to a superior to maintain his position on the ladder.

What's the alternative to this shabby charade? Simple: Avoid the narrow ladder altogether. Concentrate on serving clients, customers and the international business community at large, through activity in multiplier groups. Of course, you should serve your own organization first, as they're the ones who are paying you, but don't fall into the trap of playing the traditional corporate pyramid game at the expense of honest, outward-looking productivity, initiative, and awareness of your personal goals. By keeping yourself free of this game, you'll have the time and mental energy to scan the horizon for islands, plumb the depths for channels, and make changes in course when necessary or desirable.

Whether stateside or overseas, one of the beautiful things about the international business community is that it offers so many more chances to chart your own course, have a rich and productive life, and stay clear of the narrow confines of career ladders and so-called fast tracks. Since most international managers and executives have to rely on their own initiative and ability rather than self-promotion or an old-boy network when facing the problems and challenges of international business, they look at substance, not style. (This is one reason that international career environments tend to be remarkably free of the buzzwords and jargon that proliferate in the domestic sector.) In addition, they have a greater need for group support to deal with foreign competitors, governments and legal systems that often are unsympathetic, if not actively hostile, to outsiders. As a result, both through multipliers and through your daily business activity, you have the chance to develop contacts across a far broader spectrum of business, commercial and industrial sectors than would be possible in a domestic career.

**A**fter observing hundreds of U.S. and foreign business people, diplomats, politicians, and others in international situations, it's become clear to me that success in the international career marketplace calls for some fairly definite characteristics, including the ability to observe and adapt, and a strong drive to internalize the realities of the career environment rather than to merely learn them or learn about them. *Simply doing something doesn't imply expertise; after all, even parrots can learn to talk.* The important thing is not to know what to say or do, or even when to say or do it; this is merely part of the traditional career ladder style. To find real success, to create the maximum number of high-quality opportunities for yourself, you've got to see how things fit together, to understand *why* things are done and, even more importantly, find out why they aren't. This is especially important in the international environment where natives are sensitive to foreigners' blunders, but also receptive to those who understand their cultures.

International successes, like heroes, are made, not born. There are several principles you can use to develop the qualities and perspective that you need to put yourself in the international success category. They aren't always easy, because you're likely to meet a lot of resistance from others (who may see your efforts as a threat to their own agenda) and from your own inertia and ingrained thought patterns (which have to be shaken up to meet new challenges). If you want the rewards, you've got to rattle your own anchor chain, knock the rust off, and get under way.

## MAKE TOTAL COMMITMENTS

**W**hen you need total results, you have to be willing to put yourself in intensive or total immersion situations. You can't undertake a voyage to success with one foot on the dock. If you're only interested in a series of jobs, you can delay commitment forever by following a linear development toward a fairly restricted goal. If your intent is merely to climb the career ladder, you'll have plenty of time on each rung to pick up the limited additional skills or seniority you need to inch your way up to the next one. For real success in the international marketplace, however, you'll need broader and more intangible expertise, a repertoire that can only be accumulated through intensive and/or extensive exposure and effort.

In my own experience, this has been confirmed time and time again. To learn Japanese, I went to Japan. At the time, there was no Japanese language offered anywhere nearby, and actually precious litte anywhere in the United States.

The commitment to total immersion has produced results that I couldn't have gotten otherwise. In addition to the language and its psychological and social roots, I made almost involuntary discoveries about Japanese thought processes, attitudes, and values, which have been invaluable in consulting. Finally, my knowledge of the language, which I started learning at a time when absolutely nobody had the slightest interest in the country as a source of business, got me an excellent job in Japan in the 70s and was a major factor in at least three major career breaks since then, including my present position. To get all these results, I had to make a major commitment, go against the well-meant advice and opinions of virtually everyone I knew ("Why on earth do you want to go *there*, of all places?"), and dedicate a year of my life to the project.

Just plunging into something isn't enough to acquire expertise, of course, and *the success of any total immersion experience depends on the scope you give it.* What you need to do is go beyond the immediate activity (language study, an overseas technical training program, a trade mission) to get an understanding of the surrounding context. This approach pays off at all levels.

For example, each time that I've been involved in language study overseas, my desire to understand the people and the culture of a country has been at least as important as my intention to learn the language. For this reason, I've been told by host-country nationals that my use of their language, although not as elegant as that spoken by many foreigners with better training or longer residence, sounds more natural than most. More importantly, because I've tried to understand the psychological source of words and usage, rather than simply learning them, I'm also told in every country I've worked in that my whole approach to business in the foreign environment is more effective. *Speaking well can be done with mere style. Knowing what's behind the words, which requires substance, is the real measure of success.*

This may sound all too obvious, so let's take a look at what value implies. To have maximum value in the international career marketplace, you need to have a set of skills that's not only in demand, but also in relatively short supply. Winemakers are in demand in Europe, but there's an

## UNDERSTAND YOUR INTERNATIONAL VALUE

ample supply. MBA's are in short supply in China, but because of the politico-economic system there's not much demand. But a winemaker in China might just have a chance to help develop a new export industry, something the Chinese are always looking for. (And the MBA in Europe? Who knows?) The point is that value is relative, which means that an MBA or other advanced degree isn't necessarily the ticket you need. Your Big Picture should reflect the relative value of your skills and credentials in different international contexts.

Skills that seem very similar may have very different values. In my own case, proficiency in Spanish was useful, but not terribly career-enhancing after a certain point, because there was plenty in supply. When I used Spanish as a springboard into fluent Portuguese, however, bingo! Less demand, for sure, but virtually no supply, so even though my formal credentials in Spanish (which included both a B.A. and an M.A.) far outweighed those in Portuguese, it was the latter that caused my stock to shoot up. The result was a couple of years in Rio de Janeiro, Brazil, on a U.S. Agency for International Development (U.S.A.I.D.) project which led to a faculty position at the University of Minnesota, which later created a consulting opportunity. You get the idea. Japanese, as I noted earlier, has also been good to me, even though my formal credentials are virtually nonexistent. More proof of the pragmatic, results-oriented character of the international career environment.

*Value changes not only with place, but also with time.* Since Japanese has been so valuable to me and many others, there are now some 25,000 Americans studying the language. The probable result? Massive oversupply, even though demand is increasing. If you've decided to use language as your main entrée into an international career, you might want to pick something other than Japanese.

**I** stress the tactical importance of the word *offer* throughout this book because it's essential to your career success. *Basically, think in terms of what you have to offer to others rather than what they can offer you. This isn't altruism, but common sense.* After all, what's a potential

## WORK FOR THE COMMON GOOD

employer, client or partner going to consider — all the good things the business can do for you, or the things you may be able to do for the business? If you're thinking the same way, you'll put yourself far ahead of the fleet, and you'll gain a perspective that will let you spot and develop far more opportunities. When looking at any company, any organization, any job offer, you immediately transform yourself into a potential asset simply by asking yourself, "How can I help these people get where they're going?" In the process, you'll start moving along a lot faster yourself.

**W**ithout calculated risks, truly successful careers are virtually impossible, and great careers are absolutely out of reach. You can never totally eliminate risk, and if you try to keep it at a minimum in all situations, you might as well resign yourself to the bottom rungs of the career

## TAKE CALCULATED RISKS

ladder or to a bench in some public park. To live, and to increase your value to yourself and others, you have to take calculated risks. Remember, you have your Big Picture, you know where you're headed, and you're tacking to take advantage of conditions. Under these circumstances, a calculated risk may turn out to be far safer than simply hanging on to the tiller and running smack into a reef that's blocking your passage.

When I took the U.S. Agency for International Development (U.S.A.I.D.) job in Brazil, I took a calculated risk along with it. I had to withdraw from a full federal scholarship at Stanford, where I was studying for a Ph.D. There was no guarantee that I'd get the scholarship back or get myself back in the difficult grind to complete the degree. Most of my friends and instructors urged me to play it safe and stay where I was. But I wasn't just rushing off blindly after a target of opportunity. The whole purpose of the federal scholarship program was to train Latin American experts, and one condition of participation was to undertake work in the field after receiving a doctorate. Would the government refuse to reinstate me if I spent a couple of years on a project that matched the goals of the scholarship program? Wasn't it in their interest to have good students complete the program — thus increasing their value to the government — rather than wash them out for taking a working sabbatical? No one could answer these questions for me, but I answered them for myself and went to Brazil. As I saw it, the opportunity outweighed the risk, and I was right. This type of reasoned risk-taking is an important factor in building a career that gives you the life you want.

## BE WHERE IT'S HAPPENING

The trade winds of opportunity are stronger in some places than in others, and you can do wonders for your career by putting yourself in the right place at the right time. The trick is to find the spot where you can get exposed to the most opportunities at once. You might find that there's more opportunity in a multiplier, or in a specific industry or company. A particular geographic region might be the best place to fill your sails. The point is to position yourself to get the most exposure to the greatest number of opportunities; the better you do this, the easier for you to build a career that gets you where you want to go. The international career marketplace isn't perfect, and at times it can be very clubby, but once you're perceived as a sincere contributor to the common good, rather than an opportunist or carpetbagger, you'll gain access to a network of interconnected channels, each one leading to different career opportunities.

Be sure you're properly equipped, of course. You may use education to put yourself within the range of overlapping opportunities, as it can if you remember to make education a means, not an end. The idea is to be an international manager (for example) who happens to know several languages (each of which gives you value in a different country), or who has a background in economics (which gives you value in many countries) — not a linguist or economist who's decided to have a go at business.

Instead of using education to prepare you for a selected spot, you may want to let your present abilities and expertise determine where opportunity is for you. You can get a fix on the best position by taking a good look at what you do well, what you like to do, and what you have to offer. You'll quickly spot these areas in the international career market where your background and abilities can do others the most good and thus have the greatest value and marketability. If you find that you've been sailing up the wrong channel, you'll have to be extra creative, and firm with yourself, to get headed in the right direction.

**I**nternational career winners have to be flexible, adaptable, and not afraid of risks. But calculated risk-taking doesn't mean getting yourself up a creek without a paddle. Sure, every once in a while you'll have to plunge into something before you lose the opportunity, but far more often you'll have enough time to look before you leap. To quote an old Asian proverb, "Measure twice, cut once." When contemplating involvement with an outfit you've never heard of before, it's well worth a small investment of patience to avoid potential losses of time, energy, money and future career opportunities. Do your homework, and check references very, very carefully.

## BE SELECTIVE

**Y**ou're not getting a job, you're building a career in one of the most vigorous, challenging, and rewarding environments in the history of the world. You can't make things happen unless you're willing to be creative. Everything out there, including potential employers, is a resource. You should use these resources to build your career like you'd build a business.

## USE AGGRESSIVE ENTREPRENEURSHIP

Successful entrepreneurs are confident that they can take on any task related to their business, regardless of whether or not they have formal training or credentials. Adopt this attitude toward your career. In the international career market, you have to free yourself from roles you've been assigned by other people. *As far as your career goes, your job is what you do, not what you call it, and you're the boss. Your career is your business.*

**O**ne secret of successful entrepreneurship is getting multiple value out of everything, as when a company publicizes the name of their primary product (such as beer or soft drinks) by putting it on a secondary product (hat, T-shirt, ice chest, or whatever) that is then sold. The company gets double value: profit from sales of the secondary product, and increased publicity for the primary product. You can get the same

## LOOK FOR MULTIPLE VALUE

double value in at least two ways. One is to emphasize skills — say, science plus a foreign language — that double your chances of success by covering two bases for potential employers. The other is to select jobs and activities that can give double value by leading to two (or more) types of career advancement. Involvement with an international trade association, for example, can lead to a job either as a member of the association staff or management, or with a member company. Working in a bank lcts you create opportunities in other banks and financial institutions and also with the bank's corporate clients. If creating multiple value calls for forging links between two or more elements in your own background, take the initiative to do so. The international career environment is an ideal medium in which to make your skills and abilities do double duty.

Finally, enjoy. It's a major factor in international success.

# 3

# GLOBAL STRATEGY, CREATIVE TACTICS

**I**n today's international career market, there are a lot of new truths in the old saw about the world getting smaller every day. Because of increased economic interdependence, actions in one country create reactions in another. As late as the 1970s, U.S. business reigned secure at home and supreme abroad. Sure, U.S. multinationals were concerned about things like currency fluctuation and unitary taxes, but in general the U.S. economy (like the Titanic) cruised majestically ahead, unchallenged and supposedly unsinkable. Even the oil shocks of 1973 and 1979, and the economic problems they caused, were soon dismissed as temporary aberrations, and indeed, in the light of what happened to OPEC and oil prices in the mid-1980s, they appeared to be.

In an entirely different area, however, far stronger forces were building. Japan, that nation of tireless international strategists, had mastered all the basic industrial production methods and technologies and, armed with a number of production, management and marketing techniques conceived but not used in the United States, was ready to make a bid for international economic supremacy. And right behind Japan were Asia's "Four Small Dragons"— Korea, Taiwan, Hong Kong and Singapore — who had observed the Japanese economic miracle and were keen to make use of their own educated, productive (some say workaholic) populations to equal or surpass it.

Suddenly, in the space of a few short years, international business was up for grabs. In everything from steel and ships to semiconductors and software, U.S. industry was fighting for its life, and everything overseas became intensely interesting. Were the French working on a cure for AIDS? A U.S. lab wanted part of the action. Was a new airport being planned in Japan? U.S. firms, backed by senators and congressmen, were clamoring for participation. This increased international awareness, slow as it's been in coming, is now providing exceptional international career opportunities.

Meanwhile, back in the United States, internal fiscal problems and intense competition from abroad are producing one of the most massive industrial and corporate transformations of this century, a change that has put tens of thousands of domestic careers on pretty thin ice. In fact, so many careers have been put at risk that in the mid-1980s the U.S. Congress commissioned a special study* to examine the economic plight of people who formerly could expect satisfying career progress but now find themselves facing minimal gains or even substantial losses. The results? Times are so tough for U.S. career builders that in some ways, the study concludes, 1973 was the last good year!

With a global career strategy, you can do an end run around many of the economic problems and uncertainties that are giving headaches to career builders in the United States. Just as many U.S. companies have found that international trade and business enable them to expand their operations and increase their profitability even during domestic slumps, more and more Americans are becoming aware of the tremendous possibilities awaiting them in international careers.

One associate of mine, who was forced out of a budding domestic consulting business a few years ago by high interest rates and other changes in the U.S. economy, redirected his career onto an international path. With a new Big Picture and aggressive tacking, he was able to *triple* his annual earnings in less than five years, during a decade in which others in his age group saw their incomes shrink by almost 15 percent. This is what a good global strategy and creative tactics can accomplish.

## THE RIGHT MOVES

With increasing numbers of U.S. companies plunging into new international activities (including marketing, manufacturing, sourcing, joint venturing, licensing, technology transfer, research and development (R & D), services, and a host of others) and expanding existing international operations, you'd think that international career opportunities would be jumping into your boat like flying fish escaping from a hungry shark. Not quite.

In the first place, a lot of the companies that are establishing or increasing international operations are expanding their stateside support bases rather than their offshore presence. This means that

*NOTE: Study commissioned by the Joint Economic Committee of the U.S. Congress, Representative David Obey, Chairman. Authors: Frank S. Levy, Professor of Public Affairs, University of Maryland, and Richard Michel, Director, Income Security and Pension Policy Center, Urban Institute, Washington, DC. In 1973, the average 30-year-old male earned $23,580 in constant dollars. By 1983, constant-dollar earnings of the average 30-year-old male had dropped to only $17,250. And males 25 to 35 constitute the most upwardly mobile class of wage earners!

many of the new jobs that are being created in their international departments or divisions are no more exotic than filing shipping documents or typing telegrams, while at higher levels, you can have "international" in your title and never leave Peoria. Especially in the case of small- and medium-sized companies, the business of cultivating overseas contacts, finding new sources and markets, and putting together and closing deals—the kind of rewarding, high-stakes, high-profile activity you're aiming at—is contracted out to international consulting firms and brokers.

However, don't make the mistake of shunning such positions in your determination to go for the glamour and the gold. Remember: tacking plus your Big Picture. You're moving in an overall direction, not a blind rush in the "damn the icebergs, full speed ahead" tradition. Keep a mix of potential opportunities in your career portfolio, and analyze any stateside-international job in terms of its ability to add useful career components to your background while you make contacts and increase the value of what you have to offer. What kind of contacts? All kinds, but especially clients, customers, and international business and trade multipliers. Any of these people, including those overseas consulting firms and brokers I mentioned, may provide the point where you make your next tack.

In the second place, the pull demand created by U.S. companies' new international activities tends to draw new people into these companies at relatively low entry-level positions, the higher positions being filled by existing staff, managers, and executives. This isn't necessarily the most productive or effective policy, of course, since many of these top people have no idea of what goes on overseas or how international business is conducted. As far as your career is concerned, the bottom line is that in many cases, you'll be facing in-house competition which is the toughest competition there is. However, here's where the special structure of the international career market comes to your rescue. If you're demonstrably better prepared and more knowledgeable about things international, and *if you have something to offer* that meets a need that few or no people in the organization can fill, you can create and occupy your own niche instead of displacing someone else.

One of the keys to building your international career is the ability to recognize and create opportunities. Luckily, you can develop this ability through practice, since without it a hundred books on career development won't do you much good. How do you get the practice? As one inter-

## SPOTTING OPPORTUNITIES

nationally successful acquaintance put it when asked to explain how to create an international career, "There's no big secret; just get out there and do it!" So let's get started.

As a first step, get the barnacles off your mind. You've got to get away from the conventional, career-ladder, corporate-pyramid mentality. You're an entrepreneur, an adventurer, an explorer. You're setting out to conquer new worlds. Now hang onto this perspective and take a fresh look around you. You're going to start developing a new Big Picture.

Use logic, common sense and creativity to make up a list of international career opportunities in your community. It doesn't have to be anything fancy; even if you live in a small town, you can come up with a simple listing of companies or other organizations in which you (or anyone) might be able to create an international career. After each name on your list, put down some ideas on what sort of international activities you might be involved in if you worked there. If you believe that the organization where you presently work offers international opportunities, list those, too. In any case, feel free to be inventive.

This list is just for your reference, and it doesn't commit you (or anyone else) to anything. Don't worry if you have trouble coming up with opportunities, or if your ideas seem vague or far-fetched. Remember, just a few years ago the whole concept of an international career sounded pretty far-fetched to most Americans, but now everybody wants to get on board. And don't worry if your list is short. Since the international opportunities in your community are always changing, your inventory will never be complete, so don't try to create the ultimate list. Keep it simple, and hang onto it. You can revise it any time. Just keep observing and thinking. Talk to people in your community to get their ideas. I don't mean formal interviews, but intelligent casual conversation.

By stepping back and taking a creative look at your surroundings, you can come up with possibilities that haven't occurred to you before, and very likely haven't been considered by the business community, either. At the same time, you'll develop your international career judgement, which is important in making the commitments required for major breakthroughs. If you have confidence in your career judgement — and you will, as you hone your skills — you can make the right moves at the right time.

Whether you're launching a search for your first international job or contemplating a mid-career change, this exercise is a must for developing the global strategy and creative tactics you need to develop a truly great international career. The more information and leads you discover, the more you'll realize what tremendous opportunities there are out there if you're willing to accept the freedom and the responsibility of charting your own course, creating your own jobs, and choosing your own route to success. The farther you get into this process, the more excited you'll get about the end-

134317

less possibilities in the international career environment. What an enviable position you can put yourself in! There's a whole new world of opportunity out there, and very few companies or individuals — even those in stateside-international jobs — are equipped or trained to take advantage of it. If you seize the initiative and lay your own groundwork, you'll be one of the select few who can profit fully from the coming internationalization of American commerce and industry.

## PRICE, VALUE AND CAREER COMPONENTS

During the course of my international career, I've met a lot of very successful people who've created their own international careers literally out of nothing. How? In the first place, they've custom-built their careers by using key components, accumulated one or two at a time, to create (if we may borrow an expression from manufacturing) a high value-added end product. Maybe each skill in itself was nothing extraordinary, but by developing the right skills to match their interests and goals, they were able to come up with a set of unique international qualifications.

The second thing that many of these people have done is *use a value approach — rather than a price approach — to analyze each job or position* and how it would help them attain their overall career objectives. Suppose you have an advanced degree from an American university, and you've been working in the same field you majored in — say, marketing. Now, however, you want to get into an international career, but you can't seem to find much in marketing, and nothing that would give you the same salary and benefits you're getting now. Finally, you spot a potential opportunity in international marketing, but at a lower level of salary and responsibility than your present position. Do you take it? Conventional domestic career wisdom says no, but if you understand the international career market, you know that the answer is, "It all depends."

Although salary and responsibility are among the most important factors in reaching a decision, in the international career environment they're far from being the only ones. Remember, unlike much of the domestic market, in the international market you're not stuck to the linear format of a career ladder or track. Since you're tacking, it makes perfect sense to accept a temporary decrease in one area in order to advance your entire cause by gaining ground in another. After all, salary and perks, which are elements of price, can always be negotiated upward, either in your new position or in the one after that. But skills and international expertise, which are elements of value, can't be negotiated. They must be acquired, and either you have them or you don't.

If you think in terms of price (salary) and value (skills, expertise or career components), the decision-making process becomes a lot easier. In many cases, a move to lower pay (or responsibility, or status) is an investment in expertise — a tradeoff between price and value. The present reduction of price should, of course, be commensurate with the anticipated increase in future value. And, as with any other investment, the greater the risk, the higher should be your anticipated return.

During my last year in the international real estate and investment business, I earned a nice income, over $50,000, plus a sizeable increase in worth. However, high interest rates had put the writing on the wall, and I knew it was time to change course. As I soon discovered, however, the traditional domestic business community wasn't too enthusiastic about entrepreneurs, especially if they'd been in California real estate. I had to figure out a new approach.

As luck would have it, an executive of a local multiplier organization knew of my international abilities, and offered me a position as director of a newly formed international division. Responsibility? Yes. Salary? Less than half of what I'd made the year before. Sounds pretty unattractive, doesn't it? But let's look at *all* the facts.

In the first place, I was preparing to leave a shrinking industry. Major firms were going down like sampans in a typhoon, and on my own ship the planks had buckled and red ink was seeping in through the cracks. So there wasn't much point in comparing the income I'd previously enjoyed in this high-risk, high-reward environment with what I'd just been offered. OK, what about going back to college teaching? After all, I had an excellent record, and as a faculty member I could probably make $35,000 or more for only eight or nine months work. Hour for hour, this would have given me about what I was getting before, with more security and far fewer headaches. Besides, I could do consulting on the side (as I'd done before) if I wanted to increase my cash flow.

The problem here was that I'd be limiting myself to a fairly narrow circle of possibilities. I could do well, but I'd never really get anywhere. It would be like ending my voyage on a pleasant, but confining island instead of using all my expertise in new and different ways to keep moving on to bigger and better things. And the longer I stayed, the harder it would be to get up the energy to set sail and go on. In contrast, the job I'd been offered would be unparalleled, both in terms of acquiring expertise and credibility, and making contacts and spotting opportunities. Instead of teaching about international matters, I'd be actively involved in working with them. I took the job.

How did it work out? Within six months, I negotiated a 20 percent raise — clearly not enough to get me back to my former income level, but certainly a good start. My employer wasn't too happy to give it to me, but even after that short time on the job, we both knew that I'd added enough *value* to my career background that I could command as much or more elsewhere.

Another year, and I was negotiating another international job, not that I didn't like the one I had, but I'd used up all the growing room it had to offer. Shortly thereafter, I was overseas, with a salary and benefits package that came close to doubling what I'd made the year before, and put me very near to what I'd gotten in the industry I'd abandoned. *There was absolutely no way that I could have been considered for this job if I hadn't earlier taken a drastic cut in income (price) in order to gain expertise and increase my value.* Within two or three more years, I'd moved up to a level of financial reward and personal satisfaction significantly above my former peak. More importantly, I had at least doubled my long-term future value because of the exposure and expertise I'd acquired.

As you can see, salary and benefits aren't always the most important things to consider when analyzing an international career opportunity. In some cases, you're wise to look at a job almost the way you look at your education: a bargain at any price, because it prepared you for bigger and better things. This kind of pragmatism can put you far ahead of the competition.

## TAKING YOUR CAREER INVENTORY

Every once in a while, it's a good idea to inventory your own career components in the light of your career goals and the international opportunities in your community. Some of these components will be pretty obvious, others less so. Just as you'll revise your list of opportunities as new possibilities occur to you and others prove undesirable, so too, you'll change your inventory of career components as you discover more clearly what you have to offer. Often, you'll find that the discovery or *redefinition* of a career component generates a new opportunity, and vice versa.

What constitutes a useful, valuable career component? Virtually any skill or ability or unique combination of skills for which there is demand, and especially those in short supply. If you speak

Urdu, you undoubtedly have little competition, but you're in a limited demand situation. If you're a computer designer, there are more people with similar skills, but the demand is also high. In many cases, the international career market will place considerable value on general international and business skills, including language, previous experience overseas, and proven management ability. The exact mix will, of course, depend on the position.

To analyze your inventory of career components, you may find it useful to imagine that you need to produce a concrete plan to create an international career (or to change the international career you're in now). If you actually write down a list of the components you might need, and the steps that you could take to get them, you can get a much clearer picture of where you are and what your next move might be.

Begin thinking in terms of selective expansion of your inventory of career components, with the goal of creating as much additional value as possible. For maximum value, be sure that the components fit each other. In language, for example, there's more general demand and opportunity for speakers of Japanese than for those who speak Portuguese, but if you're knowledgable about tropical hardwoods and are interested in a career in that sector, Portuguese (the language of Brazil, a major exporter of tropical hardwoods) could be a better match.

## APPRAISING CAREER COMPONENTS

It's also important to be aware of the many ways in which your career components can be combined to create totally different careers. Often, different possibilities will be a function of differences in overall economic or technological development, or the growth, decline or evolution of specific industries in a country or region. For example, in an LDC (lesser developed country), a knowledge of science and a foreign language might be the right components for a position as the head of a scientific institute, an R&D (research and development) facility director, a senior professor, or a head researcher. In a NIC (newly industrialized country), these same components might have the most applicability and value in a technology transfer or technological manufacturing situation; in a technologically advanced country they would be more suitable and valuable for marketing technical and scientific equipment. Any additional career components including management, grantsmanship, manufacturing expertise, or marketing skill that you might need in order to qualify for each of these opportunities would have to be selected to create the appropriate component mix.

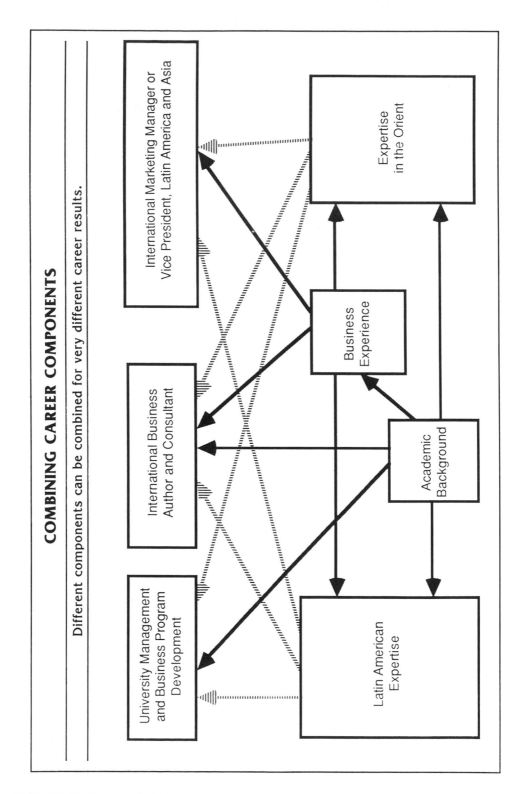

## COMBINING CAREER COMPONENTS

Different components can be combined for very different career results.

International Marketing Manager or Vice President, Latin America and Asia

Expertise in the Orient

Business Experience

International Business Author and Consultant

Academic Background

University Management and Business Program Development

Latin American Expertise

Even if you haven't yet put much detail in your Big Picture, you should, from time to time, give some thought to the value that each of your career components might have in totally different careers or jobs. One way to do this is to write each career component and each potential career in your Big Picture on a small card (say, half of a three-by-five-inch card), lay them out on a table, and move them around in different combinations to help you visualize just how they might be applied. Since the focus can be very general, as it is in the following chart based on my own career, you can start doing this at a very early stage in your international career planning. In the chart, for example, academic background has direct application in university management and in a career as an author and consultant. However, unless the academic background is in business (which in my case it was not), an additional component of business experience would be necessary for a top-level position in marketing.

If you assess each component for its market value in different contexts, you'll see that different business sectors, as well as individual companies within those sectors, assign quite different values to the same component. This is where long-range planning becomes important. The value you assign should reflect your own future objectives and final goals as well as the present cash price in a specific setting. A realistic appraisal will also show that you won't get all the components you need in glamorous positions. For some of the most valuable components, you'll have to forego some glitter, but if they fill important gaps you'll come out far ahead later on. *Don't fall for the "golden cage" trap: a job that looks good, but keeps you in the same spot until it's too late to go on to anything better.*

Above all, keep thinking, analyzing and restructuring your present situation to take advantage of opportunities and create a viable career. This doesn't mean disloyalty to your present employer, but simply living up to your own potential. If a job is big enough for you to keep learning, growing and prospering, stick with it. If it proves limiting, then during your tenure you've given your employer the benefit of more competence and initiative than he/she bargained for. As long as you leave your position or department or division more valuable and productive than it was when you arrived, you've given fair compensation for the opportunity.

# PUT YOURSELF IN CHARGE

Throughout your journey, *you have to rely on the quality of your own efforts*, not only to uncover opportunities, but also to create a marketable set of skills. Of course, contacts can be very useful (that's one of the reasons that I emphasize multiplier organizations), but few people will risk their professional position (or, in the case of smaller businesses, their own money) by hiring an unknown quantity, let alone a proven mediocrity. So the burden is on you to generate credibility and let others see your value in international business matters.

How can you do this? Simply by reaching out and creating your own opportunities. In the process, you'll gain valuable experience and create a background that will make you interesting to potential employers.

One way to generate your own opportunities and help your present employer at the same time is by helping your company create new international activity. You can do this either in companies that already have international business, or in those that have hung back from the international market. Many U.S. companies, content to rely on the size of the U.S. market and apprehensive about the additional effort required to make the initial move into foreign markets (even when located right next door), will resist making any moves. If you've already taken some of the initial steps, it can be a different story. By laying the groundwork on your own, you turn yourself into a *de facto*, in-house international consultant at no cost to your employer.

Suppose you work for a manufacturing or distributing company, and you have a strong desire to get into an international career. How can you parlay this desire into actuality? The key word is creativity. First of all, look at your company's product. See any international demand? Possibly. But wait—your company doesn't export. Good! This is another opportunity for you. Instead of merely giving a suggestion to the marketing manager, who may not follow through with it, you can use your idea to create an export department and launch an international career for yourself. Begin doing the groundwork on your own time and quietly stimulating management's thinking along these lines.

U.S. companies vary tremendously in their willingness to accept change or suggestions of change from management and staff. Regardless of your corporate environment, however, you can be alert for international opportunities for your company that may open new horizons for you. Even if you aren't able to come up with any proposals for new international business, if you're thinking and talking international, you're more likely to be tapped for new international activities that develop. It's happened to me, and I've seen it happen time and time again to others: when a decision is made to move into an area, someone will recommend you for a role in the project if you've displayed a consistent, intelligent interest in international business possibilities. And if you recommend yourself, your established interest will make it a lot more likely that you'll be accepted.

## SEAMANSHIP PLUS LEADERSHIP

To take advantage of the tremendous opportunities in the international career environment, you've got to take the initiative, and to get the maximum benefit, you've got to be entrepreneurial. This requires not only innovation and resourcefulness, but also a healthy dose of self-confidence, strength of character and leadership. To make key moves, you often run the risk of antagonizing someone from the career-ladder school of thought, who will be intensely resentful of your drive to create and develop your own opportunities instead of staying on your assigned rung, or going whichever way the wind and currents carry you.

If you're honest and straightforward, who could you possibly offend? Any number of people. Your employer or anyone else in a higher position in the company might feel threatened by your display of initiative and ability. Don't try to steal the show. As the saying goes, there's no limit to what you can accomplish as long as you don't care who gets the credit. Your goal isn't kudos, but new responsibilities, new expertise, new opportunities.

The other main problem area will be the domestic departments or divisions that fear their relative importance will be reduced as international activities generate new business outside their sector. If you were trying to create a new opportunity for yourself in the domestic side of your company, this perception, and the resulting resistance, would be a major, perhaps insurmountable, obstacle, but thanks to the unique character of the international market as a separate structure existing alongside the traditional corporate pryamid, you generate much less friction when you try to create something international. In the first place, you're not trying to push anyone off the ladder, or squeeze them aside to make room for yourself. Instead, you're creating an entirely new niche. If existing staff and management aren't qualified to function there anyway, they're losing nothing. If they are qualified, or close to qualified, you've created a new opportunity for them, as well as for yourself.

Furthermore, many domestic departments will see their importance actually increase as a result of your international initiative. Billing, shipping, advertising, customer service, and many other areas may all experience a higher level of activity and increased staff levels. You're actually creating more power for the people who run these departments, as well as more prosperity for the entire organization. In short, your initiative has value for everyone in the company. To help it gain acceptance, you may want to present it in this light.

## CAPTAIN OR CREW?

The bottom line, however, is your own career. You may find it impossible to get your ideas implemented or accepted with good grace. Your supervisors and colleagues may find it impossible to conceive of any system or career strategy that goes beyond the narrow, zero-sum confines of their career ladders. At this point, it's decision time. Do you want to spend your life as a deckhand under someone else's command, or take the helm and build a satisfying and rewarding career that can eventually make you the skipper? Stepping on others to get where you're going is bad, of course, but letting them decide your every move will do just as much damage to your self-respect, your image, and your career in the long run.

If you hesitate over this question, maybe another one can help you answer it. How independent do you want to be? Not everyone is cut out to be an entrepreneur, and many very talented and capable people function better within the more secure environment of a large corporation. If you're ambitious but don't like the idea of drawing your own maps, determining your own compass heading, and trusting your own seamanship to get through uncharted waters, you may be better off in a large company, where your overall direction is mainly determined by the organization.

You can take this route and still have an international career. After all, for decades the only U.S. companies involved in international business were America's largest corporations, and these companies still account for the lion's share of the U.S. exports and offshore investment. Keep in mind, however, that choosing this path involves a trade-off. You may spend your entire career in the United States. If you go overseas, you may be sent to places you've never heard of before, and never want to hear of again. You may find yourself impatient with your lack of career progress, and hemmed in by organizational rules and the sheer dead weight of size. And the longer you remain in the necessarily bureaucratized environment of a large organization, the more dependent you're likely to become.

If, on the other hand, you enjoy a little excitement, don't mind taking calculated risks, and have a positive attitude toward change, you may enjoy the challenge of creating an international career to your own specifications. It won't always be easy, but with initiative and perseverance you can live where you want and do work that's meaningful and rewarding. Above all, you'll never be bored.

For many people, the creative aspects of international career building are as important and rewarding as the financial and professional results. These people get an extra thrill out of developing the broadly based expertise, which may include market research, PR, language, forecasting, and product development, needed to take their international careers to the limit. Furthermore, by stimulating personal and professional development across the board, the more independent type of international career — which is ideal for growing and moving ahead, rather than just getting to the top of the heap — puts you in position to spot more and more new directions as you move along.

## GETTING UNDER WAY

If the idea of a largely self-generated career appeals to you, you can test your desire and aptitudes before you actually push off from the dock. There's no better place than where you are, and there's no time like the present. Regardless of the results you get on the first attempt, and regardless of what mode — from solo sailor to one of a huge crew — you decide to use later in your career, you'll gain useful experience.

If you work for a company that has domestic business (and don't forget that even if your company exports, it may be overlooking the international potential of its domestic products) try to identify domestic product or service lines that could be marketed internationally. Use a mixture of market knowledge, intuition and logic to come up with an initial list. Refine your list by reading trade publications, keeping a sharp eye out for related articles in more general business publications, and talking to people in the industry. You may want to check with local multiplier organizations to see if their opinions coincide with yours.

If you're not presently employed, or if you work for an organization that does only international business, analyze the domestic products or services of another business in your community. See anything that appears to have international market potential? Try to identify possible markets. Use the sources mentioned above (publications, industry contacts, multipliers) to confirm or modify your initial opinions. Can you come up with something that has potential for your own company, but that your company is not now marketing abroad?

If all this seems pretty involved to you, that's good. It shows that you're thinking of some of the many factors that might affect a final international marketing decision. (What's the competition in the target market? What sort of tariff and non-tariff barriers will our product face there? How about exchange rates? What's the long-term outlook for the country or region in question? How do we handle the paperwork involved? What sort of terms and conditions of payment should we establish?)

Don't succumb to "analysis paralysis"! You can answer all these questions later. The purpose of this exercise is to get you thinking creatively about new international possibilities. For now, concentrate on expanding your awareness and exercising your creative business sense. As you'll soon see, it's a lot of fun, especially when you have absolutely nothing to lose. Short term, it's an awfully interesting way to spend your time and (why deny it?) a very appealing conversation starter. Long term, it can lead you to the type of business intuition I used to envy in self-made international millionaires — the kind of entrepreneurs who could wash up on the beach in an unknown country with no money, no language skills, and no contacts, and come skimming out a couple of years later in their own custom built hydrofoil with a wad of cash.

I don't expect you to come up with a concrete plan of action, but just to look around, do some thinking, and start gaining new international perspectives. While you're at it, let yourself feel the thrill of the limitless, untapped potential all around you. It's there, and it's waiting — that's what makes international careers so exciting.

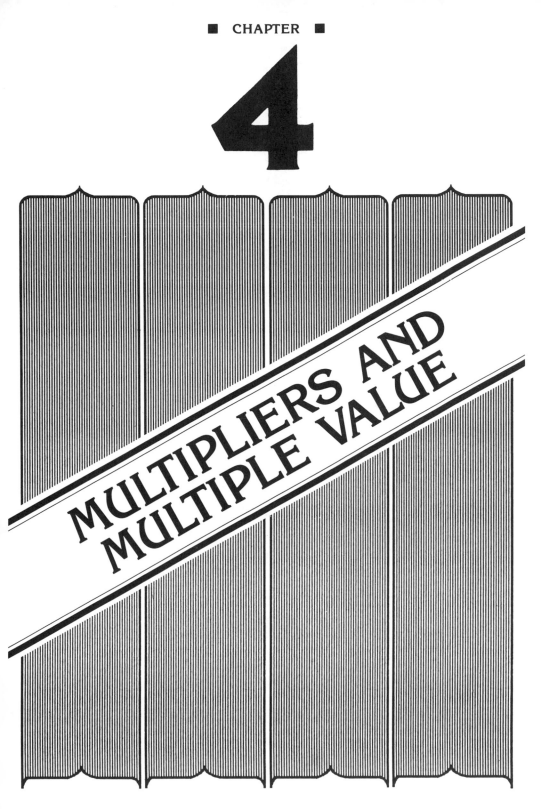

# 4

## MULTIPLIERS AND MULTIPLE VALUE

**I**n the course of my career as an international business consultant, I've provided counseling and international business assistance to executives, managers and representatives from all sorts of companies, from small to very large. These men and women have considerable international business experience, yet they often lack even the most rudimentary knowledge about key factors in the international business and career environment. This not only hampers their business activities, it reduces their chances of creating more rewarding careers for themselves.

The most common problem is a sketchy idea of the resources available to them in their specific environments. They often are amazed to learn, for example, that the U.S. Embassy can provide them with information and services ranging from market reports and investment seminars to assistance with trade disputes and trademark violations, or that AmCham can brief them on the challenges facing virtually any business sector in the country, or provide data on wages and living costs. In short, they don't know what opportunities are available because they don't understand what major international organizations do.

In building your international career, you'll soon discover the truth of the old adage that knowledge is power. If you dedicate a high percentage of your efforts to learning what's out there, you'll uncover new opportunities and put yourself far ahead of the rest of the fleet. If you're content to rely on familiar, convenient contacts and the traditional, sector-specific type of old-boy network (which often keeps you circulating in the same industry you start out in, changing jobs and perhaps commanding higher prices but not really going anywhere or acquiring significant value), you're more likely to end up becalmed, or sailing in circles in a vain attempt to get a good wind and favorable currents. It's far better to be aggressive in scouting new channels, but to do this effectively, you need information.

Because the international career market is far larger, more varied and more complex than the domestic market, you'll need to follow a consistent strategy of involvement in activities that give you multiple value by putting you in position for several career opportunities at the same time or creating links between two or more career components. Luckily, you can acquire information in large chunks and get multiple value by using a source that I've touched on already: so-called "multiplier organizations" or simply "multipliers."

## HOW MULTIPLIERS WORK

**M**ultiplier organizations are formed to multiply the effects of the members' actions (for example, in public information campaigns that benefit the members), to gain the high profile that comes from acting as a group (like trade missions), and to make it easier for the members to get information on trends and issues that affect their business. You can use their structure to get a two-way, direct conduit to many organizations or businesses without approaching each one individually. By being aware of multiplier programs and positions, you understand the needs and attitudes of the members, and by being involved in multiplier activities, you let the members see what you're all about.

Multipliers deliver multiple value by letting you get exposure while you increase your international IQ and learn of career opportunities, and by helping you create career opportunities both with member companies and with the multiplier itself. They also can save you a tremendous amount of time and energy by reducing the number of places you have to go to get information. By working with and through multipliers, you often can put yourself in a position to take advantage of international opportunities that most people (even those considered knowledgeable about international business and international affairs) never even hear about. Finally, knowledge of multipliers and their functions gives you credibility, especially if you're aiming at or trying to create a position that calls for an innovative generalist. In this respect, your participation in multipliers is like company participation in a major trade show: being there may not get you any immediate sales, but it lets the market know that you're in the game. In fact, if you're absent (or worse yet, unaware of the event), you're perceived as being disinterested or second-rate. It's better to be involved.

Even after you've established yourself in your career, you'll need to become familiar with new multipliers as your professional activity takes you into different product or service sectors, or as you're transferred from one geographic location to another. When you enter a new company or city or country, multipliers are the best source of information on who's who and what's what in international trade and business matters. For one thing, they can further your progress on any new tack by quickly getting you up to speed both on major issues and on the details of how to make things happen. For another, they put you in touch with people and companies that represent future opportunities for your next move. So whether you're just starting out or contemplating a mid-career change, it's advisable to keep active in multipliers, and maintain solid contacts in them.

You may not need to become involved in any multiplier other than the local chamber of commerce or international trading association; in fact, circumstances may give you no other choice. It's worth your while, however, to take the time to identify all the multipliers in your community (or nearby metropolitan area) that are involved in international activities as well as those that you believe could or should be.

To decide where you can best direct your efforts, talk to key people in the international section at each multiplier. Often, you'll find that secretaries and other staff people are the best sources of information. Find out what kinds of projects they're working on, and what their organizational goals are. Ask what relationships each organization has with the others you've identified. Are they working on any joint projects? How about relations with organizations outside the immediate area? For example, does your local chamber of commerce ever promote joint trade missions with other chambers of commerce? The more you know about what's going on in local multipliers, the sooner you'll spot new opportunities for yourself.

Each multiplier organization offers you two distinct career-enhancing possibilities: activity as a member, or employment in a staff or managerial position. Both can give you a high profile, and you may find that one leads to the other, especially in a community or an industry where international activities are in a growth phase. As an active member, you're well positioned to spot or create opportunities within the organization, as well as in member companies.

Technically speaking, multipliers are private sector associations. However, they're often discussed together with public sector agencies such as state trade offices or the Foreign Commercial Service (FCS) because their activities are both overlapping and complementary.

If you're considering employment with a private sector multiplier, you should be aware that even small multipliers have some of the same career characteristics of public bureaucracies. Working for a private sector multiplier, like working for the foreign commercial service (FCS) or other business support agencies, gives access to many private sector businesses, but you're always one step removed from the actual business decision-making that's an essential ingredient in private sector careers. This separation from the bottom line relieves you of a lot of stress, and the encompassing nature of the multiplier gives you a higher profile and more diverse contacts than you could make in a private sector firm. The trade-off for this high value is the same low price (salary) and restricted advancement that makes short stops out of many public sector jobs.

Which multipliers and agencies should you contact, and which ones should you contact first? There's no single good answer to this question. As you can see from the following discussion, some multipliers are primarily sources of information and contacts, while others have greater job potential for you. Of the multipliers and agencies where you might find employment, some offer more in terms of price (including both salary and advancement), while others are definitely weighted on the value side. Rather than try to establish a prioritized list (which might be perfectly valid for me and utterly backwards for you), I've discussed multipliers more or less according to organizational structure and size, with large, internationally active American ones first.

## AMERICAN MULTIPLIER ORGANIZATIONS

For variety of experience, breadth of contacts and creation of credentials, work at an internationally oriented multiplier organization is hard to beat. As international trade, investment and related matters become more important to all American businesses, virtually every type of multiplier, from industry associations to chambers of commerce, is becoming aware of the need to have at least some international expertise on board to keep abreast of developments, do research, advise on policy, and deal with specific international issues.

Is a foreign country planning to change the regulations on electrical appliances? The U.S. appliance industry association needs to know about it. Is there a chance to increase international business or investment in your community by establishing relations with one or more foreign chambers of commerce? There may well be and you can be the one to get the ball rolling. You can play these and similar key roles far more easily, and gain far greater acceptance, if you're employed by a multiplier organization. Even if there's not enough demand to create an international section, you can develop an international specialty or orientation within an existing unit. Most multipliers have some sort of economic research section or business development section, which is an ideal environment for developing internationally oriented activities and programs, perhaps as modest as an occasional column on international business in the multiplier newsletter, or as ambitious as a multinational trade and investment mission.

Because your duties may range from organizing a conference to handling trade documentation, or anything in between, you'll develop all kinds of skills to enhance your future marketability. Be aware from the start that these organizations, being nonprofit and relying on member dues or contributions for funding, often don't pay as much as profit-making companies, and you many find yourself earning only two-thirds to three-fourths as much as you might at an individual firm. However, keep in mind the important difference between price (salary) and value (the worth of the contacts and expertise you gain). Since work with a multiplier can give you expertise and exposure in many areas, time and energy spent here may lead you to a much wider range of opportunities.

## OVERSEAS ORGANIZATIONS AND AGENCIES

Unless you've recently won the national lottery, or are the type who can pick the daily double by throwing darts at the racing form, you're probably better off if you line up a job before heading overseas to work. However, if you're already in a foreign country as a student, a teacher, or even as a tourist, you certainly can and should touch bases with multipliers and government agencies there. Why? Because there's an awful lot of business activity going on overseas that you simply can't get a feel for if you're in the United States.

The process of learning what's out there can be frustrating and tiring. Like doing sales work, it's often hard to see results, and you may start asking yourself is there are ever going to be any. The solution is to keep your eye on long-term value. While making the rounds to find out what exists, you'll make contacts and increase your general expertise. And you may get a pleasant surprise if, as often happens, someone later calls you to let you know of an opportunity. As with all your career-building activities, be interested in the process itself. If you're looking too hard for immediate results, it'll be obvious to others. You may come across as too eager, or even worse, self-centered. If you enjoy what you're involved in, it'll show. And meanwhile, you're learning a lot about international business and related activity. In fact, you're liable to wake up one morning and realize that you've become an expert.

Overseas organizations can supply valuable information for future use, and perhaps a few near-term contacts. This is particularly true if you'll be in the country for a fair length of time, and if you have something to offer.

For example, if you have a strong background in economics, you can make a contribution to the work of, say, an American Chamber of Commerce (AmCham) banking committee. If your background is in science, or in law, you have a possibility of doing the same thing in the field of intellectual property rights, which is a very hot topic in several foreign countries where massive counterfeiting and piracy of U.S. books, films, computers and software, pharmaceuticals, and other products is a major problem.

Of course, you have to present yourself in such a way that your worth to the group and its members is evident. The main thing is to have a clear sense of purpose (besides looking for a job so you can "stay in this beautiful country"!) that communicates itself to people in the organization. This purpose could be anything from a research project on local business to addressing an AmCham group on the latest business-related developments in a given field in the United States. Above all, you need to have a sincere interest in advancing the group's goals rather than just your own. Believe me, it'll be noticed, and it may turn into a lead or an offer, even after your return to the United States.

Even if you don't visit any of your target countries immediately, you can use many overseas organizations as sources of information and ideas by mail. In person or by mail, you should always ask about new trends and developments. Are new state representative offices being opened? What U.S. companies are coming into the country? What business sectors appear most likely to expand? Does the host-country government have plans for new educational or industrial centers? These and similar questions can give you ideas that lead to opportunities.

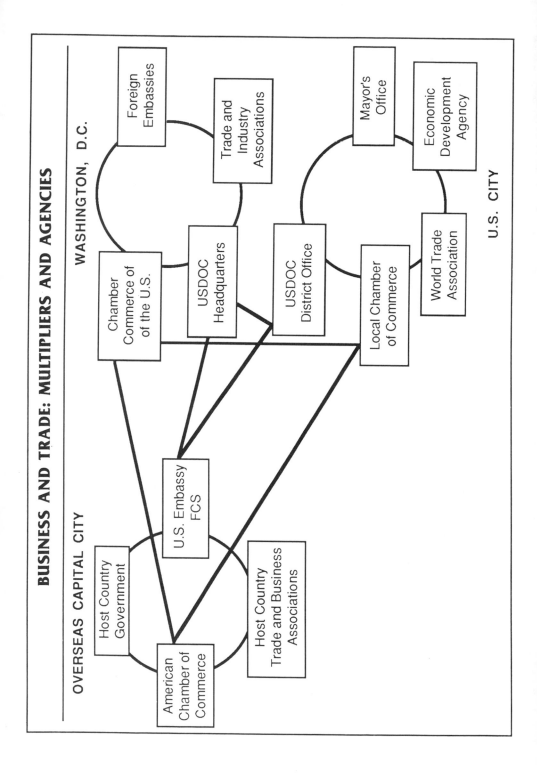

## BUSINESS AND TRADE: MULTIPLIERS AND AGENCIES

**WASHINGTON, D.C.**

Foreign Embassies

Trade and Industry Associations

Chamber Commerce of the U.S.

USDOC Headquarters

**OVERSEAS CAPITAL CITY**

Host Country Government

U.S. Embassy FCS

American Chamber of Commerce

Host Country Trade and Business Associations

USDOC District Office

Local Chamber of Commerce

Mayor's Office

Economic Development Agency

World Trade Association

**U.S. CITY**

# U.S. EMBASSIES AND CONSULATES

**A**lthough you might never go after a job involving service at an embassy or consulate, they're so important to all international business and trade (not to mention diplomacy), that you should know something about them. As is true with so many other aspects of the international career world, this knowledge may have unexpected value later when you're planning or executing a move.

With any U.S. Government agency including embassies and consulates, your efforts and contacts won't usually produce much besides information because most hiring is done in Washington, and because it's rare for a U.S. Government employee to make a recommendation for a job from the private sector. Don't neglect this activity, however. After all, not only your value but also your ability to market it are largely determined by what you know.

Embassies are located only in capital cities in foreign countries. (I once earned the wrath of a very insistent gentleman who was furious at my failure to provide him with the address and telephone number of the U.S. Embassy in Los Angeles, California.) Their main functions are contact with the host-country ("foreign") government, and representing the legitimate interests of U.S. citizens abroad. An embassy is under an ambassador and his right-hand man, the Deputy Chief of Mission or DCM (who as *Chargé d'Affaires* runs the embassy in the ambassador's absence).

The major sections of an embassy may include political, consular, labor, administrative, public affairs (this is the United States Information Service which includes press relations and cultural affairs), economic, commercial, and agricultural. These last three are particularly involved in matters related to U.S. economic, business and trade interests, including marketing assistance. They also work closely with AmCham. Depending on their size and location, embassies may have a wide variety of additional offices, including science, military, customs (U.S. Treasury Department), U.S. Agency for International Development (USAID; foreign aid) and others.

Consulates are sort of mini-embassies located in major cities outside the capital where U.S. interests require permanent official representation. Each consulate is under the direction of a consul (or, at a larger and more important consulate known as a "consulate-general," a consul-general). Consular staffs may be as small as a handful of people; offices represented vary according to the importance of various issues and interests in the country and city in question. Normally, there's at least a consular section (for passports, visas and citizenship services), and economic (or economic/commercial) section, and an administrative section. Because most consulates are located in less heavily urbanized environments, the atmosphere at a consulate, particularly a smaller one, is often less hectic than at an embassy which means that officers are more accessible.

Clearly, you're not going to serve on any committees or get any job offers at embassies or consulates; the only way to get in here is to take the Foreign Service exam or apply through the appropriate agency headquarters in Washington. There is, however, valuable information to gain here.

## THE COMMERCIAL, ECONOMIC, AND AGRICULTURAL SECTIONS

These have the most immediately useful business information: market reports, economic trends reports, import and export regulations, Am-Cham and host country business directories, and similar information that can give you further ideas and leads. If you have some legitimate business interest other than job hunting — be it research for a university study, preliminary groundwork for a stateside chamber of commerce or international trade association mission, scouting markets for one or more U.S. exporters — you should also be able to get some time with one of the Commercial, Econ, or Ag officers to get a better picture of business activity that might translate into opportunities for you.

Keep in mind, however, that many embassy officers are also looking for private sector opportunities, so if they sense you're a competitor, or that you have no potential to generate an opportunity for them, they may be reluctant to give you more than a couple of minutes. Another problem is awareness: you may run into an officer who's spent too much time on the cocktail circuit, or a professional bureaucrat who has neither the ability nor the desire to control his career, let alone give you information that will improve yours. If you think that you've encountered any of these types, rather than press the issue, try to find an officer who may be more cooperative or more aware. Again, if you've been active with Am-Cham, discreet inquiries there can generate a good idea of who to talk to at the embassy.

Either the commercial section or the economic section can also give you a free list of attorneys. (Actual preparation of the list is usually done by the consular section.) Since attorneys are involved in a lot of different types of business situations, a few minutes of conversation with one (over lunch, perhaps) can give you a world of leads and a good idea of what it's like to function in the host country. This sort of contact is easier to make via an AmCham meeting or through the local expatriate (expat) network, but if you're a consultant or represent any U.S. or host-country firm, you should be able to generate a meeting on your own. After all, there may be business in it for the attorney in the future.

T his is a good source for much non-commercial information. If you need to get information on cultural events, education, and the news media, a few minutes' chat with a USIS officer can be a big help. In addition, USIS reference libraries are very valuable when you're overseas and want to do

## UNITED STATES INFORMATION SERVICE (USIS)

research on topics related to education, journalism, and other areas of primary interest to USIS. If you're in any of these fields, you should be able to talk to an American officer about what's going on in the country. Be sure to find out if any retired USIS personnel are teaching at host-country universities or working for host-country media; they sometimes do, and they're often quite accessible and willing to share information with you.

## U.S.-BASED AGENCIES

E mbassies and consulates are a sort of multiplier in that they house many different agencies and provide a one-step source of information on many different companies and industries. For actual employment, of course, you need to apply to each agency separately, usually in Washington, DC.

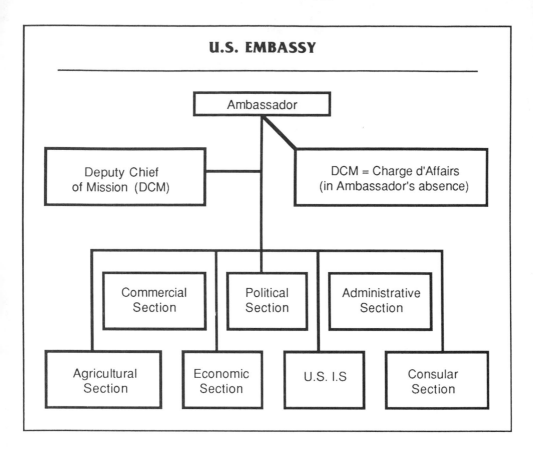

# U.S. EMBASSY

```
                    ┌─────────────────┐
                    │   Ambassador    │
                    └─────────────────┘
┌──────────────────┐            ┌──────────────────────────┐
│   Deputy Chief   │            │  DCM = Charge d'Affairs   │
│ of Mission (DCM) │            │  (in Ambassador's absence)│
└──────────────────┘            └──────────────────────────┘

      ┌─────────────┐  ┌─────────────┐  ┌─────────────────┐
      │ Commercial  │  │  Political  │  │ Administrative  │
      │  Section    │  │  Section    │  │    Section      │
      └─────────────┘  └─────────────┘  └─────────────────┘
┌─────────────┐ ┌─────────────┐ ┌──────────┐ ┌─────────────┐
│ Agricultural│ │  Economic   │ │ U.S. I.S │ │  Consular   │
│   Section   │ │  Section    │ │          │ │   Section   │
└─────────────┘ └─────────────┘ └──────────┘ └─────────────┘
```

The U.S. Department of State, which is the major organization at all U.S. Embassies and Consulates, is possibly the most well-known of the numerous international career possibilities with the U.S. Government. I'd advise most people aspiring to an international career to take the State

## DEPARTMENT OF STATE

Department Foreign Service Examination, which is given once a year (early December) in major cities throughout the United States and around the world. (Contact your local Federal Office Building, embassy or consulate for details, sample questions and application forms.) Be forewarned that most people don't pass the exam on the first try, and for those who do pass, there's usually a lengthy waiting period (a year or more) for a job opening. Taking the exam is a good experience, and passing it gives you both an iron in the fire and increased credibility with other potential international employers.

Foreign Service officers serve in Washington, DC, on various other assignments within the United States, and at U.S. Embassies, U.S. Consulates and U.S. Missions around the world.

What sort of Foreign Service officers is State looking for? Critics say that the main criterion is a suitably preppy image, preferably ivy league. Although this assessment may be extreme, many observers agree that much of the process of training and personnel evaluation at State seems geared toward cultivating an air of gentility and conformity to pseudo-partrician values and behavior. Certainly many State officers overseas make no bones about their distaste — often bordering on disdain — for commercial work with American businessmen.

Whatever the value system, one good thing about being a Foreign Service officer is that you're guaranteed to go overseas. If you stay in long enough, you can expect to do a series of two to four year tours in different posts (the more difficult or unpleasant the country, the shorter the tour), punctuated by occasional tours in Washington, DC. State also has a wide variety of training programs (including language), and a number of programs through which you can be placed on loan with other government agencies (federal, state and local) to provide international expertise. All in all, they take good care of their people.

Overseas, most Foreign Service officers work in U.S. Embassies or Consulates. (There are also a very few officers in such places as the U.S. Mission to the U.N.) Assignments vary according to the track or "cone" (which is State's way of making the good old corporate pyramid sound hollow) to which you're assigned when you enter the Foreign Service. There are several such cones, including Political (political contacts and reporting), Economic (macroeconomic reporting and analysis, some commercial work), Consular (passports, visas, birth and death records, assistance to U.S. citizens), and Administration (in charge of logistics, supply, services including motor pool, and similar functions).

In general, the Political cone is the route to stardom, since virtually all career ambassadors come from this cone. As a result, everyone with any ambition is fighting to get into it. Obviously, not everyone succeeds. On the other hand, once inside, you'd better like it and make a go of it, since after a few years there are few directions you can take besides becoming a political science professor. However, if you can acquire enough expertise (including language capability) in an exotic or difficult country or region, you may find other openings in the private sector. Most of these opportunities seem to involve remaining in your adoptive overseas habitat forever, to take advantage of the host-country contacts you've developed.

For most Foreign Service officers, the next choice is Econ. The work is interesting (you're dealing with bankers, Ministry of Finance officials, and some host-country legislators) and has some applications in private sector businesses, particularly banking and financial services. In smaller embassies and consulates, Econ officers also do commercial work, which provides more experience and contacts in the business world.

Very few people want to be consular officers, so State humanely lightens their load a bit by making all new officers take a turn for a year or eighteen months when they come on board. This is real galley slave work: day after endless day facing equally endless lines of huddled masses yearning for a visa, and willing to do almost anything (including fraud, threats and bribery) to get one. Consular officers are also the ones that get to visit U.S. prisoners in foreign jails, locate the missing, and provide assistance to the indigent. You'll get through this trying period, of course, but it is a long time to spend dead in the water.

The Administration cone is a real blind channel. Most Admin officers, although likeable enough, appear to have run aground long ago. Happily adjusted to life on their limited atolls, they pass most of their days making sure the sails are properly patched, brass polished, and anchor chains free of rust. If you're the type who loves supervising handymen, this is the job for you; you won't have to work very hard, and you can give yourself the best housing and furniture that the embassy or consulate has available. The Admin section also houses Personnel, Budget and Fiscal.

Personnel officers have little responsibility, since all hiring, firing and promoting of Foreign Service officers is done in Washington. However, embassy Personnel officers are responsible for these functions for nationals (Foreign Service Nationals, FSN's).

Budget and Fiscal (B&F) is responsible for financial records (including payroll) and the accounting function of the embassy. Since U.S. Government accounting is done by methods and procedures that would probably lead a private businessman to ruin, long exposure to them does little to qualify you for work with a private sector accounting firm.

## NEGOTIATING SALARY

Status, responsibility, and salary level in the Foreign Service are based on a system of grades (for responsibility and authority) and steps (for salary level) much like the domestic Civil Service system, except that the numbers are backwards. In the Foreign Service, you climb the cone toward FS1, which corresponds roughly to the GS15 of the Civil Service system. Entry-level positions for college grads are usually at the FS5 grade. Within each grade, there are fourteen steps corresponding to fourteen different salary levels arranged so that the higher steps of each grade pay more than the lower steps of the next grade above. For example, an FS3, step 14, makes more than an FS2 step 5—but even though the FS2/5 makes less money (lower price), he/she is still above any FS3 in terms of authority and responsibility (higher value). Therefore, if you're negotiating for anything other than a standard entry-level position, you should consider trying for the higher grade, even at the sacrifice of salary. You'll be able to accomplish more and accumulate more expertise and contacts for your next tack. *Whether your priority is salary or grade, it's important to get all you can going in, since after that your destiny is controlled by committee,* and the only arguments you can present are in writing on your annual performance evaluation.

Promotions are based on annual performance evaluations written up by your supervisor (rating officer) and reviewed, with comments, by a higher level officer (reviewing officer). You may make comments or rebuttal before the completed forms are sent to Washington for judgment by a committee. Since not everyone would be promoted even if everyone did an outstanding job (remember, you're in a cone, so each move up means fewer people), you can't expect to get promoted every year. If you remain more than a certain number of years in any grade, however, you are "selected out."

Salary levels in the Foreign Service range from about $22,000 at the lowest entry level (FS5, step 1) to about $70,000 at the top (FS1, step 14). In addition, while overseas you get free, furnished housing, bonus pay (from 5 to 15 percent, depending on proficiency) for ability in designated "hard" languages (presently including Japanese, Chinese, Korean and Arabic), and hardship and/or cost of living allowances at difficult or expensive posts.

Most overseas agencies of the Federal Government operate under a grade and step system virtually identical to the one used by State, and use a similar system to determine country and post of assignment: you submit a bid list (based on a list of open assignments provided by your agency) and an assignments panel does its best to match you, your qualifications (including language), and your list with the available positions. At least, this is how it works in theory; in practice there's a lot of behind the scenes arm-twisting and horse-trading going on, as upper level managers fight for talented officers or tout their favorite protégé for a choice assignment.

Since 1980, the U.S. Department of Commerce (USDOC) has had primary responsibility for promoting U.S. trade, business and commercial interests overseas. (Before that time, the responsibility rested with the State Department.) Sections of USDOC that deal with international

# DEPARTMENT OF COMMERCE

matters include the U.S. Travel and Tourism Administration (USTTA), the International Trade Administration (ITA) and the Foreign Commercial Service (FCS). Of these, FCS has the largest overseas staff (about 170 Americans).

Some slots in the Foreign Commercial Service (FCS) are reserved for so-called "limited appointments", mid-level appointees (based on old-boy connections) who don't have to pass any sort of competitive exam. These appointments, whose maximum duration is five years, provide a superb chance to increase foreign and American contacts and get positioned for a tack back into the private sector. Other FCS officers are chosen through a competitive examination and assessment process somewhat similar to the one for State Department Foreign Service officers, and waiting times for actual employment can range up to one year. Once selected, the FCS officer normally serves in a U.S. Embassy or Consulate overseas. Assignments are also available in Department of Commerce (USDOC) District Offices, located in major U.S. cities (contact the nearest Federal Building or FCS, Washington for details), and in Washington, DC.

*One of the biggest advantages of the Foreign Commercial Service (FCS) over State is the tremendous breadth of practical business experience that FCS officers acquire. In many respects, it's far superior to going through an MBA program, and you're drawing a good salary the whole time.* In contrast to State, which does most hiring at the entry level, most FCS positions are middle management slots at the grades of FS4 (about $27,000 to about $40,000) and above. The salary range and supplementary benefits (including free housing) are the same as those for State Foreign Service officers.

FCS officers cover the entire spectrum of international business activity. In the FCS, you may be involved in putting on trade shows, doing market analysis, working on the reduction of tariffs and elimination of trade barriers, acting as intermediary in trade complaints, combatting counterfeiting of U.S. products, helping formulate marketing strategies, organizing trade and investment mission activities, and all the other things that go into creating and maintaining profitable business activity in a foreign country.

74 ■ INTERNATIONAL CAREERS

There is no other activity that can give you comparable expertise, and after a few years you'll be highly qualified to move on to more specialized career activity in marketing, placing direct investment, or running some phase of international operations for a U.S. company. If you have the sense to eschew the petty in-house politics engendered by the bureaucracy and instead make a strong commitment to helping your business clients, you'll generate a lot of opportunities in the private sector.

The FCS also generates excellent opportunities in trade, both import and export. Virtually every business case you handle can give you ideas on trading opportunities that would never occur to you otherwise. Of course, conflict-of-interest regulations prevent you from using insider information for personal gain, but you'll add whole new sections to your Big Picture that you can use later in your career, whether with a U.S. or foreign manufacturer, a trading company, or as an independent international trader or consultant.

■ **U.S. Department of Commerce District Office.** These U.S. Government offices, located in major U.S. cities in most states, are prime sources of information on international business trends and specific data on business opportunities in various countries. In some cases, they are amenable to the presence of interns (usually recent college graduates or graduate students) who, although working at no salary, acquire invaluable experience, knowledge and contacts that often generate job offers. These offices provide close liaison with commercial sections in U.S. Embassies and Consulates worldwide, and export counseling, information and other services to U.S. exporters, particularly small- and medium-sized businesses. Emphasis is on new-to-export and new-to-market (i.e., exporters that have experience, but have never tried to penetrate a given market) firms.

Although positions in USDOC District Offices are theoretically awarded as the result of open competition, the fact is that slots are often filled on the basis of political or in-house connections. At the same time, the larger network of the nearby stateside-international business community (especially major multipliers) often plays a decisive role. If the members of an influential world trade association are behind you, for example, you're far more likely to get the nod.

Salary scales are the same as for the Foreign Commercial Service: an entry-level position pays about $23,000, and an office director makes close to $70,000. Since these jobs, like most bureaucratic positions, offer high security but snail-like advancement, they're beneficial in terms of experience, exposure, and credibility rather than rapid forward progress. In addition, they may help you get overseas with the FCS. Although there's no direct transfer between the two organizations, it's far easier to pass the FCS entry examination once you've done a couple of years in a USDOC district office. In the meantime, you become very knowledgeable about international trade and business, you make excellent contacts—both in-house and through your role as government consultant to local exporters—and you may have opportunities to go abroad with trade missions or on temporary assignment to an FCS post.

**B**ecause food exports are vital to the U.S. economy, the Department of Agriculture has officers in the Foreign Agricultural Service (FAS) promoting sales of U.S. food products around the world. In essence, Foreign Agriculture Service (FAS) officers do the same thing in the agri-

## DEPARTMENT OF AGRICULTURE

cultural sector that Foreign Commerical Service (FCS) officers do in the area of services and manufactured products. In fact, the two often cooperate in areas of overlap (say, forest products and building materials), or in cases where FAS has no officer available to help a U.S. agricultural exporter.

Service with FAS can lead to international marketing positions with private sector agribusiness concerns, both individual companies and industry cooperatives. FAS officers with a flair for salesmanship may also get into the very lucrative area of international commodity sales, usually through a trading company specializing in agricultural products. As is true of other multiplier and consulting-type services, every day exposes you to new career possibilities.

If you have a solid background in agronomy, you may become one of the experts that the Ag Department sends overseas to help other countries develop their agricultural potential. These assignments may lead to work with the United Nations, other international food programs, or programs of foreign nations.

The Department of Agriculture also has offices in cities where agriculture is an important part of the local economy. These offices are connected with Agricultural Attaches and Agricultural Trade Offices in U.S. Embassies worldwide. Employment here can create excellent contacts in agribusiness, and lead to a variety of overseas assignments.

Customs offices are located mostly in cities that are ports of entry and exit. ("Port" includes highways and international airports.) U.S. Customs Service (USCS) is responsible for controlling the flow of goods in and out of the United States, including shipments of high-technology and military items to foreign powers. Stateside offices maintain liaison with customs agents at U.S. Embassies overseas.

## U.S. CUSTOMS SERVICE (DEPARTMENT OF THE TREASURY)

Like most bureaucratic agencies, USCS (which has civil service entry procedures and salary scales) offers slow advancement. However, it's a good place to learn about U.S. Customs law and procedure, and get a first-hand experience of the problems facing both importers and exporters dealing in high-tech or restricted products. This experience, in turn, can be parlayed into a position with an exporter, importer, custom house broker or import agent. Some enterprising ex-customs service officers go into business for themselves or with foreign freight forwarders, providing consulting on how to get products into the United States. With U.S. protectionism on the rise, this secondary tack should be increasingly in demand.

U.S. Customs Service officers serve in a variety of overseas assignments, including monitoring illegal diversions of high technology and military equipment to the Soviet bloc and other areas. They also control the export of counterfeit items from foreign countries to the United States. Because the Department of Commerce (USDOC), which has the authority for controlling exports, has no powers of arrest, U.S. Customs provides the muscle for export control. Customs also works closely with the Drug Enforcement Administration (DEA) in monitoring and attempting to control the flow of illegal drugs into the United States. Customs work ranges from the boring (office routine or inspecting incoming travelers' luggage) to the very, very dangerous (making an arrest on an international smuggler). Service with USCS, which gives you a good picture of what's happening in world trade, can create good contacts with U.S. and foreign companies that need help with import procedures and export controls.

## U.S. AGENCY FOR INTERNATIONAL DEVELOPMENT (USAID)

USAID administers a variety of development assistance programs around the world, often through contract teams from American universities and other organizations. USAID programs embrace such diverse activities as redesigning a foreign educational system, providing food aid under the Alliance for Progress in Latin America, and giving grants for the construction of major projects. A major employer in the 1960s, when in many countries the USAID mission was larger than the U.S. Embassy, USAID has shrunk dramatically as former aid recipients have become more self-sufficient and U.S. deficits have led to cuts in the U.S. foreign aid program. Most USAID assignments overseas are for specific projects that may last a few months or two or three years, usually in very underdeveloped countries. For this reason, the main value of USAID experience often is limited to general foreign awareness and some language proficiency. Pay and benefits are comparable to the Foreign Service and Foreign Commercial Service (FCS).

## U.S. INFORMATION AGENCY (USIA)

This Washington-based U.S. Government agency is responsible for promoting a favorable image of the United States around the world. For some reason, overseas the organizations called U.S. Information Service (USIS).

USIS handles liaison with the media at U.S. Embassies and Consulates abroad, and operates cultural centers which usually include a library and facilities for art shows, exhibits, recitals, conferences and other cultural activities. In addition, there are special USIS programs to further close relations with students, academicians, journalists, and other groups in the host country. After USIS, your career can proceed to virtually any aspect of public relations management, or to educational or academic affairs.

Because its mission is to reach out to the people of a country (which is different from the embassy or consulate mission of providing liaison with the host-country government and representing the interests of Americans), USIS has branches not only in major cities, but in smaller cities as well. Within this broad presence created by relatively large numbers of small offices, USIS keeps American staff at a minimum; in fact, a USIS officer is often the only American in the office. This means fewer employment opportunities, but those who are hired enjoy much more responsibility and independence than is available to other U.S. Government officers overseas.

## OTHER U.S. GOVERNMENT AGENCIES

**A** wide variety of other U.S. Government agencies (including the Department of Labor, the Drug Enforcement Agency (DEA), CIA and others) offer international career opportunities. Contact the nearest Federal Office Building to get the Washington addresses of various agencies so you can write for information. Try to talk to local agency officers as well.

## CHAMBERS OF COMMERCE

## U.S. CHAMBER OF COMMERCE

**D**on't make the common mistake of confusing the U.S. Chamber of Commerce (COCUSA), which is a private-sector organization made up of dues-paying members, with the U.S. Department of Commerce (USDOC), which is a branch of the U.S. Government. U.S. Chamber members are local chambers of commerce in cities throughout the United States, and American Chamber of Commerce chapters overseas. Like all national multipliers, the U.S. Chamber is both a clearinghouse for information and a voice for the membership. Because of its huge, widely scattered membership, the U.S. Chamber won't normally be a source of specific, direct leads for you. You'll use it mainly to identify member organizations and to discover useful international currents by noting the major concerns of member organizations.

Let's suppose you have expertise that you're sure could give you an international career based in Indonesia (or any other specific country). You speak the language, you've studied the history, you know what the economy's doing. You may even have been there, but at the time you didn't think about international career opportunities. How can you help turn your expertise into meaningful business contacts that can contribute to your career?

In this type of situation, the U.S. Chamber is a good starting point for you. At a bare minimum, they can tell you the name, address and contact person of the American Chamber (AmCham) in your target country. They may also have knowledge of the membership (including directories), which will give you a very complete picture of American business activity there. (U.S. companies aren't forced to join AmCham, of course, but virtually all of them do.) They can tell you whether or not the AmCham in Indonesia belongs to a regional AmCham association. (In fact, it does: APCAC, the Asia-Pacific Council of American Chambers of Commerce.) Finally, they may have copies of position papers and reports from Indonesia (and APCAC) that will give you a very good idea of the problems, issues and concerns of U.S. businesses in both the country and the region. You can use this information to plan your strategy in targeting and approaching companies with present or potential business interest in the region. As you can see, this is a perfect example of how multipliers become sort of a one-stop clearinghouse of opportunity via information.

# AMERICAN CHAMBER OF COMMERCE OVERSEAS (AMCHAM)

The overseas branches of U.S. businesses usually start local chapters of a U.S.-style chamber of commerce called "AmCham" in any foreign city where there's a significant U.S. business presence. The U.S. Chamber of Commerce in Washington, DC, or the U.S. Embassy or Consulate in the foreign city can provide you with the address, telephone number, and name of the appropriate contact person at the overseas American Chamber (AmCham).

An AmCham chapter functions very much like a local chamber of commerce in the United States, but committees and activities reflect the particular problems of doing business in a foreign country. Each chapter normally has volunteer committees organized to deal with problems and issues ranging from local labor laws and taxes to joint venture procedures and the protection of patent rights. AmChams work closely with the commercial and other sections of U.S. Embassies and Consulates, in much the same way that a local chamber of commerce in the U.S. cooperates with the mayor's office.

Contacts with AmCham can be among the most useful that you make, but don't waste their time and yours by going after a position with AmCham or a member company unless you're truly qualified for it. In addition, I usually advise against making any moves to get a position through AmCham connections until you've spent at least several months working with AmCham and letting the members see what you're made of. If you approach AmCham staff or members before you've made it evident that you have something to offer, you run a real risk of defeating your own purpose.

Unless you're overseas, or planning to be there, don't expect to generate specific opportunities through AmCham. From a stateside location, what you should be looking for is information: membership directories, names of key committees, membership in regional AmCham umbrella associations, articles and position papers that will give you a reading on the major trends and issues in the country in question. Virtually all AmChams put out a monthly publication; these range from slick, bound, four-color glossies to stapled black-and-white printouts, but all have a lot of useful information. If you're going to be in a specific country, or if you're concentrating you efforts on landing a job there, you may want to become an associate member of the local AmCham and receive the publication.

If you are overseas, AmCham membership is almost a must to help you develop your career. You needn't be affiliated with a large company, either; you can join as an individual or associate member. Just as you would with a local chamber in the United States, get involved in committees where you have or want to develop expertise. Many AmCham members have told me that being active and committed to the organization got them offers that they never would have received otherwise.

If you have expertise on business-related topics (actions taken by stateside multipliers to open up host-country markets, new U.S. rulings on counterfeiting, new reverse investment plans by host-country companies, and so on), consider making a presentation to the appropriate AmCham committee or at a general meeting of a smaller chapter. The members are always eager to learn of the latest internationally related business developments in the United States, and a good, solid presentation can go a long way toward establishing you as a credible international expert.

In the United States, local chamber of commerce members are local businesses and individuals, with most businesses represented by their chief executive. In general, the local chamber of commerce speaks for the mainstream local business community, and works to promote policies

## LOCAL CHAMBERS OF COMMERCE IN THE U.S.

that will improve the local business environment. Naturally, the scope of chamber activities varies enormously from one city to another, but chambers are involved in lobbying for favorable business tax rates, promoting the construction of stadiums, convention centers, and other community facilities, investigating the advisability of international trade facilities, attracting new capital investment (both from within the United States and from overseas), developing tourism, and similar activities.

Within each chamber, there are normally a number of committees or divisions (taxation, tourism, and so on) that correspond to the members' major areas of concern. In larger cities, the chamber of commerce usually has some sort of international division, that handles functions like trade and investment missions, international conferences, and seminars on international business topics. If you become a member and play an active part, you'll be in frequent contact with local businesses that have international interests and give them a chance to see what you have to offer. If you're involved in projects that help their business, they're getting a no-risk, no-obligation demonstration of your capabilities, and you're turning yourself from an unknown quantity into a potential staffer, manager or executive of proven value.

If the chamber in your city is small, or lacks an international division, rejoice! This is a perfect opportunity for you. Most smaller communities are keenly aware of the importance of economic diversification, including international trade and investment. If you have international expertise or are willing to develop it, you can take the helm and provide the leadership needed to get your community moving in an international direction. In the process, you'll put yourself in a choice position to take advantage of the opportunities you'll help the group develop. In any city, big or small, chamber membership can do good things for both your awareness and your image. There's no way to get involved if you're on the outside looking in.

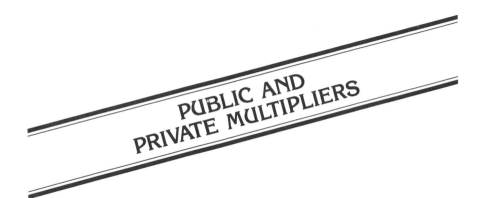

Although they go by many different names, these offices at all levels have similar objectives: to stimulate regional or local economic growth by promoting trade and international investment (so-called "reverse investment" or "inward investment") in their areas. As with private multiplier organizations, a position in one

## TRADE, BUSINESS, AND ECONOMIC DEVELOPMENT OFFICES IN THE U.S.

of these offices can give you excellent exposure and very, very useful contacts; in effect, every business you assist is a potential future employer. Your duties may include organizing trade and investment missions, attracting groups of foreign buyers to state or local trade shows, organizing participation in overseas trade events, counseling businesses on export opportunities, and assisting foreign businesses that want to set up manufacturing in your state or region.

These are usually only in state capitals and one or two other major cities in the state. They promote trade and investment to create jobs and increase prosperity in the state. In addition to providing export consulting services, they mount trade and investment missions overseas and host visiting delegations.

## STATE TRADE DEVELOPMENT OFFICES

Some of the staff and managerial positions are political, while some are not. The size of the staff and the salaries paid vary enormously according to the state's commitment to international trade and business, and the amount of money in the budget. Many people say that these positions combine the best of comparable government and private sector positions: less bureaucracy than the Department of Commerce (USDOC), and better experience and exposure than in a chamber of commerce. Furthermore, since many states have overseas offices in major market areas, a stateside position with a state office often leads directly to a stint overseas. Many of them pay even less than chamber of commerce positions, however (sometimes on the order of $20,000), so you may find yourself going for value rather than price.

Surprisingly, it's not always necessary to be a native or even a resident of the state to qualify for one of these positions, so don't limit your inquiries to your own state. The big problem in these jobs is usually politics: you may have to know someone to get the job, and your tenure may end when your patron falls from favor. This is by no means universal, however, since many growth-oriented areas realize that professionalism, not politics, gets the best results. Because of the variety of procedures among the fifty states, you'll have to talk with in-state sources to find out how the hiring procedure really works. As in almost every area, activity and contacts in multipliers can do a lot for you in this regard.

Depending on how aggressive your state is, these jobs may offer considerable overseas travel. Future career moves may include switching to an overseas office run by your state, entering the Foreign Commercial Service (FCS) or the Department of Commerce (USDOC), and many private sector businesses including trading companies, companies that organize international conferences and trade events, or firms that want to export their own products. You may also find attractive opportunities with foreign firms that you've helped to locate in your state.

**M**any of the same public sector agencies that have stateside offices also have positions in overseas locations. Although foreign language ability is a prerequisite for many of these jobs, some of them don't require it. The most common overseas offices are those run by individual U.S. states, and by local or regional port authorities trying to increase use of their ports by foreign shippers.

## TRADE, BUSINESS AND ECONOMIC DEVELOPMENT OFFICES OVERSEAS

The commercial section of the U.S. Embassy or Consulate in a foreign city should have a directory or listing of individual states' offices. Contact these offices to find out what companies from your state are doing business in the host country, and what sectors and activities seem to be the most promising for business expansion. The state reps are usually far more personable and less bureaucratic than embassy personnel, so you may develop good contacts here. Although you may come up with specific leads — and certainly you should always try to do so — more often these offices will be important as sources of general information that will increase your ability to add to your Big Picture.

Because the level of expertise required is usually much higher than for a stateside office, these jobs pay considerably more. Again, there's a considerable range, but $60,000 or so (including overseas incentive pay and cost-of-living) isn't uncommon. Some states use an innovative incentive method: they give the overseas rep enough to run an operation (say, $250,000 per year, including salary and all office overhead and expenses) and let the rep decide how to allocate it. As long as set criteria of contacts made and business generated are met, there is a lot of leeway. If the rep falls short, he/she is out of a job.

Because people in these positions are at the center of their state's international business activity, they can tack to many different private sector jobs without difficulty. After all, every day they're exposed to new international career possibilities through their work on behalf of business clients. However, since they have tremendous freedom and responsibility, plus a good income and a very interesting life, few of them seem to want to do so. Because of this low turnover, most new openings are in new offices, and access is often through previous experience in a stateside office.

International trade associations, like other multipliers, provide their members with information (seminars, conferences and regular publications on international trade and business matters), conduct trade missions and trade shows, and make their members' needs known to larger multipliers (including the chamber of commerce) and to government. Their areas of concern include such things as foreign trade zones, customs clearance problems, government assistance to exporters, and local port facilities.

## LOCAL WORLD TRADE ASSOCIATIONS OR INTERNATIONAL TRADE ASSOCIATIONS IN THE U.S.

The members of these multipliers are local businesses and individuals interested in international trade and business. Many or most of them also are members of the local chamber of commerce.

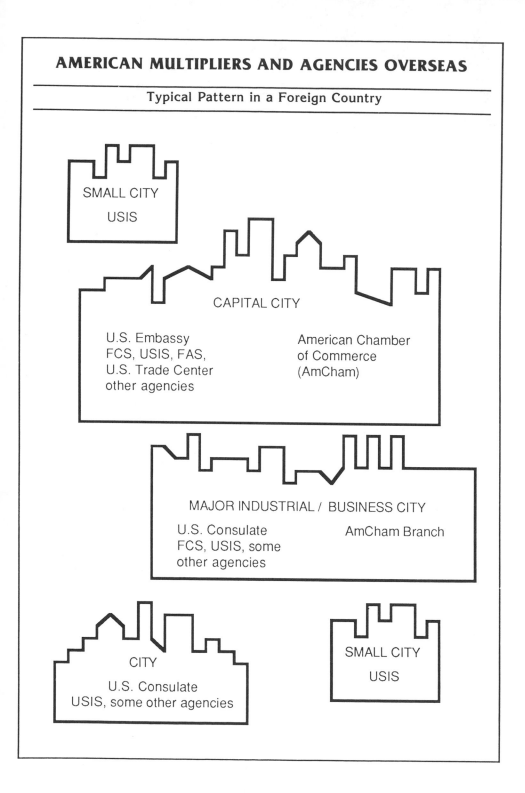

# AMERICAN MULTIPLIERS AND AGENCIES OVERSEAS

## Typical Pattern in a Foreign Country

SMALL CITY
USIS

CAPITAL CITY

U.S. Embassy
FCS, USIS, FAS,
U.S. Trade Center
other agencies

American Chamber
of Commerce
(AmCham)

MAJOR INDUSTRIAL / BUSINESS CITY

U.S. Consulate
FCS, USIS, some
other agencies

AmCham Branch

CITY
U.S. Consulate
USIS, some other agencies

SMALL CITY
USIS

Typically, larger local businesses are represented by international managers or VP's; smaller businesses (especially service businesses like freight forwarders, custom house brokers, international consulting firms, and others) are often represented by CEO's, including owners. This means that many of the career opportunities you can create are no higher than middle management levels, since the people you deal with in the trade association will normally be hiring subordinates, not equals. However, I've also seen international trade association involvement lead directly to higher level spots (including a VP international and the director of a trade promotion institute) when outgoing top executives recommended fellow trade association members to be their successors.

If you're the entrepreneurial type, international trade associations are also a good environment in which to make contacts leading to a position as a partner, or as an associate or employee on a retainer-plus-commission basis. Most aggressive trading companies, exporters and consultants belong to an international trade association, and they're ready-made vehicles for putting your own ideas into practice. Basically, they provide an address and the credibility of a going concern, and you provide new ideas on sources or markets for products or services. Using their name and office facilities, you do much of the legwork to generate new business for them and for yourself. This is an especially good approach for attorneys, teachers (who have a steady income and considerable free time) and housewives, military, and other people entering the career market after a prolonged absence. It can be especially effective if you're returning from overseas with foreign contacts and a specialized knowledge of foreign markets and products.

Because of mushrooming American interest in international trade and business, there's always the possibility of founding an international trade association if your community doesn't have one already. This action can be part of your strategy to create or expand the international activities of the company where you're employed. At first, the results may seem small compared to the effort, but don't let that stop you; even though it may take some time, the need is there. There is no community in the United States that couldn't profit from more international business activity. I've seen international trade associations idling at the dock for lack of members, and then have the membership shoot up so fast that they could barely keep up with it. One of the best success stories I've seen happened in San Diego, where a hard-working but tiny group that went through years of virtual anonymity suddenly exploded into an organization with over 600 member firms and a voice so loud that U.S. Senators pay careful attention to what it's saying. This growth has created opportunities for a lot of people, including the founders.

These include organizations such as the National Machine Tool Builders Association, National Sporting Goods Manufacturers Association, and many others. Most major industries have some sort of industry association, to do for a specific industry what chambers of commerce do for their cities: promote the welfare of

## BUSINESS AND TRADE ASSOCIATIONS (NATIONAL AND LOCAL)

the members' businesses through lobbying, providing information, and organizing member participation in conferences, seminars and trade events. Even smaller industries like manufacturers of hunting knives or archery equipment have active associations. Smaller industry associations often are members of a larger association, so that their members can enjoy the leverage of the larger organization.

Like their members, many of these organizations are just beginning to discover the advantages of international activity. This means few ready-made opportunities as a staff member, but many chances to play the role of consultant by creating international programs. If you contact an industry multiplier to get information on their membership profile and international concerns, you'll be able to form a picture of the possibilities.

You might convince an organization to promote its members' participation in an international trade fair with you as coordinator of the project. You might work with an export management company (EMC), either as an employee or as a consultant, to generate exports for the members of a specific association. On an individual company basis, you can use the association directory to locate members in your area, and work with them (perhaps through the chamber or international trade group) to develop their international business. This is an area in which you can develop your entrepreneurial spirit of exploration with the flexibility and diversity of the international career market to come up with totally new tacks.

If the industry you're employed in has an industry association, use it to develop your international career potential. Find out what activities they're involved in, and see how you can participate in existing international programs, or help create new ones. You may be able to develop joint activities with a local international multiplier such as the creation of a specific industry committee within an international trade group, or a jointly sponsored trade mission.

If you come up with practical ideas to help increase exports, the Department of Commerce (USDOC) District Office should be interested in cooperating with you, perhaps by recruiting companies for a trade mission or trade show.

Not every community has all the organizations in the following list, and some may have ones that don't appear here. I've discussed in some detail the most important ones and some of the ways you can use them to further your international career goals.

## OTHER ORGANIZATIONS AND AGENCIES

And the less important ones—is it really necessary to check them out? Yes, at least to be aware of their existence and scope of activities. It's like knowing that Europe exists and being able to locate it on a world map: you may never do business there, but if you don't even know of its existence, your international competence in every area will be subject to doubt, and justifiably so. Although the creation of your international career involves an exciting and fascinating voyage of discovery, keep in mind that you're not the first person to sight the new territories beyond the horizon. Small though their numbers may be, the informed members of the international business community—the ones who may be called upon to pass judgment on your fitness for a top-notch international position—already know about the international agencies and organizations at home and abroad. Since they consider this knowledge to be a minimum requirement for professional competence, you overlook it at your peril.

You can raise your level of competence by knowing something about every local group involved in international activities. It's up to you to assess their potential usefulness and budget the time and energy you spend on them accordingly. As you explore and discover, you'll meet internationally active people, all of whom know other internationally active people. The name of the game is contacts—special contacts—and you never know when one is going to open a door for you. *Who you know is part of what you know*, so don't disdain knowledge of any organization; they're all made up of people who can help you.

■ **Mayor's Office.** The international section of the mayor's office handles the political and protocol aspects of the city's international life. In general, the mayor's office works closely with the chamber on all issues, including international ones. (The relationship between the mayor's office and the local chamber of commerce is similar to the one between a U.S. Embassy or Consulate and an overseas American chamber of commerce chapter.) Any position here is likely to be political, but you may get tips on international activity that you can become involved in as a means of building a network and keeping abreast of developments.

■ **Sister City and Sister State Societies.** These organizations promote relations with designated sister cities and states (or provinces) in various countries. Foreign counterpart groups often attach more commercial importance to these relations than do American members, but increasing numbers of Americans are beginning to see the business possibilities. If you're active in the local sister city society, you're in an ideal spot to meet visiting foreigners whose business plans may mean opportunities for you. If you have expertise on a country where your city has a sister city relationship, a lecture or seminar to the society can give you a higher international profile and generate potentially valuable contacts.

Check with the mayor's office in your community to find out where they have sister cities. Again, your objective is to get involved and acquire knowledge.

■ **Port Authority.** On the international side, the port authority promotes use of the port by foreign shippers. The port authority may also have land and facilities that they're eager to sell or lease to foreign interests for warehousing, packaging and assembly operations. If you're a real estate broker or consultant, knowledge of such properties can make a major contribution to your international potential. Appointment to the port authority itself is political, and staff and management positions are few but it never hurts to find out what there is.

Many port authorities have overseas representatives (usually foreign nationals) in major foreign port and industrial cities, and participate in trade and investment missions, especially if the port is associated with a free trade zone or foreign trade zone.

■ **State offices dealing with international issues.** These are especially active in states bordering on Mexico and Canada. Some states have special offices to deal with international issues of particular importance to the state. There's not much here in the way of direct employment, but through involvement in conferences and other activities, you can make good contacts.

■ **Convention and Tourism Bureau.** As the name implies, this agency works to attract tourists, including those from abroad, and major conventions to the city or region. It cooperates with the mayor's office, chamber, and economic development agency. Employment opportunities are limited and specialized, but possible future tacks include the Travel and Tourism Administration (USTTA), and the international hotel and resort industry.

■ **University center for international studies.** The U.S. academic community is right in step with America's increasing involvement in international trade, business and related matters. Many U.S. colleges and universities have special centers and programs dealing with specific geographic areas overseas, and more are springing up each year. These centers can be valuable sources of information and opportunities, and can also do a lot to enhance your local profile and contacts if you have sufficient expertise to be featured as a speaker or give a course on some international topic.

■ **Foreign Trade Zone (FTZ).** An FTZ allows foreign manufacturers to bring parts, components, and partially finished goods into the United States, do assembly or other value-added processing, and ship them out again without paying duty. Often an FTZ is located in, and administered by, a port authority. Because of the large numbers of potential industrial tenants in an FTZ, it's another attractive possibility for commercial and industrial real estate experts.

■ **Economic Development Agency.** This type of agency may be city-wide, county-wide, or regional in scope. The purpose is to attract new business investment to the area. These agencies are usually quite small, but since they often make special efforts to attract foreign investment, they can be a very good place to develop an international career. Salaries are usually similar to those paid by chambers of commerce ($25,000 to $60,000 for managerial positions). Economic development agencies work closely with (and in some cities are part of) the chamber of commerce.

■ **Foreign embassies or foreign consulates.** Foreign embassies (Washington, DC only) and foreign consulates (major U.S. cities) represent the interests of foreign governments in the United States. They offer very limited staff and management opportunities, but if you can get a position, it can be valuable in terms of generating contacts, especially in the foreign business community.

■ **Foreign government agencies, in the United States or overseas.** Foreign government agencies, including embassies, trade offices, and the like, need foreign (to them) employees (that's you), mainly to deal with the public, handle routine correspondence in English, correct English translations, make summaries of the English-language news, do market research, and similar jobs. Although the level of work may not be very high (just as in the U.S Foreign Service, the better managerial positions are reserved for citizens), it gives you experience, exposure, and credibility. Especially if the job is overseas, you have the additional advantage of learning a language for later professional use.

If you have control over two foreign languages plus your native English, you may be able to create a three-way situation like working at a Latin American embassy in the Orient or an Asian embassy in Europe. Since English is not only the world's most widely spoken language, but also the language of international business and diplomacy, your ability as a native speaker satisfies one of the main requisites for this sort of job. A second factor in your favor is the relatively advanced state of language teaching in the United States, especially in exotic or "hard" languages like Japanese, Korean, Chinese, and Arabic. Since most smaller or third world countries offer few chances for such study, businessmen and diplomats from those countries are often totally adrift overseas.

In the Orient, for example, some businessmen and diplomats from Latin America and elsewhere speak neither English nor the language of the host country. In this type of situation, there's a crying need for a qualified person to bridge the language gap — often at a higher level of responsibility than would normally be available to a foreign staffer. Furthermore, since few of the host-country businesspeople will speak a third-world language (many of them have all they can handle with English), this unique role makes you virtually the only channel of communication for business transactions in both directions. The future career possibilities that derive from this strategic position are obvious, since for many businesses you've become their only link with their interests and contacts in the other country.

Salaries usually aren't high. Many start somewhere in the $20,000 range, depending on the country doing the hiring, but there are higher priced positions to be found, and the value is almost always exceptional.

■ **Foreign government trade offices.** Top management positions are usually reserved for their nationals, but there are lower management and staff positions involving economic analysis, market research, promotions of foreign imports (including trade shows and trade missions), and facilitation of foreign direct investment and joint ventures. Salaries are low (perhaps starting in the low 20s) and long-term advancement limited, but the value is definitely there; you'll learn about trade and international business, make contacts, and become very marketable both to foreign companies doing business in the United States and to U.S. importers, operators of Foreign Trade Zones, and others. These positions are usually filled by an open application procedure, but if you've been active in local ethnic community multipliers associated with the country in question, you may have an inside track.

■ **Other foreign government offices.** Examples include travel and tourism offices and other specialized offices dealing with specific sectors such as fishing. Each foreign consulate should be able to tell you exactly what offices their government has in your community and nearby metropolitan areas.

■ **Foreign multiplier organizations.** In larger U.S. cities, you can find organizations like foreign chambers of commerce, foreign residents' associations, and similar multipliers. Like foreign companies operating in the United States, these outfits don't offer much in the way of in-house advancement, and, like American multipliers, they may lack the financial resources to pay impressive salaries. At the same time, they combine the advantages of foreign companies and American multipliers: credibility, exposure, and variety of responsibilities.

As foreign direct investment and manufacturing activity increases in the United States, you can expect increasing opportunities with foreign multipliers. If you've made contact with foreign companies in your community through existing multiplier activities, you may even be the catalyst for the creation of a new multiplier (with a position for you to occupy) to meet the needs of foreign companies. If there's a large enough foreign chamber of commerce or foreign merchants' association in your community already, any contacts you've made there may lead to a position for you, especially if you have language skills. Possible duties might include liaison with other local multipliers, researching business opportunities for members, and organizing meetings and functions (overseas travel will probably be nil). Although you'll probably be limited to part-time work, the additional contacts you'll make in member firms and other organizations will be invaluable.

■ **Private-sector liaison organizations for business.** In some countries, bilateral organizations have been formed to promote investment and business contacts between U.S. interests and their foreign counterparts. Short term, there's little that this type of organization can do for your career in terms of concrete leads. However, you can identify the corresponding outfit in the United States for future contact there. Like much of the information you should acquire, the mere knowledge of these organizations is important because if you lack it, you're clearly ignorant of what's going on in the field. Your objective is to be a specialist, an expert with unique skills and talents. If you don't know the other players, their positions, and their assignments, you probably won't be selected by any team.

# 5

PUBLIC SECTOR VS. PRIVATE SECTOR

**B**y now, I'm sure you're getting an idea of the variety of international career opportunities that are waiting to be developed, especially through internationally oriented multipliers. Before you go charging off through the breakers after them, however, I'd like to give you a bit more in the way of general information — charts and maps, as it were. Otherwise, you'll spend more time shipping water and running aground than enjoying what should be an exciting and rewarding cruise toward your destination.

To refine your tactics, and to have an even better idea of the ports of call, you need to study the private sector side of the international marketplace, learn how it's structured, and find out what general categories of opportunities exist. Once you know what's out there and what interests you, you can focus on the points where the lines of interest and opportunity cross. These are the Xs on your map, the places where you can find your bonanza.

**W**e're living in an information age, and to succeed in building the kind of career you want, you've got to keep current on factors in the international career environment that affect your chances of reaching your goal. Raw information isn't enough, of course. To make sense of the great variety of opportunities available, you've got to analyze, evaluate, and categorize. In the case of multipliers and government agencies, much of this work has been done for you by the organizations themselves: they're broken down into clearly defined functional subdivisions whose names (example: "U.S. Travel and Tourism Administration") give you a good idea of what they do.

For private sector businesses, you have to dig a little deeper, mainly because private businesses have to follow the flow and keep pace with the changes in the international environment. It's not enough to know what a company does; you also need to have some idea of trends that affect the company and the industry of which it's a part.

To understand the environment and develop your Big Picture, form the habit of seeing everything in terms of different international career possibilities. When you read international news and business articles, think about the specific opportunities and positions behind the people and organizations involved—in other words, what's happening, and how you might fit into it. You'll find it useful to start a list of general possibilities (examples: "Brazilian aircraft industry", "Mongolian yak breeding") that interest you. Later, you can refine your general list and target specific opportunities, but to understand what those opportunities really mean in career terms, you need to consider ways to assign them to career categories. At the same time, you need to weigh the relative advantages of the public sector and the private sector. After all, the environment in which you work can have an overwhelming impact on your career.

# PUBLIC OR PRIVATE SECTOR?

In many ways, comparing the two sectors is a real apples-and-oranges exercise. In contrast to the relatively constant and predictable nature of the public sector (where even the financial crises, which are always resolved, occur like clockwork at the end of the fiscal year), understanding the private sector is like getting a fix on a moving object while you yourself are in motion. However, this difference of kind—which explains why planned economies don't work, and why bureaucrats and entrepreneurs almost never see eye-to-eye—can be the basis for examining the two sectors as career environments. Each has its distinct advantages and drawbacks, and each can add different valuable components to your international career.

In general, the public sector is more protected. You're sheltered from almost every type of storm, from layoffs to arbitrary actions by foreign officials. On the other hand, the shelter of a snug harbor doesn't give you much room to maneuver, and if you're the type who likes the sensation of an occasional high-speed, high-risk tack with one hull out of the water and waves curling off the bow, the private sector may be a better environment for you. If your choice isn't that clear-cut, you can often find a middle course, either by going with a larger private sector outfit, which will give you both relatively high job security and reasonably good career mobility, or by getting into a smaller office overseas with a public agency (local, state or federal), which gives you similar security while allowing you, in some cases, to be the captain of your own ship. Let's examine these options in some detail.

# BUREAUCRACY VS. INITIATIVE

To many people, the public sector is synonymous with bureaucracy; indeed, it's hard to think of any public organization worthy of your career attention that isn't highly bureaucratized. Certainly any agency of the Federal Government, from the Department of Commerce to the CIA, is run by a rule book several volumes thick (for most federal agencies overseas, it's the Foreign Affairs Manual (FAM) in eight volumes plus supplements), which is backed up by mountains of forms that have to be filled out in duplicate, triplicate, or quintuplicate before anyone will make a move. One amusing thing about this paperwork is the existence of a series of forms with the designation "OF" for "optional form". Try to exercise the option of not using the form, and see how far you get!

Since this sort of formalistic overkill is anathema to most dynamic, upwardly mobile international careerists, many of them automatically head for the private sector. Is the situation there any different? Virtually all large U.S. corporations are ruled by equally thick manuals, which in many cases are far less clear or consistent than their public sector counterparts. Furthermore, as any frustrated international manager can attest, the bureaucratic layers in U.S. multinationals can often match the U.S. Government when it comes to sluggishness and inflexibility.

However, while public sector bureaucracy seems universal and absolute, private sector bureaucracy tends to be proportional to the size of the company. This means that in the private sector, you often can choose the degree of regulation and regimentation in your professional life simply by targeting companies of a certain size. Governments, on the other hand, are big, period, and since even smaller public agencies are part of the same massive whole, they all suffer from excessive bureaucratic restraints.

Another factor contributing to the bureaucratic nature of public sector agencies is the fact that they have no bottom line to worry about. Unlike private industry, they face no stockholders, make no profits, suffer no losses. They can and do incur deficits, of course, but no nonelective employee is likely to lose his/her job because of them. *This basic lack of accountability does more to kill creativity in public sector organizations than any other single factor.* Worse, initiative of any sort may be viewed as a threat because it implies change, which in turn implies more work. Since there's no profit motive, and promotions are based mostly on seniority, more work is just more work, not a chance to advance the fortunes of the organization or one's career.

If you think that you can make more headway by using your individual initiative and creativity, then you'll probably want to set sail for the smaller islands in the private sector archipelago. Here you can maneuver more freely, acquire a variety of experience, and have more chances to create new programs or products.

If, on the other hand, you believe that the vast resources and name recognition of a larger organization can provide the best site from which to launch your international career, you may well do better to sign on with a larger outfit, either public or private sector.

And therein lies a paradox: by opting for a smaller, private sector organization, you may find more freedom of movement, but if you go for a larger outfit, you have your choice of public or private sector.

In many cases, the unique characteristics of the international career environment can resolve the paradox and give you the best of both worlds. The secret is in the dual structure that evolves in many international organizations. On the domestic side, there's the familiar, bureaucratic corporate pyramid, but the international side tends to be more open and less rigid. In addition, in many companies the international division shows a similar environmental difference between the stateside and overseas parts of the operation. Managers and executives in stateside-international positions in the home office may enjoy more freedom than those in purely domestic slots, but they still are bound by many of the bureaucratic constraints that stifle creativity and initiative in domestic positions. If you're in the field overseas, however, you're often running your own shop, subject only to guidelines and reporting requirements rather than extensive supervision by the home office.

There's a lot of variation, of course. Some overseas managers and executives have a virtually free hand in everything, including planning marketing strategy, selecting partners and agents, and choosing office and manufacturing sites. At the other end of the spectrum (especially in the case of multinational service companies like banks or airlines) are companies that insist that the overseas manager follow fairly detailed plans issued by the home office. But even in these cases, as an overseas manager or executive, you generally have more autonomy than your stateside colleagues. In fact, the international environment even gives more flexibility to some public sector situations, and allows the size factor to come into play: officers at smaller overseas posts (consulates, Information Service branches, state trade office representatives) generally have far more freedom of action than other government employees, whether stateside or overseas. In both the public and private sectors, many overseas employees pursue the status and glamour of an embassy position, or the heavyweight image of the main in-country office of a company, so that smaller office positions—which have a lower profile but more freedom of choice—are often easier to come by.

## WHAT'S IN A NAME?

A larger organization usually offers something that few small companies can provide: prestige, or at least name recognition. My first international job, right out of college, was with the Bank of America, at that time the world's largest bank. Because I didn't believe that the bureaucratic environment in their international program was the best place for me to advance my career, I left after a relatively short stay. On several occasions, however, having that big name association in my background has done far more for me than later stints with smaller, unknown outfits. Never mind that I stayed longer, added more functional value, and learned more on these later jobs. The big name has the image.

The same thing is true of government work. The Commerce Department, my most recent employer, has a miserable reputation among the U.S. business community. A lot of it isn't Commerce's fault; it's served as a dumping ground for virtually any government function that needs a home. (How else can you explain Commerce's surrealistic, Jack-of-all-trades role as custodian of the National Aquarium, keeper of the Population Clock, and administrator of the International Trade Administration?) But many business people—and even other government officials—complain that Commerce headquarters is big, sluggish, unresponsive, and ineffective, and that many of these negative traits are affecting Commerce's overseas arm, the Foreign Commercial Service (FCS).

In spite of this, my tenure with the FCS has given me a far wider range of choice than I'd have had if I'd spent the same length of time with a little-known company. Logical? Perhaps not—or maybe it is recognized that the FCS is a cut above the head office. Whatever the explanation, name recognition is a powerful reason to give serious thought to starting or enhancing your international career with some time in a big, well-known organization.

# WHAT COLOR IS YOUR LIFEBOAT?

**W**ithin a given range of size and name recognition, there are some other notable differences between public- and private-sector careers. Until fairly recently, one major advantage of a public sector international career was security. Like tenured university professors, officers in organizations like the U.S. Foreign Service could pretty much count on being retained until retirement age, when they could retire on a modest but adequate pension.

The public sector still offers a higher degree of security, but things are changing. Some international public-sector careers may be more secure, others less so, but the trend is to increasing selectivity. In addition, the pressures of the federal debt and America's enormous trade deficit have increased the chances that even in the Foreign Service and other international federal jobs, employment conditions will be subject to increasing strains. In fact, there seems to be movement in that direction already, as fewer officers are able to make the higher levels of the Foreign Service, and the retirement system is being changed to reduce the level and duration of payments. Current Foreign Service policy, for example, calls for more hard-nosed adherence to a long-standing policy often known as "up-or-out": if you get passed over for promotion more than five or six times, you're "selected out" (a gentlemanly way of saying fired or forcibly retired). Promotion is theoretically on the basis of merit, but there are less objective factors that force successive cadres up — or out — more or less in unison.

In many ways, it's the same old corporate pyramid game, plus the bureaucratic disincentive of patronage and sympathy promotions. Nevertheless, because of the increasing importance of international trade, business and diplomacy, you generally enjoy more job security in the international public sector than in domestic goverment jobs.

How about private sector careers? In general, the chances for sudden termination are greater, since in addition to the risk of failure to make the cut at some point (one major international accounting firm has a policy of reducing each cadre of managers and executives by 33 percent at each round of promotions to keep the management structure from become top-heavy), there's always the possibility that your company or division will be sold. If this happens, there may not be room for you in the new organization, or the new ownership may decide to do away with the entire operation in which you've been involved. Even international managers or vice presidents can find themselves on an involuntary new tack after being forced off the old one as the result of a buyout.

Generally, public sector international careers tend to offer more opportunities for training and ongoing education (including language), and to be more secure but less financially rewarding. In virtually any U.S. Government position, for example, there are pay caps that keep even the top officers permanently in the middle class, and because both the civil service and foreign service promotion systems are designed to move everyone along at more or less the same rate, there's little chance to reach the top at all. Of course, in this environment there's not much financial reward for outstanding performance. I remember a group of foreign service officers chuckling wryly at a statement by a private sector multinational manager who said he planned to leave his huge company because even a remarkably successful year of service would be rewarded by at most a 10 percent raise in salary. In the foreign service and other government bureaucracies, the biggest raise you can get is less than a quarter of that!

Government bureaucracy presents some other drawbacks not usually encountered in the private sector. Most personnel matters, including hiring, promotions, assignments, and other actions of vital interest to your career are handled by faceless committees. In many cases, regulations make it impossible for you to discover the identity of these groups, let alone negotiate with them directly as you normally could in the private sector. As a result, many ambitious people in government bureaucracies quickly turn to in-house politics, a web of personal contacts, and all the zero-sum activities that make a truly outstanding international career impossible.

On the other hand, these same personnel systems—which often allow dead wood to float along at much the same speed you do—do protect you against the grossly inconsiderate or unfair actions that may cause rough sailing in the private sector. In the public sector, it would be virtually impossible, for example, to be hired away from a good overseas position, brought back to the United States for training, and dismissed six months later as part of a reorganization. Yet this sort of thing can and does occur all too often in private sector companies. And in general, the private sector pyramid is much steeper, with the result that even during stable periods more people are pushed off earlier in their careers. To compensate for this uncertainty, the private sector offers higher salaries and more generous perks and allowances, and provides greater incentives and opportunities for talent and individual initiative.

## SHELTER FROM THE STORM

**O**verseas, the public sector offers some major advantages. If you're in the Foreign Service (including FCS, FAS, USIS and other embassy or consulate agencies), you have diplomatic status, which can relieve you of many tension headaches. For example, you aren't subject to host-country taxes, so you're spared the hassles of figuring out how local tax regulations apply to you. (You file only with the I.R.S.) Diplomatic immunity, although pretty badly battered by everything from terrorist activity to smuggling by the diplomats of various countries, still gets you through customs and immigration faster, and keeps you from being shaken down by the police in countries where that sort of thing is common.

Your job's a lot easier, too, since you don't have to deal with the cantankerous reality of doing business in a foreign country. Your job is only to advise and assist, so regardless of the success or failure of negotiations with the local authorities, you can sleep at night. Not so in the private sector, where your career could take a quick turn for the worse if you're unable to resolve a problem generated by host-country policy changes.

There's literally no way to know when this sort of lightning will strike your ship — or right next to it. One friend of mine is living proof of how dicey private sector career life can be: while he was on his way to a meeting to sign a major contract for merchandise to be exported to the Philippines, the government closed the country to all imports because of political turmoil. If he hadn't been listening to the radio — or if the news had reached him just thirty minutes later — he would have committed his company to a huge purchase that had no chance of being sold. His fault? Not at all — but he's the one that would have had to walk the plank. To a U.S. diplomat or FCS officer, however, this type of arbitrary foreign government action isn't a business or career problem, but merely the subject of another reporting cable.

The long and the short of it is that many businesspeople who spend years overseas end up with mixed emotions about the professional side of it because of the hassles they've been subjected to, while most government types just don't feel that way. It's not a question of adaptability, but exposure: *international government jobs usually come with massive support systems, and the people in them simply aren't subjected to the daily buffeting that those in the private sector must face.* It's a lot tougher when you have to go off to turn a profit in someone else's home waters—especially when (as is often the case) they're full of sharks and pirates.

Luckily, you don't have to make a permanent choice between the two sectors. In many cases, it's highly advantageous for you to acquire skills (like the extensive language training available to members of the Foreign Service), contacts and exposure in one sector, and transfer them to the other sector in a tack that puts you closer to your career goals. You may make several of these changes during the course of your career. In fact, some U.S. Government agencies encourage their international specialists to do a stint in the private sector from time to time to broaden their background, and increasing numbers of international companies can see the value in letting managers acquire government contacts by spending a couple of years in the public sector.

All in all, the public sector (or a private sector multiplier) seems to be a better place to acquire general international skills, including language, overseas experience, understanding of foreign government procedures, and management of foreign personnel, while the private sector tends to foster more specialized expertise. Our discussion of multipliers covered public sector careers in detail, so let's look at some of the factors involved in international private sector careers.

## CAREERS WITH PRIVATE SECTOR FIRMS

**M**ost international career opportunities in the private sector are still in traditional manufacturing, marketing and service activities. As international business follows the shifting tides of world production, trade and economic development, new openings are constantly being generated. Sometimes, you'll find exceptional opportunities created by new expansion of well-traveled channels, as when rapid development and increasing prosperity in the Pacific basin produced dramatic increases in U.S. trade with longtime partners in established industries like automobiles, textiles, and other consumer items. On other occasions, new channels for career advancement appear as the result of significant shifts in production capability (such as PCs from Korea or Brazil) or the relocation of service industries (like the expansion of medical treatment centers and banking and financial services in Singapore). Additional opportunities are created if previously protected economic sectors or occupations are opened to foreign participation (for example, stock brokerage and the legal profession in Japan).

There are also increasing numbers of newer, specialized career possibilities. For example, you may set your sights on a career with a company that organizes trade fairs in the United States and overseas. Although this activity has a long history in Europe, it's fairly new in the United States, and should be a growth area for international employment over the next few years. In terms of wending your way to your international goal, it represents a very interesting leg of the journey, since it will give you exposure to the marketing side of a wide range of international businesses , both U.S. and foreign.

As the examples I've cited show, at present the majority of new international career opportunities are appearing in organizations active in the Pacific basin, especially in Northeast Asia (Japan, Korea, China) and the ethnic Chinese economies of Hong Kong, Taiwan and Singapore. The reasons aren't hard to understand: Latin America and Africa are unstable, and Europe (which until the 1980s was the region of greatest U.S. trade, investment and business presence) is generally characterized by flat economies, mature markets, and high concentrations of international expertise in virtually every field. In short, low demand and adequate supply. The Pacific basin, in contrast, offers a wide range of economic development (which means low cost land, labor and materials at one end of the spectrum and technological sophistication and significant buying power at the other), some of the fastest-growing economies in the world, and many unfilled career niches in all sectors. A classic case of low supply and high demand, the kind of international career-building environment you're looking for.

However, don't neglect possibilities elsewhere in the world. There are attractive niches everywhere, and by taking a little-used channel, you may come out far ahead of the competion. Latin America, for example, presents an overall scene of economic and political confusion, but certain countries, among them Brazil and Argentina, have surprising strength or potential in a number of sectors, including electronics, avionics, and vehicles. In Europe, the 1986 accession of Spain and Portugal to the European Economic Community (the E.E.C., or "Common Market") will generate new career opportunities for years to come. Even business disasters like the tainted wine scandals that hit Austria and Italy in 1985 and

1986 can create sudden, unexpected openings (in this case, for competing wines and other alchoholic beverages) in normally stable markets. Daily reading of one or more major international business publications (like *U.S. News and World Report* or the *Wall Street Journal*) can help you develop a feeling for where the opportunities are likely to be for you.

Whatever specific regions or industries you target, here are the major categories of private sector employers you should consider when planning your international career.

*W*hether presently engaged in international business or not, American companies are prime candidates for your next career tack. In the first place, you speak their language, and understand the thousands of cultural intangibles that shape their thinking. Secondly, there are no problems with

## AMERICAN COMPANIES

work permits and similar documentation. Finally, because of America's historically domestic orientation, there's tremendous potential demand—unrealized and unfilled.

Even a company with no international plans can be your starting point, if the company offers products or services with a significant international market. According to the U.S. Department of Commerce, *there are tens of thousands of American companies that could profit by exporting, but don't yet export.* Although the size of this still untapped career market makes it impossible to create a comprehensive list, you can develop ideas by asking the nearest Department of Commerce office and state trade offices what types of industries offer the best prospects in specific countries or regions. In addition, the short, current lists of new-to-export companies and products announced in regular Department of Commerce publications will give you a good indication of trends and currents that can help you get where you want to go.

To these companies, you can play the same role that Columbus did for the Spanish crown: discover new worlds of business for them to conquer by starting an international operation within the company—and an international career for yourself in the bargain. One friend of mine, who had a knowledge of the construction business and some contacts in the Middle East, did just that for a small, strictly local hardware and building supply wholesaler. He approached the owner, convinced him of the possibilities for sales into the lucrative Middle Eastern construction market, and signed on as the company's VP for international marketing, on a retainer-plus-commission basis. Low risk to the owner, possibly high rewards for all concerned.

This approach from the outside (as opposed to developing international opportunities from inside the company where you work), has limitless variations. Another professional acquaintance, for example, did something very similar after spotting some interesting possibilities while overseas on a study program. On his return to the United States, he contacted a hometown trading and international consulting company, presented his ideas, and worked his way into a very lucrative and exciting international position. What's the common denominator? Creativity, initiative, and *offering* something of value (the possibility of new business at little cost) *instead of asking* for a job handout.

When U.S. business began its overseas expansion in the 1950s and 60s, most executive and top managerial positions went to Americans. Later, however, as local nationals gained experience, it became less and less cost-effective to keep a U.S. citizen overseas when a local would do just as well, and considerable substitution took place, especially in countries where language, extremely difficult living conditions, or nationalistic sensibilities created problems for American managers. Nevertheless, there will always be career opportunities in U.S. companies overseas for aware, adaptable, linguistically competent Americans, but normally you'll need to offer more in the way of expertise than you would for a stateside-based position.

Since you have to offer more, you can expect to command a higher price. The package of benefits for overseas positions usually contains a number of items not normally found in stateside agreements which can run your total compensation up to double your normal stateside salary. The most important is housing; you should expect anything from a cash housing supplement to free, furnished quarters with all utilities paid—a benefit worth well over 50 percent of your base salary, in some cases.

In general, the less developed the country, the more luxurious the accommodations. In places like the Philippines, parts of Africa and South America, or the Asian subcontinent, these may include a spacious (5-bedroom or more) house, tennis court, pool, and landscaped grounds. This won't always be the case, of course. In the People's Republic of China, a nationwide housing shortage dictates that you'll live in a hotel. Additional perks often include a car and, in countries where the prevailing wage scale is low, a driver. Some companies may substitute a transportation allowance (say, $600 per month) in lieu of actually providing a car. If you have school-age children, you also can expect an education allowance to cover the cost of a private, English-speaking school.

Because long residence abroad involves not only inconveniences but extra expenses, many companies are willing to pay up to 10 or even 20 percent as overseas incentive pay, and if conditions are considered difficult, you should be able to negotiate a hardship bonus of as much as 20 percent of your base salary. If essentials are expensive or hard to come by, you should receive appropriate compensation in the form of a cost-of-living differential allowance.

Sometimes places that should be cheap, aren't. The People's Republic of China, for example, seems to have a national policy of gouging foreigners, and Lagos, Nigeria, of all places, is often rated the world's most expensive city because the scarcity of virtually everything means you have to make most of your purchases at exorbitant prices on the black market. If it appears that a host-country currency may soar against the dollar, you'll need to have some protection written into your agreement.

What kind of positions might you target? To help yourself sort out the virtually endless possibilities, subdivide them into categories, including the following.

■ **Manufacturing.** Many U.S. firms, under pressure from low-cost foreign competition, escape the relatively high cost of U.S. production by setting up their own factories in overseas locations with low labor costs. Some of these operations are joint ventures, others are 100 percent American invested. A great variety of industries are involved, but most are engaged either in some sort of labor-intensive production, including electronic components, sporting goods, shoes, textiles, toys and similar items, or the manufacture of products (like pharmaceuticals, chemicals, packaging including bottles and cans, fertilizer, fibers and others) that have a good market in the country or region and are either uneconomical to ship or face import restrictions.

These firms need resident U.S. managers to keep manufacturing costs down, oversee quality, coordinate the production of new lines, and help fight off the pirates and counterfeiters that inevitably try to copy successful products and trademarks. The problem with many of these jobs is that manufacturing sites may be located far from any major population center, which often means a lack of activities and services, including education. To get around this, some U.S. managers are forced to commute long distances, or live apart from their families during the week. In addition, you're pretty much tied to the plant or plants; this means you have to observe local working hours, most of which tend to be longer than in the United States. Most of these jobs are also straight salary (in the $40,000 to $60,000 range, plus allowances), but some have bonuses for maintaining high quality and low costs.

■ **Services.** The U.S. economy is primarily a service economy, and U.S. companies in transportation (including airlines), shipping, leasing, banking and financial services, insurance, hotels and others are very competitive internationally. The major U.S. firms in all these sectors have U.S. managers and representatives in principal cities of the world. Employment abroad in almost any service sector will bring you into contact with a wide variety of U.S. and host-country firms, which will increase your odds of spotting still further new opportunities. In some sectors, like hotels and airlines, you're virtually guaranteed to be the most popular expat in town; everyone wants to get close to the person who can get visiting firemen a discount at a good hotel, or give them an upgrade on their international airline flights. Salaries vary widely, but will be about the same as in the United States, plus overseas allowances including housing.

■ **Major projects.** This special category includes major construction and engineering works like power plants (conventional or nuclear), subways, highways, bridges, airports, dams, and other civil engineering projects. In addition to the construction and engineering aspects, many of these projects involve extensive opportunities for U.S. suppliers of goods and equipment. Nuclear power plants need security and safety equipment; subways need fare collection systems; airports need electronics, navigational aids, and a host of items for customer service. Each one of these peripheral product sectors creates the need for U.S. company presence that may range from one or two visits of a few weeks to a series of longer visits or a single stay lasting one or more years to supervise assembly, installation, and training. Salaries are usually the same as in the United States, with additional overseas allowances.

■ **Marketing.** Although most U.S. firms are unable to penetrate foreign markets successfully without strong host-country representation in the form of a local agent or distributor, many of them also maintain a resident U.S. manager or executive to oversee and coordinate marketing activities, and to look out for the company's best interests. As with manufacturing, the list of product categories is virtually endless. This type of position is a logical extension of the U.S.-based international marketing function; after a company has tested the waters and developed a degree of market presence in a foreign market, the next step is to set up an office there so that the American marketing manager can promote and coordinate sales throughout the region.

If you're an innovative self-starter, this type of position offers incredible possibilities. It's a real thrill to create an operation in one country, build it up, and then use it as a springboard to expand and build an empire in nearby countries. Moreover, you aren't tied as tightly to the home office as you are with sourcing and manufacturing, where you're basically responding to demand from the U.S. side of the company. Finally, there's a greater chance to determine your own income level by working for salary plus commission on sales. A reasonable arrangement for a small regional office would be a base salary of $40,000 to $60,000, plus allowances and a commission of about 2 percent. Of course, a larger operation would warrant a higher salary.

■ **Sourcing.** More and more U.S. companies are obtaining parts, components and finished products offshore. Particularly in the case of complicated or large items, this generates positions for Americans on either a long-term or short-term (up to two years) basis. In this sort of job, your duties range from finding suppliers to setting up a captive manufacturing operation (under which a foreign factory agrees to produce only for your company) or overseeing production and checking quality. Products might be anything from stuffed toys to computer parts or offshore oil rigs.

Sometimes, these positions evolve by accident. I've met people who came overseas to order and inspect a single shipment of parts or equipment, and ended up staying years because their company decided to place additional orders and needed someone on the spot to supervise things. In most cases, you'll be on straight salary, which will probably be somewhere between $35,000 and $50,000, plus additional allowances for housing, hardship, education, and cost of living.

■ **Capital equipment.** The sale of capital equipment to foreign manufacturing companies generates the need for U.S. technicians and some managers to install equipment, get it running, and train local personnel in operation and maintenance. In addition, after-sale service contracts create further opportunities for return visits. Most of these overseas career experiences are fairly short, from a few weeks to a few months, but they often can help you discover entirely new areas of opportunity that would never occur to you in the United States. As with major projects, you'll normally draw your regular stateside salary, plus additional expenses.

# FOREIGN COMPANIES OPERATING IN THE U.S.

**U**ntil just a few years ago, this category of opportunity was almost nonexistent. Ironically, recent U.S. protectionism (which aims to shut out foreign competition) has resulted in a surge of international career opportunities by stimulating foreign direct investment in the United States. (This, by the way, is the type of trend you should be on the lookout for.) The most publicized of the new arrivals have been from Japan, but other countries anxious to protect their presence in the U.S. market are right behind them. At the same time, foreign industries eager to develop technology have established smaller operations that serve as listening posts and conduits for technology transfer in high-tech areas like California's Silicon Valley. Finally, in spite of protectionism, foreign-owned banks, trading companies and marketing groups will continue to expand and prosper in the U.S. market.

At present, the opportunities with foreign companies in the United States are somewhat limited, but the experience of U.S. multinationals, who hired increasingly high percentages of local managers and executives as time passed, indicates that things should change for the better. Although many Asian companies in the United States—the most active investors of the 1980s—are in the earlier stages of the U.S. multinational pattern (in Japanese companies' U.S. operations, for example, over half of the executive directors and over a third of the managers are Japanese rather than American), the pursuit of economic efficiency should cause them to increase the number of Americans, especially whenever a weak dollar makes it more attractive to hire in the local (U.S.) economy.

Even in foreign outfits that reserve upper-level advancement for home country nationals, entry-level to mid-level positions can be very attractive because of the exposure, contacts and credibility the experience provides. Most of these jobs won't move you overseas, but they can get you into U.S. companies that will. After all, what better way to become knowledgeable about the foreign competition than by working for them?

How can you find out about foreign companies operating in your area? If the company where you work has international business, you can begin to meet more frequently with foreign partners, customers and suppliers. By getting to know them better, and learning more about their companies' plans and needs, you may well identify a good new tack.

Whether or not you're employed in an internationally active company, multipliers are another useful vehicle. Use the local chamber of commerce or international trade association (if your company doesn't belong, take out an individual membership) as a listening post and point of contact to learn more about international business in your community. If local possibilities are limited, consider making periodic trips to programs offered by multipliers in nearby metropolitan areas. You can increase your own chances of success by organizing a small group of local business and professional people from a local multiplier to attend such meetings as a group. The host organization will be flattered, and each member of the group – including you – can get much higher visibility and make more contacts than you could as an individual.

If you're just setting out on your career, inquire at foreign consulates and local multipliers to identify foreign importers, manufacturers, banks, and other outfits. At first, the work you do might not be very international in flavor (you see one computer terminal, you've seen 'em all), but that's OK if it meets your purpose, which is to put yourself in position and headed in the right direction.

## FOREIGN COMPANIES OVERSEAS

It's usually harder to break into a foreign company abroad (they don't know what to do with you, especially if you aren't totally fluent in the language), but there are some opportunities. If you work in a company with international business, or if you have access to international multiplier organizations, you can make contacts and develop leads using the same approach that I've discussed in connection with foreign companies in the United States. Foreign service companies, (including banks, accounting firms, brokerage firms, insurance companies, shipping companies, and others) are often especially attractive career targets because they need nonlocals (you) to deal with English-speaking client companies, and to assist the increasing numbers of host-country firms that need to understand U.S. financial and other practices in order to do business in America.

Likewise, host-country advertising agencies with certain types of accounts (for example, host-country hotels catering to foreigners, or foreign firms selling in the host country) need creative foreigners to service them. Since most large cities overseas have one or more English-language newspapers, and perhaps a couple of English-language radio and TV programs, there are usually opportunities in this area, which often offer the added advantage of high turnover among the expat population (your competition). Luckily, the most common language in the world is the one you speak — English — so your chances of employment are much better than nonEnglish speaking foreigners, and the relative lack of local competition can often get you in at a much higher level of responsibility and future opportunity than would be possible in the United States. Most of these opportunities aren't in Europe, but in lesser developed countries (LDC's) or in countries, many of them in Asia, where language is a major barrier. As elsewhere in the international career market, your own creativity and self-confidence are your only limits.

Don't disdain less glamorous jobs, however. If you lack significant management or other professional experience, you may find your work limited to correcting someone else's English in translations and business correspondence, doing editing or proofreading for local staff writers, or something else that's less than breathtaking. Be it ever so humble, this kind of experience can add considerable value to your inventory of career components, and will certainly contribute to your language resources and overall ability to handle yourself in a foreign environment. In addition, if you maintain an outgoing and creative attitude, you may well work your way into something better. Just as you would in the United States, use multiplier organizations to make contacts, spot opportunities, and prepare for the next leg of your international career voyage.

Because they're geared to host-country nationals, foreign (host-country) companies won't normally offer the overseas incentives, housing, and other allowances that you should expect to get from an American firm, and in many countries the salaries they pay are lower than in the United States. In addition, you'll be expected to work local hours, which in many countries run about ten hours a day and at least a half day on Saturday. As a result, you should be prepared to "go native" and like it. Employment with a foreign (host-country) firm will give you a good exercise in weighing price (salary and perks) against value (the irreplaceable expertise you can gain).

■ CHAPTER ■

# 6

## STATESIDE VS. "OVER THERE"

**A**s you build your international career, you'll be faced with a continual string of choices, including where you want to be based. Just as it's perfectly feasible to have a long and successful international career without ever living overseas, some people find they prefer to build their entire career and perhaps even retire in foreign settings. If you follow the strategy of tacking from one point to another, you can have ample opportunity to sample both stateside and overseas career environments, and steer a course that puts you wherever you can best meet your personal and professional goals.

## "INTERNATIONAL" MAY NOT MEAN "OVERSEAS"

**R**ecently, over lunch, the new country manager of an international trading company expressed envious admiration for my Foreign Service life. "It must be rather exciting, isn't it? Adventure, diplomatic parties, all the James Bond stuff . . ." Coming from him, this was a real surprise; after all, here was a guy who'd parlayed his job as private tennis instructor for foreign businessmen and their families into a business career that most diplomats would envy. But his comment got me thinking.

Just as being based in the United States has its advantages and limitations, so being overseas for long periods of time will have an effect on your career in any organization. Fairly early in your international career planning, you need to think about where you want to be based, and you'll want to make your decision a rational one. It's important to realize that life overseas — whether as a diplomat or a private sector businessperson — can often be as dull as yesterday's paper. Sure, when you first hit the beach in Tokyo, Rio or Casablanca, it's exotic, and the lift that you get from exploring a whole new country — customs, language, food, business practices, and all the rest — can give you a prodigious ability to ignore personal frustrations and leap professional obstacles at a single bound. But inevitably reality dawns. After the thrill is gone, your daily work routine might as well be taking place in Tuscaloosa, Rochester, or Chicago. In the morning and evening, you may be a traffic-jammed tollway commuter or a straphanger caught in a tempestuous, surging sea of chain-smoking humanity (most places overseas have yet to discover the joy of clean lungs). In between, your office environment may be just like any you'd find in the United States, complete with a local staff so fluent in English that you find your hard-earned command of the local language slipping away from lack of use.

Of course, there's no denying that many overseas assignments offer more glamour than comparable domestic or stateside-international positions. If you're in the diplomatic corps (as all Foreign Service 'officers, including FCS, FAS, and USIS are), you'll be invited to a steady round of parties and receptions. Commercial officers and overseas-based state trade representatives spend a lot of time hobnobbing with visiting U.S. mayors and state governors, and political and econ officers squire around visiting U.S. Senators and congressional delegations (or CODEL's, as they're known in State Department and embassy jargon). High-level contacts and galas aren't limited to the embassy set, either: American business-people often can play much more prominent social roles than they could at home, and foreign business customs (especially in the Orient) often call for a tremendous amount of extravagant after-hours socializing. But — unless you're a hard-core social butterfly with a cast-iron stomach and a liver to match — this, too, eventually becomes old-hat or physically debilitating. In any case, it's a pretty fragile hull upon which to float an international career.

This isn't to say that your career course shouldn't include a couple of tacks that take you overseas. On the contrary, you should always be open to the possibility. But it's important to realize that many excellent international careers involve little or no extended residence abroad, and some may offer only infrequent travel. In fact, it may well be that your personal style and professional opportunities fit in far better with a stateside-based career, and that occasional international travel may give you a fresher, more valuable perspective than you could get as an expatriate.

It's awfully easy to slip into a pleasant, but limiting routine in a foreign country. You may choose to become part of the local expatriate or diplomatic scene (build up a circle of local and expat acquaintances, join the right clubs, spend time in the right hangouts), you may "go native"

## A WINNING COMBINATION

(have mostly host-country friends, avoid the typical expat stomping grounds and watering holes), or you may follow a middle course. In any case, the risks are similar. As time passes, you fit more and more easily into your place in the local society, but — unless you have an absolute genius for language and customs — you won't be fully aware of the subtle changes taking place in the host country, and your infrequent visits to the United States won't allow you to keep pace with developments there, either. After a few years, although you're likely to believe that you're more valuable than ever before, you're actually living in the past, increasingly out of sync in the host country, and out of touch with your own. To avoid ending your career in this sort of Flying Dutchman mirage, *I strongly recommend working in the United States for at least one year in every four or five.*

A U.S.-based international career may actually let you create more new tacks and more rapid career advancement. If your stateside work in a chamber of commerce, international trade association, or state or Department of Commerce trade office puts you in constant touch with a group of regular U.S. clients and contacts, you may develop better professional relationships and future career possibilities than you would on an overseas assignment, where you'd meet with them only once or twice a year when they came over on business. If you work with the U.S. international business community as a U.S.-based freight forwarder, customs house broker, banker, attorney, or other provider of services, the same is true. And in any field, you'll learn about business conditions and opportunities in many countries, rather than limiting most of your expertise to one country (or at most a few countries in one region) as you usually must when working overseas.

On the other hand, if you spend all your time in the United States, it may be harder to develop the kind of in-depth, country-specific or area-specific expertise that can make you absolutely indispensable to a company's plans. For this reason, you might want to lay out a U.S.-based career course that zigs in the same way that an overseas-based course zags: at least one year abroad for every four or five spent in the United States.

One of the main advantages of being in (or fairly close to) the head office of a U.S. outfit is that you can make yourself seen, heard, and known. You may call this "company politics," but the fact is that many (most?) people base their entire career on it. Moreover, decisions including promotions, assignment locations and job responsibilities normally are made in the home office (often with little or no input from the field). If you're in the home office, you at least have a chance to influence the decision-makers and maybe even impress them with your brilliance and competence. On the other hand, your weak points may be more noticeable, and you run the risk of getting in the way of some competing individual or faction.

In the field (particularly overseas), you tend to be safer from company politics. In fact, people may forget who you are, which tends to slow your meteoric rise to the top. However, you have the advantage of building up direct and irrefutable knowledge of international business realities. It's pretty hard for anyone to argue with someone who's "been there." All too often, however, it's "out of sight, out of mind," and your expertise, which may be deferred to once you return to a stateside position, is ignored as long as you're abroad.

Even worse, your relations with the home office will often get caught in a reciprocal time warp. Just as the extremely rapid pace of change in America makes it hard for you to keep abreast of new corporate thinking there, the people in the home office tend to retain outdated images of the political, economic, and business reality of the country and region in which you're operating. U.S.-based executives may remember Europe or South America as it was during the heyday of the U.S. tourist in the 60s, or the Asia they saw during the war in Viet Nam, or even the Korean War. As a result, you may recommend or follow strategies whose relationship to overall corporate strategy has been weakened by events in the United States, and they may be unable to understand the changing factors overseas that force you to modify your tactics there. This sort of situation produces a perception gap that swallows up communications like the Bermuda Triangle.

This combination of factors often produces a bizarre situation in which an executive, passed up for promotion because of a long overseas assignment that supposedly has left him/her out of touch with company priorities and strategy, is hired into a senior position at another U.S.-based company because of the expertise acquired through long experience overseas.

T his discussion, of course, doesn't answer the big question: should you plan your international career, or major stages of it, around a stateside, or an overseas base? Clearly, that decision is yours, and yours alone, but here's a compass check that can help you decide. Examine the relationship

between your present tack, your objectives (including the next two or three possible moves) and your background and abilities. If you have or are developing all the expertise and career components you need to keep moving forward for the foreseeable future, you're on course. If things don't look as clear as you'd like, try dividing your skills into three categories: those that you can build on best in the United States, those that probably need to be developed overseas, and those that can be developed and used in either setting. By comparing these with your Big Picture, you can get a fix on what your next tack might be.

If intensive overseas experience needs to be part of your Big Picture, when's the best time to get it? The answer to this question will depend on circumstances, but all things considered, I'd recommend working it in at the earlier stages of your international career, perhaps after a couple of years of stateside experience in the same sector. The longer you wait, the harder it may be to create, or take advantage of, an overseas opening. The older your children get, the more difficult it will be for them to adapt to life abroad, and the more their education may be compromised. A four-year-old can thrive almost anywhere; not so a fourteen-year-old, so playing Swiss Family Robinson has its limits.

On the professional side, you may become so involved and so important in the stateside operations of your department or division that your company doesn't want to interrupt the rhythm by letting you pull up stakes. This might be flattering to your ego, but you may find yourself at a disadvantage later when competing with someone who's acquired the special, indefinable polish of international expertise. You may have done a great job of keeping the sails trimmed and the ship on course, but if a returning expat knows how to handle the foreign buyers better or keep the margins up in the offshore manufacturing operations, you may find him/her taking the helm.

If you take an overseas assignment in an unfamiliar country when you're deeper in your career, you may run into a similar problem: if you're running the office, you may be so tied up with management that you have little time or inclination to delve into the language and culture of the country you've been assigned to.

For this reason, it's often advantageous to do your first stint overseas before you rise too far in the company. As an assistant manager, you'll probably learn more on an overseas assignment than your boss will, and you're almost guaranteed to have more fun. Later, you can decide whether you'd rather stay overseas (when your boss leaves, you'll be the most qualified to be number one, and if your company doesn't see it that way, there's a good chance that another one will), go back to the United States to rise higher in your company, or go after a position with another outfit. You may decide to use your international expertise to go into business for yourself.

## GULLIVER HAD IT EASY

If you're going overseas, you'll do better if you're aware of the changes that the move may cause in your personal and professional life. Some of these changes are subtle, while others will almost jump out and grab you. Almost none of them are what you might expect.

One of the most misleading phenomena of the post-World War II era has been the superficial westernization (or Americanization) of much of the nonwestern world. American businessmen, politicians and others going overseas are continually tripped up because they equate fast food outlets, U.S. hotel chains, and three-piece suits with "westernization." Because they see some things that look familiar, they expect the locals to think, respond and proceed like Americans. Since this never happens, the inevitable long-term result is confusion, frustration, and a loss of efficiency.

Let's start with the "easy" places: England, Canada, Australia, New Zealand. Same language, same culture, right? Should be a snap. Not by half! In each of these countries, the evident similarities cover a world of differences. In the United Kingdom, for example, you're facing an ingrown, self-assured business community in which a typically American approach will get you branded as brash and self-indulgent, and where it can take years to understand ordinary native speech in some regions—to say nothing of prevailing attitudes toward labor, management and business in general. Canadians, superficially the most similar, have an entirely different national agenda (for example, they were happily doing business with the People's Republic of China at a time when the United States classified such activity as trading with the enemy), and are deeply resentful of perceived and actual U.S.

domination of Canadian culture and the Canadian economy. The Canadian business picture is further clouded by the issue of language and culture in Quebec, which has business practices (including compulsory bilingualism) all its own.

How about Down Under? American managers in Australia agree that unless you can put aside your hard-driving notions of how to run an office or deal with partners, suppliers and customers, you have little chance of success. The sense of priorities and timing, and the resulting relations between coworkers, colleagues, and labor-management are completely different from those you're accustomed to in the United States. New Zealand, of course, is different from both the United States and Australia—and you can't afford to forget it.

For most American expatriates, the next level of difficulty is Europe. To Europeans, who admire subtlety and generally have a team approach to business projects and problem-solving, Americans seem hopelessly individualistic, undisciplined, and abrasive. As in the English-speaking countries, the management style that American business writers often refer to as "take-charge" or "no-nonsense" is regarded as dictatorial and self-centered. American business also has earned a reputation for impatience and impulsiveness. Even if you're able to adapt to local realities, you'll have to overcome these and other stereotyped impressions before you can be effective, and, of course, you can't simply ask: "How am I doing?" To top it all off, business style and ethics differ widely from one country to another, and woe to the unwary American who, after finally coming to grips with the basics of the business world in, say, France, tries to apply the same skills in neighboring Spain (or Switzerland, or Germany).

In Asia, things are even more difficult. In general, all the comments I've made thus far hold true, and then some: in various countries, U.S. businesspeople are perceived as too profit-oriented, unreliable over the long haul, unwilling to adapt to local standards of performance, sloppy, disorganized, and insensitive to local needs. Not all of these perceptions are logical or fair, of course, but they exist, and you'll have to deal with them. In addition, you'll have to struggle your way through business cultures in which directness of word and deed is avoided, and where almost every aspect of life, including business, has rituals that can't be ignored without giving offense.

And then there's the Arab world (where letting a business contact see the sole of your shoe will end the relationship forever), Latin America (20 countries, each with its own set of priorities and practices), Africa . . .

I could go on for several hundred pages, but I think you get the idea. No matter where you go, things are very different. In one country you're expected to inquire about your partner's wife and family; in another to do so would be a serious insult. In some countries, government is the closest ally of business; in others, they appear to be mortal enemies. In still others, bribes, payoffs and kickbacks are commonplace and necessary, yet in many of those same countries, business and social practices that are accepted in the United States can land you in jail. In many places, there's the additional handicap of a double standard: one set of rules for local business, another for foreigners (including you). Unlike America, you'll often encounter enforcement of regulations that aren't on the books, or that you aren't allowed to see, while rules that you've scrupulously adhered to turn out to be meaningless. At times, things can seem so topsy-turvy that you fully expect your compass needle to point south instead or north. And virtually everywhere, the business style and philosophy that you've been brought up with and taught in business school—all the good American virtues of honesty, openness, compromise, efficiency and others—may turn out to be totally counterproductive.

## HOME OFFICE 1, REALITY 0

**A** related problem is the inability of the home office to believe this when their overseas executives and managers (you) tell them about it. They're determined to believe that any problems you're having can't be due to the local government passing ex post facto laws (we don't do that, it's unconstitutional!), local businessmen changing their minds and their adherence to contracts on a daily basis (but we have a written agreement!), or any other reality that's markedly different from what they're used to.

In short, many international companies aren't sufficiently aware of the fact that it's far more difficult to do business in some countries (or even specific areas within countries) than in others. In fact, they're so out of touch that many overseas managers rate home office misconceptions as their number one management problem. At first, this may seem like a minor inconvenience, but it can have a devastating impact on your effectiveness, and ultimately on your career.

One major issue is results. The home office, where careers are determined, tends to look at gross productivity figures (sales, profitability, and so forth) without taking into account what it took to attain them. All they can see is that you, in some far corner of the globe, didn't show as big a bottom line as the fellow in Chicago or

New York. Never mind that your office was shut down half the year because the power was out, or that you couldn't get the raw materials you needed because of host-country import restrictions or a ten-month dock strike.

To eliminate mistaken impressions, you should be prepared to spend extra time and effort to keep the head office fully informed of any unusual difficulties you face. Of course, this doesn't mean making up an endless string of excuses. Just point out the facts. Often, you can use clippings from local English-language newspapers or international publications to support your comments on changing government regulations, shifts in the local economy, problems experienced by your major suppliers or customers, and other factors that affect your operation.

AmCham and the commercial or econ section of the U.S. Embassy or Consulate should have reports or position papers describing in detail — and from the all-important American point of view — the major handicaps and problems facing foreign business in general. These can be very valuable in helping the home office understand why you have to spend so much time and energy on things like the protection of your designs and patents, or why in your host country you can't just hire an attorney when you need to force compliance with an agreement. Of course, you can and should report difficulties in detail in your own words, but the generic experience will reinforce what you have to say and make it clear that the problems aren't of your own making.

When it's time to report the bottom line, use extra statistics to present a more accurate picture. For example, express annual productivity in terms of production hours available, or compare your operation's profitability or increase in market share with the industry as a whole, with other foreign companies, or with other U.S. companies in the same area. Much of the data you'll need is available from AmCham and its members, the U.S. Chamber, the Department of Commerce, and U.S. Embassy offices. Again, if you've been saving relevant clippings from the media, you can use them (or summaries) to buttress your arguments.

Another problem is style, not in a superficial sense, but the entire complex relationship of awareness, attitudes and actions. To be a successful international manager or executive overseas, you must internalize — not merely study or know about — local business and social practices. In so doing, however, you'll be forced to displace some of the typically American patterns and responses that foreigners find offensive. As a result of this evolution, your relationship with the home office will change. Increasingly, you'll view them with much the same critical eye as host-country businesspeople do. When top management comes over from the United States, it may take all the tact and patience you can muster to keep from cringing at their repeated social and business blunders. Meanwhile, they may begin to perceive changes in your style—perhaps less confrontational, more indirect, more sympathetic to the claims of host-country staff or even the competition—that can lead them to believe that you've lost your drive or "gone native."

These changes tend to occur even if you're working with other Americans. In fact, unless you're careful, criticizing the latest dumb move of the home office or a stateside branch can become a favorite pastime. The result may be the development of an "us against them" mentality that can have even more negative effects on your career. The best antidote for negative thinking is awareness and occasional rotation back to a stateside position, but over the very long term there's probably no cure for the perception and culture gap. After all, explorers from Marco Polo to Columbus and Captain Cook have had the same problem: how to get the folks at home to understand a world they've never experienced (although you can't say so, the CEO's annual junket definitely does not count as experience). To date, no one's found a solution.

## OUR MAN IN ONGA DONGA

There are overseas assignments, and overseas assignments. The problems that you have with the home office are compounded if you're somewhere out in the boondocks, especially out in the boondocks in a country or region that's of relatively minor importance to your company's international operations. In this situation, your existence—and your career—may be reduced to the status of a pin on the headquarters' map. "What's this one?" "That one? Oh, yes, that's our man in Onga Donga. Can't remember his name." To avoid this sort of mid-career shipwreck, you should pay attention to just where you're likely to end up overseas.

Once you've established the broad outlines of the overseas phase of your international career (for example, public or private sector, or electronics rather than widget splicing), you'll want to consider details that will vary according to specific areas within the general sector you've chosen to target. In many countries, for instance, certain types of production facilities tend to be located in remote or newly developed areas far from management bases. If you like a more sophisticated living environment, this type of situation can have you climbing the walls in no time. And (just as in the United States) you'll often find different types of industries concentrated in different parts of the country. For most countries with a significant U.S. business presence, a little time with the AmCham membership directory and a country map will give you a pretty fair picture of what's located where.

Corporate headquarters are often concentrated in or near the capital city, but manufacturing may be at the other end of the country. If you're sourcing steel pipe, supervising quality checks on an oil rig, or manufacturing shoes or a thousand other things from IC chips to soft drink cans, you may be living and working in an industrial city hundreds of miles from your in-country headquarters — and from all the top managers and AmCham activities that could help give your career the next decisive turn. Given the trend of increasing U.S. investment in offshore production facilities (to overcome trade barriers and to take advantage of exchange rates, lower labor rates and other cost differentials), these differences seem likely to affect an increasing number of international careerists. You'll want to research the geographic distribution of positions you go after in any region or country, but accept the fact that if you're already overseas in a carefully selected, cosmopolitan metropolis and your company opens a new branch office or other operation somewhere in the hinterlands, they may tap you to set out from the big city to run it. You may choose to make a change instead.

Similar geographic differences exist in public sector careers. In some countries, for example, the political and business centers are one and the same. From a diplomatic post in, say, Paris, you can develop any kind of private sector contact you want to. If you're posted in Bonn, or Beijing, or Brasília, however, you'll find yourself far from the centers of commercial and industrial life which means fewer chances to establish the kind of in-country network with expat managers that can create rewarding new opportunities for you. If this is important to your planning, you may want to try for Hamburg or Frankfurt, Canton or Shanghai, or São Paulo or Rio instead of the capital cities.

There's also the issue of quality of life. In the United States, United Nations agencies are concentrated in New York, and in Europe they're in some of the nicest areas on the continent. Embassies are located only in capital cities, but don't let the intimate and livable environment of Washington, D.C. mislead you into thinking that all foreign capitals are as pleasant. Some are huge, gridlocked, smog-covered concrete jungles (or jumbles, if they're among the many that have yet to discover urban planning or zoning).

For this reason, if you're aiming at an overseas government post, for example, and want a relatively stress-free lifestyle, even at the expense of some big-city glitter, you may be happier in a consulate (rather than an embassy) or in an Information Service (USIS) assignment in a smaller city. The bad news? Unless you do some research, you may wind up cut off from potentially useful contacts in larger cities or manufacturing centers, or in an unhealthy, grubby backwater with nothing but your collection of VTR cassettes to break the monotony. Check the AmCham directory and read the State Department Post Report for signs of intelligent life before you bid.

# CAN YOU DRINK THE WATER?

Life overseas can be rewarding, but it can also be frustrating. In the first place, few foreign countries place as much emphasis on popularity as the United States does, and many Americans find host-country nationals rather unsociable. National tendencies may be exaggerated by the fact that you're a foreigner: just as in the United States, many people don't feel totally at ease around foreigners (especially if they aren't fluent in the local language).

Even if the natives are friendly, they may not allow you to get very close, especially in countries where family ties are important, or where the local ethos (such as Confucianism in the Orient) has created a well-defined structure into which outsiders don't fit well, if at all. At work, you may find yourself without any close friends, and in your neighborhood the situation may be much the same. In this type of social environment, it's often all too easy to become too reliant on the expat community, which can reinforce a cycle of alienation from local reality.

There may be other personal adjustments, ranging from a sense that the host-country society is overregulated (like Switzerland and most Oriental and Iron Curtain countries), underregulated (many Latin American, Middle Eastern, and developing countries), too clean, too dirty, too noisy, too quiet, too fast-paced, too boring. The list is endless. You may have problems with the food, the transportation system, the role of women, treatment of children, cruelty to animals. The only way to cope is to remind, or perhaps convince, yourself that the American way isn't the only way, and that many of the people whose habits are offensive to you are equally offended by some of your actions. Whatever you do, avoid overt expressions of distaste; they only serve to widen the gulf between you and the locals. Americans have marvelously expressive faces, but a grimace in a restaurant or a shop can lead to a sudden decline in the service you get, and at work it can sour a lot of things, including your career.

In many countries, you'll need to change your expectations. One of the biggest mistakes made by Americans abroad is to try to find American style (or worse, hyphenated American ethnic) food and other consumer experiences. After all, even if you're lucky enough to hit upon prime rib in Pakistan, enchiladas in Kuwait or sushi in Lesotho, is it really rational to believe that they'll be anything like what you're used to? In all likelihood, you'll pay an outrageous price for a thoroughly unsatisfactory meal. Better to discover your taste in local fare, and learn to do without many food products and other items that you considered essential in the United States.

A more serious drawback in many countries is the lack of medicines and adequate health care facilities, especially in countries with exotic diseases. In such places, you'd be well advised to do the overseas portion of your international career while you're young, healthy, and able to bounce back quickly from disease or injury. To be on the safe side, you should line up a good physician as soon as possible after your arrival in an overseas assignment. Don't be roped into settling for the resident expat doctor that everyone else has always gone to; in many cases, his practice may be based on popularity, force of habit, and the fact that he speaks English, not on professional competence.

Education for your children also can be a real problem. (For example, many Americans and other foreigners working in the People's Republic of China send their children to boarding school in Japan, which is the closest place they can get a full education.) Even if the school is of good quality, an adolescence spent abroad, especially in a series of two to three year assignments such as you'll get in the Foreign Service, can translate into adjustment problems, both overseas and back in the United States.

If you have property or other investments in the United States, being overseas for long periods of time can create a special and very frustrating set of difficulties. Bank and credit card mixups, problems with tenants, decisions on disposition of assets — all become far more difficult and expensive to take care of when you're ten thousand miles away. A situation that could be resolved with a phone call or two in the United States may require correspondence lasting months (keep in mind the common minimum turnaround time of two or three weeks for a single exchange of letters) and a hundred dollars or more in telephone calls, many of which must be made in the middle of the night because of time zone differences. (On company business, it's the same story: for some reason, it always seems to be the overseas manager — never the home office staff — who has to stay up half the night making and taking international calls.)

Fun? Hardly. But if you're prepared for it, it's an acceptable cost associated with the overseas portion of your career.

# BURIED TREASURE

There are also very real benefits. I've already discussed the free housing or substantial housing allowances, cars (some with driver), and salary differentials provided by most overseas international employers. In addition, in many countries, the low prevailing local wage means that you get a lot more mileage for your dollars: not just spacious houses, but also domestic help (maids, cooks, drivers, gardeners) at bargain-basement prices.

The intangibles—the real buried treasure that jacks up the value of your international career—can be just as important, especially if you believe that there's more to life than a big house and servants. To me, the greatest thing about living overseas is that every day is a learning experience. At the office or plant, a combination of patience, observation and an open mind will teach you a multitude of things, not just about the locals, but about management, operations, and human nature in general. The problems of organizations, hierarchy, and productivity are the same worldwide; it's only the solutions that are different. In any country, no matter what the level of development, you can learn a lot of new ways to do business and relate to contacts, colleagues, supervisors and subordinates.

Because of the small size of the foreign community in many overseas locations, you're able to make contacts and connections (both personal and professional) that you couldn't make in a lifetime in the United States. In the first place, if you make efforts to attain the unusual status of an internationally competent American including language skills and most importantly a sincere interest in understanding the host country's point of view, you'll stand out in the eyes of host-country big-leaguers, whose friendship can mean an exponential increase in the value of your foreign assignment. I'm not talking about jobs or contacts for jobs (nothing alienates an International Fortune 500 director or CEO faster than a job hustle), but a perspective from a much higher level than most people ever reach.

Something similar happens with the expat community. Even in a major metropolis, if you're active in AmCham, you'll become acquainted with a much broader spectrum of international managers and executives—often including non-American expats, who join AmCham because of its size and clout—than you normally would at home. Since you all face much the same set of special problems in doing business (host-country regulations, lack of protection for industrial property, difficulties in finding and retaining qualified local staff, struggling with culturally induced management and administrative problems), you'll find many more occasions to cooperate on committees or in informal situations. And because you're all in the same boat vis à vis the host-country government and host-country competition, you'll find that distinctions based on nationality, title or levels of authority often fade into the background, even more than in the U.S.-based international business fraternity. For this reason, you often can develop a network of contacts of various nationalities, and if you're in a lower managerial or even staff position, you'll find it a lot easier to develop business and personal rapport with upper management, including VP's, than it would be at home. This not only helps you in your present position by giving your employers positive feedback from their peers on your performance and potential, it creates a lot of possibilities for your next tack.

## LOOK BEFORE YOU LEAP

It costs an organization a lot of money to send an employee overseas, and it's a tremendous expense and inconvenience to bring you back if you decide you can't take it after a few months. Naturally, abandoning an overseas assignment after a relatively short time can be very traumatic for the employee as well, particularly since it implies some damage to long-range career plans. The bad feelings are likely to be compounded by the policy of many organizations requiring you to pay for a substantial portion of your transporation and moving costs if you come back to the United States before a specified minimum time (usually one year) has elapsed. This can mean thousands of dollars out of your pocket.

To help avoid this unnecessary difficulty, make up a list of things that you *and the members of your family* feel you just can't live without, and a companion list of things you cannot tolerate. Be sure to include items related to health, safety, your children's education, and general freedom of activity. Could you and your family stand two years or more in a dictatorship? How about life in a country where women aren't allowed a full range of activities? These are important issues, and I've seen many careers (not to mention marriages) get pretty frayed around the edges because of them.

# 7

## CREATING OPPORTUNITIES

ne of the great advantages of the international career environment is its amazing capacity to generate new opportunities. Thanks in part to the efforts of Department of Commerce (USDOC) District Office personnel, who are engaged in an ongoing campaign to get new-to-export (NTE) and new-to-market (NTM) companies to do business where they've never done it before, there are international positions opening up every day.

In many cases, you can create your own opportunities far more easily than you could in the domestic market. At a multiplier meeting, you hear that a local company is convinced they could do business in Eastern Europe, if only they had in-house expertise. The door's ajar. If you spot it — and your involvement with multipliers will make it far more likely that you will — you can step in and take the lead in building their Eastern European business. Or perhaps a U.S. manufacturer needs to develop cheaper sources of parts and components, but doesn't know where to look. If you know the international ropes — and once again, multipliers are among the best places to learn them — you can fill the gap.

Contrary to a common misconception, you don't have to be overseas, or have extensive overseas experience to create a good international position and career for yourself. If overseas experience were the key, the internationalization of U.S. business would be far more complete than it is. What you need is expertise — not mere experience — plus the creativity and initiative to turn it into an international career. No matter where you live, where you work, or what you do, there's plenty of raw material all around you. Organize it, shape it, assemble it, and set sail.

# WHAT AND WHO YOU KNOW

To do this, you need to combine two types of knowledge: what you know and who you know. But you do this in a special way. What you know—real-life, make-things-happen expertise—can count for much more than it does in the domestic sector, and you can land more positions on the basis of merit alone. For most American industries, the international waters are still uncharted, and skilled skippers are in big demand.

Your ability to move forward because of who you know is heavily subject to what you know. In the domestic career environment, many old-boy networks are based on the fact that most of the jobs involved could be filled equally well by tens of thousands of people. Internationally, it just isn't that way, in part because the foreign competition, which universally has had to come from behind, is a lot tougher, hungrier and more experienced at the game of international business survival than are most American companies. It's international know-how, not good ol' boys, that U.S. companies need in order to compete successfully. Luckily for you, companies that don't learn this lesson end up on the bottom, while the ones that do learn it can prosper, grow—and hire. They're the ones you want to have see you in action.

In this sense, the international career environment is like the world of high-level Research and Development, or corporate turnarounds, or any other expertise- and results-oriented activity. People in the industry all know who the top talents are, and what they're good at. The winners get opportunities because they aggressively go after them, and of course they use contacts in the process. Still, the final decision to hire or not to hire, to fund or not to fund is based on a solid, innovative proposal and demonstrated ability to get results. *Expertise plus a new, viable project equals opportunity.*

In creating your own international career opportunities, you have the benefit of multiple contacts and tactics. In the first place, you can combine domestic and international approaches. You can and should use the traditional, in-house or in-industry network, and also suggest new international products, marketing programs and other activities that will generate positions and progress for your career. At the same time, plug into the overlapping networks formed by international multipliers. Locally, your involvement in an international trade association and other multipliers will give you cross-industry contacts and opportunities far beyond the range of the industry sector you work in now. It's a perfect way to develop a network of managers and executives from many different industries, each of whom has the potential to be an asset in your next tack.

This activity also gives you cross-national exposure. Through the international activities of your local chamber, international trade association and other multipliers, you come in contact with U.S. and foreign companies worldwide, thus creating a network that spans not only different industries, but different countries. You can generate multicountry contacts not only through the missions and other activities of your local group, but also through connections with foreign multipliers and their member companies.

This is one reason that you should be aware of all the international multipliers in your community, including nonbusiness groups like sister city societies. When foreign delegations come to call, simply talking to members about their business interests can give you new ideas and potential contacts for future career tacks. This type of networking creates possibilities that are light-years ahead of anything the domestic scene has to offer, including many triangular situations where you, as an American, work with a foreign company in their dealings with a foreign firm of a different nationality. I've seen it lead to sourcing manufactured goods in one country for shipment to another, the creation of a distributorship for imports, and multinational career situations in which an American in one country recommends an American in another country to an American in the United States.

Creating a first-class international career is a long-term proposition. The truly great situations don't develop overnight, and you have to put in the time and effort to create them. Your big breaks usually won't come as bolts from the blue, but as a result of your continuous efforts to be knowledgeable, competent, and active in your community's international affairs.

Furthermore, there's no way to predict exactly when and how you'll assemble the necessary contacts and components that generate a specific opportunity. For this reason, the successful development of your international career, which in a very real sense is a voyage of discovery, requires a high degree of innovation and adaptability. You've got to continuously rechart and modify your course as you go along. Follow these tactics, and you can become one of the people that international businesses, both American and foreign, seek out for information and advice as part of their international team.

All this can be done in your local context, of course, and many people have created excellent international careers without so much as crossing the county line. Nevertheless, a tack overseas, even at a lower price (salary) than you're making now, can have immense value if it gives you expertise (including language) and contacts that you can apply later in a local context.

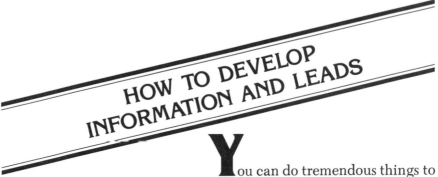

## HOW TO DEVELOP INFORMATION AND LEADS

You can do tremendous things to advance your international career if you know how to develop information and leads. At the beginning and at frequent intervals throughout your career, you should take your bearings from the high ground of multipliers and umbrella organizations, the vantage point that lets you spot opportunities, chart courses, and expose leads for followup. How? For starters, by reading their publications, taking part in their activities, and talking to their staff people.

Since your career will be far more rewarding if you aggressively create your own opportunities, you also should consider using various other sources of information to get a fix on possible tacking points. Of course, you won't ignore convenient, commonplace or obvious openings like campus corporate recruiters or the Foreign Service, but to give yourself the greatest number of possibilities and keep ahead of the fleet, keep identifying and defining others. You may get wind of these through items in the newspaper ("Argentina plans to develop shrimp farming") or track them down by persistently researching topics that relate to your own cherished career goals (you want to be the exclusive West Coast rep for a trading company specializing in rhinoceros horn aphrodisiac).

Unless you have a concrete lead (a tip on a job from one of your multiplier contacts, an announced position with the U.S. Government), your usual starting point will be a multiplier organization or an agency (such as the Department of Commerce or the U.S. Embassy) with people and reference resources to get you pointed in the right direction. To maximize your chances of success, ask for other leads and sources of leads at every step. The idea isn't to just find out where the job openings are, although you may be informed of some, but to learn what's happening in the field. This enables you to use the time-honored domestic career strategy (don't ignore dometic approaches; just be sure you go beyond them) of finding a need and filling it.

The types of leads you'll uncover are endless. They'll range from the very specific (a local company could be exporting, but they don't have anyone who knows about international trade; a builder wants to source materials offshore, but doesn't know where to look for them; someone keeps getting inquiry letters in a foreign language, but can't read and answer them) to the very general (there's been a big increase in foreign industrial acquisitions in your area; local industries could benefit by participating in more international trade events; the chamber of commerce is looking for ways to diversify the local economy).

Especially in the early stages of international career development, while you're still learning the ropes and getting acquainted with local multipliers, you may want to work on some long shots for practice. You can gain valuable skill and confidence by generating opportunities that aren't a matter of life and death, perfecting your technique as you go. This activity is particularly worthwhile in the context of opportunities that are far away or result from the newspaper and other impersonal sources. The odds are lower, but you have absolutely nothing to lose. In contrast, if you chase after too many local opportunities before you've laid the groundwork, you risk looking amateurish or poorly prepared.

The other half of the process is to work your way back downstream to develop leads and turn them into a career. Even if you've been given a specific lead, you'll want to do a little extra digging before taking action. Suppose you've been told that the export manager of a local firm is quitting to start a trading company. Right away, you're presented with a number of questions. Would you rather fill the vacancy being created, or cast your lot with the new trading company? Can you go after both positions at the same time? Clearly the export manager has initiative and ambition, but were there any other factors that precipitated his/her departure? What are the present needs and future plans of both outfits? If you're well connected in local multipliers, it shouldn't be too hard to get the answers to these and other important questions, perhaps from the export manager, or from other people at the first company.

A second step in this sample case is to formulate some sort of proposal or plan of action, based on what you've learned, that meets the needs of one or both companies. This can be anything from marketing to operations to smoother handling of paperwork. Again, your contacts in local multipliers can give you a lot of information. Was the export manager frustrated by inefficiencies in the shipping and billing departments? You'll be a lot more attractive as a replacement if you come in with some ideas on the subject. Does the new trading company plan to be active in handicraft imports? If you have useful knowledge of any country or area where such products originate, there can be a place for you in the new organization.

When ready (that is, when you know exactly what you're after and what you have to offer), contact the target company. *Personal contact is best, and contact in the context of a local international multiplier is even better.* This is where your contributions to multiplier goals can pay big dividends. You're not only a known quantity, you've proven your ability. Your ideas and your future on the company staff or management team will get favorable consideration because of it. If you've developed a multiplier network, now's the time to use it. Let your close contacts know you're interested in the job in question. They may surprise you by going beyond a recommendation and suggesting additional opportunities or offering you a job in their own companies. Incredible as it sounds, this actually happens. Everyone wants you if you're good, but they'll usually wait for you to make the first move.

Of course, sometimes you'll go after a position where your network can't provide direct help. This is often the case when you're trying for a long shot job overseas, or when you're overseas and aiming at a position in the United States. At the very least, try to get an indirect reference through your local contacts and multipliers. If you've been active there, you may find a heartwarming desire to help you make the tack you want. I've seen people get job offers because of a second- or third-hand recommendation between two people who didn't know each other, based on a careerist's activity with a multiplier. This sense of camaraderie and mutual enthusiasm for promoting talent in service of the international business community is one of the most positive aspects of the international career environment.

Finally, you'll enter into negotiations. International negotiations call for a very well-developed sense of timing: distance creates time lags, and if you're dealing with a manager or executive who's on the road a lot, your communications may go unread and unanswered for weeks. Remember that in a situation involving overseas mail, it'll take about a week in each direction for the letter to reach its destination, so you may want to send key messages by telefax. (To most people, telex appears too urgent and impersonal for this type of communication.) In addition, the host-country culture may have a different sense of timing (usually slower), which can affect dealings both with host-country firms and with U.S. expats. You'll have to walk a fine line between seeming pushy and impatient, and letting things drag.

# START FROM WHERE YOU ARE

One of the most common errors made by international careerists is believing that to break into an international career it's necessary to live in a city with an international tradition or image, or have spent half a lifetime abroad. It's imperative that you avoid this conceptual trap. Unless you're living in a mountaintop hermitage, you're surrounded by international career opportunities.

In all larger cities, there are multipliers, agencies and individual businesses with international activities and the potential for even more, with the right kind of initiative and creative leadership. You can help provide it. Paradoxically, in smaller communities you may have even greater international opportunities, since you're facing far less competition and it's easier to get to know business and community leaders.

Rather than searching elsewhere for a starting point, then, you should start from where you are right now. It may not be obvious, but you're already in contact with a potential international network that's waiting to be tapped. The pieces are all there; all you have to do is figure out new ways to put them together. You say most firms in your city don't do any international business? That may be true, but they or their suppliers or distributors deal with companies that do. Your job is to examine the chain of production and distribution to discover the points at which there's an international connection. You'll often find that you can increase your opportunities greatly by moving toward the mass wholesaling (including franchising and financing) and manufacturing level, because here you'll come in direct contact with international business.

A good first step is to examine the activities of the company and industry where you work to look for international possibilities. You may find immediate possibilities in the area of trade (imports, exports or both), manufacturing, sourcing parts and components, licensing trademarks or technology, services, franchising, and a thousand others. There's literally no limit to what you can come up with, if you're willing to be creative and aggressive. Even a small town, with such common small town advantages as cheap land, low-cost labor, plentiful water (for manufacturing), and unique local products can attract international industry or create export business. Common items can succeed in unusual places, and unusual items almost anywhere. I've seen people build international careers around disposable medical supplies in Korea, hamburger franchises in Brazil, tacos in Australia, beef jerky and sea-urchin eggs in Japan, tractor parts in Mexico. Others have brokered the sale of plant and equipment to third world countries, attracted foreign investors to rural sites, or become involved in manufacturing or distribution of commodities, raw materials, parts, or finished products. The lists, like your possibilities, are endless.

You can start where you are job-wise, as well. Rather than rush out looking for an international position, or aggressively promoting new international activity with your present employer, there's something to be said for maintaining a holding pattern at work while starting or enhancing your international career through multipliers. The main advantage of this tactic is that it's risk-free. You avoid both the danger of competitive backlash in your own company and the tightrope act that's required to create an international job with another firm without alienating your present employers. By working with multipliers as a member, you can create international career opportunities for yourself while you play an active part in directing your community's international development.

Starting where you are doesn't, of course, mean operating in a vacuum, or reinventing the wheel. Use the successful programs of multipliers in other cities as a model for how things can be done. Find out what products, services and industries in your area have the greatest international potential. How? Ask Department of Commerce (USDOC) District Offices, state development agencies, larger chambers of commerce and trade associations and other organizations for information and advice. You'll find them glad to provide it, especially if you approach them on behalf of one of your community's multipliers. Talk to multiplier members and other local businesspeople, too. Many of them have ideas on international trade and business that they'd love to discuss or implement with you. Even with a severely restricted set of resources, you have the power to build an international career. Actually, the most troublesome limitations you'll encounter will be of your own making. Luckily, they're easily eliminated through forward thinking.

## LOOK AHEAD

Especially when entering or reentering the career market, or making a major tack into new and unfamiliar waters, it's essential that you view yourself, your activities, and your potential from the vantage point of the new market, not the old one. *You should relate where you are to where you're going far more than to where you've been.* The fact that your last tack was to enter college, for example, doesn't mean that you should look at yourself as just a student. If an international trader or lawyer, or industrialist takes courses for professional awareness and advancement, is he/she thought of as a student? Of course not. Look forward to your next tack, not back at the last one. A high percentage of your ability to move ahead, and your credibility with others, depends on this key point.

If you ignore your international potential and interpret your present position in traditional job-description, career-ladder, domestic-market terms, you're holding yourself back. I've seen this disastrous attitude keep the fastest ocean racers immobilized at the dock, like one brilliant international career builder I know who consistently describes himself as a graduate student doing international intern work with a multiplier. Since this is how he's painted himself into his Big Picture, this is what he is. As a result, no opportunities are going to open up until he finishes school and gets himself out of the student category in his own mind and everyone else's. He could get his career under way right now if he portrayed himself in a more accurate light: an international marketing specialist who's broadening his background with a combination of course work and government experience. This attitude certainly worked for a secretary with ten years experience in international trade who finally stopped looking at herself as a secretary and accepted the reality that she was, in fact, a very knowledgeable international trade specialist. In less than a year, starting from that realization, she was running a major international export operation.

## OVER-THE-HORIZON RADAR

**P**ersonal contact is the best source of opportunities, and you should concentrate most of your efforts in this area. However, the nature of the international marketplace often produces attractive, viable career opportunities that simply can't be dealt with except at long range. Rather than pass these up, you're better off learning how to detect and develop them. For this purpose, the newspaper can be your radar.

There are several ways you can use the newspaper to create opportunities at long range and shape all stages of your international career. For this purpose, the *Wall Street Journal* (and its overseas regional editions) is one of the best; another contender is the

*International Herald Tribune.* If you've decided on a country (or a specific foreign city or two) where you want to develop your international career, you may find it useful to subscribe to (or at least read) the English language papers from that location. Local and university libraries have reference works, including *Editor and Publisher International Yearbook*, that list most of the major English-language newspapers published overseas. These lists may not be complete, so you can also ask the nearest consulate of the target country for names and mailing addresses of English-language papers. AmCham or the Information Service at the U.S. Embassy may also provide names.

The papers you get will be out of date by the time you read them, but they'll give you some sense of what's going on in the country, and perhaps even some specific leads on opportunities (although the time lag imposed by intercontinental distances is a big handicap). Your main purpose is to analyze major trends, write down your findings, and keep a file. The knowledge you gain not only will help you see or create opportunities, it will give you more to offer prospective employers.

Use your local paper plus the *WSJ* or *Trib* and any foreign papers as part of an ongoing program to find and go after opportunities. There are two separate activities in this program: spotting and analyzing trends, and categorizing specific opportunities.

## SPOTTING AND ANALYZING TRENDS

**B**egin to pay extra attention to stories related to areas (geographic regions, product or service sectors, specific companies, or whatever) in which you're especially interested. Collect and file these stories. Analyze them in terms of what they might mean to your career, and use your conclusions to improve your Big Picture.

Beginning in the mid-1980s, for example, the news media were full of stories on the Pacific basin. The area began to be touted as the region of the future, the great economic success story for the rest of the century and a good part of the next. If you noticed the ads in the same media, you saw that seminars on doing business in China, Japan, the Philippines, and other countries in the region were sprouting up like mushrooms. Clearly, a full-blown trend was in full swing.

The broad outlines, of course, aren't enough. When you become aware of a general trend like this, start focusing on the details. The Pacific basin is a big area, with economies ranging from the advanced post-industrial, high-tech society of Japan to lesser developed countries like Indonesia and the Philippines. Within each country, some industries are expanding, some stable, some in decline. Finally, there are pros and cons to living, working and doing business in each country, which can make that country more or less attractive to U.S. companies and to you. All these factors need to be examined and evaluated to see which ones match your goals, and how. You can get some additional information from local multipliers, USDOC, and the appropriate foreign embassy, consulate or trade office; you'll also find that if a trend is really solid, and not just a flash in the pan, it will appear over and over in international news media, each time with new information. Some of the articles will be no more than fillers, but if you collect them over time, they can provide you with quite a bit of insight.

Given the complexities of international industry and trade, the possibilities are literally endless, but one example will give you an idea of the type of approach you can take. If a foreign government has announced plans to invest billions to create a local electronics industry, there should be business opportunities for both U.S. and host-country companies and career opportunities for individuals with international ambition who can contribute to that effort with technical, managerial, production, marketing and other skills. If you have skills or expertise, including international savvy that cuts across industry lines, that can be used in any part of the electronics industry, you can start laying the groundwork for a tack toward the country in question.

Start thinking in terms of helping U.S. companies get in on the action, whether individually or through multipliers. There may be firms in your area that can supply capital equipment, materials, or technology for the proposed push. Show them your potential, perhaps by giving a talk at a local multiplier. If you have country-specific expertise, or if your international expertise is sufficient to help them make contacts, set up marketing agreements or organize technical promotion seminars in the target country, they need you. Help them realize this, and you've created an international career opportunity. The local international trade association or local branch of an electronics industry association might profit from a trade mission to the country in question. You can help organize and escort that mission. Enlist the services of the nearest USDOC District Office and local multipliers for information, advice, and assistance, including arrangements in the foreign country through the U.S. Embassy and foreign multipliers.

Consider the needs of business interests in the host country, too. Maybe they could benefit by undertaking a buying mission to the United States to source the equipment, materials and parts they'll need. Your community could be a stop on that mission. Long term, they'll want markets for the new line of products. You can help establish U.S. marketing channels. The embassy or nearest consulate or trade promotion office of the foreign government in question should be interested in assisting you with this type of activity. After all, you're helping them generate potential export sales.

Clearly, much of what you can accomplish will depend on where you work, the type of multipliers in your community, and other factors. However, there's so much going on in the areas of international business, trade and finance that almost any U.S. area has a chance to become involved. A good deal of your success will depend on how well you've come to know local companies and multipliers, and how active you've been in promoting their interests. Often, you'll decide that the time isn't ripe to take action on a specific trend or opportunity. Just don't use this as an excuse for inaction. It doesn't take long to write a letter of inquiry, and if you send out just one letter every week, you'll have fifty-two chances per year to make or improve contacts. This kind of consistent effort generates a lot of opportunities.

Be sure to write down your thoughts. The most obvious idea can slip away if you don't get it down on paper. Use the information and analyses you've created and collected to target specific opportunities in relevant areas.

## CATEGORIZING SPECIFIC OPPORTUNITIES

Here is a most valuable exercise that will help you begin to see how and where you fit into the international marketplace. Study the "positions offered" section of the paper, paying particular attention to *any job that you believe you could do* (regardless of whether or not you think you meet the qualifications stated in the ad) and also to *any job that you believe you'd want to do* (again, regardless of stated qualifications). As in every aspect of your international career development, keep your mind open. One of your major objectives is to interpret your background in the light of attractive jobs that you spot, rather than pass up what could be a perfect opportunity because you don't precisely meet the requirements. At the same time, be sure to relate specific opportunities both to major trends and to your own goals. If discrepancies keep cropping up, be adaptable enough to modify your criteria. Otherwise, you may find yourself sailing in the wrong direction.

Cut out promising ads, and relate them to your own background. For each one, write down a list of all the qualifications (career components) that you believe you have, and what you need to do to get the rest. Look for creative interpretations of your expertise that will convince employers that you're right for the job. For example, if the ad states, as many do, "minimum of 5 years in international trade" and you have only two years, then you need three more—maybe. If the rest of your background is strong enough, a sensible employer won't get hung up on the five-year requirement. You should think of comparable experience that will give the hiring company what they need. You may have specialized expertise, such as language skill, long residence and contacts in key market areas, technical qualifications, that more than make up for a shortfall in the stated requirements. Categorize and file the ads. Create a priority list based on the desirability of the positions offered and the components you have that can help you get them.

At first, if you're like most people, you may be slow at relating the ads you read to your own background, potential, and international career goals. To become more proficient, try to do at least one ad each week. If you pay close attention to the process, you'll probably find that your assessment of your qualifications changes as you consider various ads. Good! This means that you're learning to shift your point of view to match your background to the job, just as you will when you go after career opportunities and interview prospective employers. This flexible perspective will enhance every move you make, including evaluating opportunities, discussing international matters at multiplier meetings, approaching potential employers, or performing at your best on the job.

If you use a U.S. paper, you're bound to run into a type of ad that's almost always a waste of time. A typical ad of this type might read like this: "Import-export company manager, full time. Fluent French, minimum 5 years in international trade. $1,600 mo." When you spot the first words of an ad like this, you're pulse is bound to speed up a bit. This is the kind of position you've been looking for! If your French is a little rusty, you start thinking of ways to brush up. Mentally, you begin to rework your resume to meet the five year requirement. And then you see the low salary. It doesn't seem to match the qualifications and the position. What's going on?

If you believe that the value of the job (experience, new contacts, credibility) makes up for the low price (salary), you certainly should look into it. Be forewarned, however, that you may not stand a chance. Many ads of this type are placed merely to fulfill a U.S. Goverrnment regulation that saves jobs for U.S. citizens. It requires employers who intend to hire a foreign national to advertise the position for thirty days and then certify that no qualified U.S. citizen was ready, willing and able to fill the bill. The discrepancy between the job requirements and the salary is intended to discourage bona fide applicants, leaving the field clear for the friend, relative or associate who wants to come from overseas to work. Even if you apply and get the job (which isn't likely), you'll probably be forced out within a short time. Check it out, but don't waste your time if the feeling isn't right.

In any case, don't ever let your hopes and expectations cloud your view of reality and don't defeat your purpose by being so eager that you rationalize where you should analyze. Keep in mind that often you'll be forced to tack not when and where you want to, but when and where you can. Go for a level and type of opportunity that makes sense now; you'll have plenty of chances to reach for your dream later.

From time to time (perhaps once a month), compare the jobs you're considering with the overview that you're developing by spotting and analyzing international trends. Do the jobs you've targeted fall anywhere near major trends in international trade and business, and do they provide possible transition points that will keep you moving toward your goals? If not, you may want to consider acquiring specific skills that will enable you to aim at more promising areas. On the other hand, you may need to be more selective, or you may discover that your Big Picture needs reworking. In fact, unless you knew a lot about international trade and business when you started, you're bound to encounter realities that call for Big Picture adjustments, because the first version of your Big Picture was based on what you knew then, not what you know now.

In one of the greatest Big Picture modifications of all time, Columbus finally had to admit that although he'd reached land by sailing west, it wasn't India, as he'd originally thought. The end result of his voyages, which led to the fabulous wealth of the Aztecs and the Incas being funneled into the coffers of the Spanish crown and the estates of a new class of Spanish millionaires, was probably far more lucrative for Spain than any trade with India would have been. Chris, however, ran his own career on the rocks by stubbornly clinging to the India version until he was discredited. Even if your initial Big Picture has some gaps and flaws, it can lead you to some very serendipitous discoveries, provided that you have the courage to follow it (at least Columbus got that right), and to modify it to fit new facts.

The more savvy and realistic explorers that came after Columbus were after success, and they got it, not by vainly yearning for the established bazaars of India or China, but by finding new sources of wealth in an unknown continent. Like them, you can create a solid and rewarding career by developing a niche in a less heavily exploited market. Remember that no career sector is static; today's small and little-known international career market could be tomorrow's bonanza, and vice versa. In 1976, for example, who could have foreseen that the People's Republic of China (PRC), which had spent over ten years vociferously supporting Vietnam against the United States while simultaneously undergoing the vitriolic, anti-Western, anti-business madness of the so-called Cultural Revolution, would offer any sort of opportunities for American international careerists? Yet by the early 1980s, anyone with expertise in the area was eagerly sought after by hundreds of U.S. companies thirsting after the potential profits inherent in the vast Chinese market. And during this China boom of the early 1980s, who could predict that by 1986 the bloom would be off the rose, and commentators would be predicting a mass exodus of American business from the PRC? The lessons are clear: no opportunity lasts forever, but by taking frequent soundings and tacking when necessary, you'll be headed in the best direction.

As you become more skillful at relating career opportunities to your background and vice versa, you'll start to find interesting opportunities that appear to be within your range. This is what you've been working for! Rather than fire off a resume, see if any of your local contacts can contribute to your approach. In particular, now's the time to redeem some of the value you've acquired by your multiplier activity. A local multiplier executive director may have close relations with a foreign counterpart, who can provide information or put in a good word for you. On overseas trips, a local international marketing VP whom you know through your multiplier activity may make regular calls on top management in the company you're targeting.

After checking with your local contacts, write to the target company or multiplier, stating your interest, summarizing your qualifications in a general way, and asking a couple of intelligent questions about the position. Based on the response, you can later create a background marketing summary (not a resume) that's tailor-made for the position. Don't be in a hurry, or too eager. You're better off using your efforts as part of a learning experience —one that may lead to an offer you won't want to refuse.

## FORGING MISSING LINKS

You can't cut corners when creating your international career. Of course, you should always be on the lookout for a new channel of opportunity, but you can't go zig-zagging all over the map. To make each change count, you've got to relate your personal goals to the opportunity at hand, and figure out the best approach for this set of circumstances.

Trying to maintain a straight course is just as bad as random tacking. If you aim straight at any single point on the horizon, you're going to ignore courses that could get you there by less direct, but surer channels. If you target only banking jobs, for example, you miss the opportunities in other financial positions, or positions that, like certain aspects of banking, are based on the ability to assess the probable success and profitability of a given business project. If, on the other hand, you're determined to live and work in a particular country, a single-minded search for a position there might leave you blind to opportunities elsewhere that could get you to your final goal more quickly. Although a direct route might appear shorter and faster, you may get lost in a fruitles search for the Northwest Passage, when the route across Panama—or even around Cape Horn—is there just waiting to be used. Of course, these routes seem longer, but they have one big advantage: they can get you where you want to go.

Suppose that you're convinced that you're best qualified to work in Germany. You know the language, and you have expertise in an industry that, according to all indications, is going to boom there and create export and in-country investment opportunities for U.S. firms. But you lack key components of international business expertise—management background, marketing savvy, or what have you—that will open the best doors for you. You could, of course, concentrate on Germany, or on the industry you know best. And short term, this approach would probably get you a job in Germany, *or* a good position in your target industry.

What you need is a link that connects the two components. This link is a job, a career tack, that gets you across the gulf that separates the two points of international business expertise (which you need) and German language and industry expertise (which you have). Once you've accomplished this, one more tack should put you where you want to be, doing what you want to do, at the level you deserve.

Dealing successfully with this very common type of situation depends on understanding a very important point: to get what you want, you have to be patient. Of course, some people have the good fortune to get hired right into their dream assignment with little or no effort. (At least I guess they do; the fact is that I've never met one.) Anyhow, the rest of us have to patiently lay some groundwork, even if it means taking tacks that seem to lead us away from our international goals. Of course, this is a lot easier if you take a long-term point of view, and concentrate on the process rather than on the results. I've certainly' seen this in my own career.

A stint teaching at a Japanese business school convinced me that I could turn my knowledge of Japanese and my previous international experience (which included some business) into the centerpiece of a viable career. On my return to the United States I did everything I could to bring this about, but somehow, nothing clicked. No matter how single-mindedly I pursued the goal, it never got any closer. Finally, I realized that I had to forge not one, but two much stronger links to connect my U.S. business background, my Japanese expertise, and my general competence in international affairs.

My next tack—one of the best I've ever made—involved turning dead away from my goal. The chamber of commerce job that I took had virtually no Japanese business component, but I figured it would give me management skills, increased international expertise, and perhaps some contacts. It did, and then some. Within two years, I was able to qualify for a Foreign Commercial Service (FCS) post overseas—not in Japan, but in Korea. I was now within sight of my goal. Since the business operating environment in Korea is in many ways similar to the environment in Japan (even the languages are similar), I was clearly gathering components that would increase my value in Japan. Meanwhile, I was able to use the geographic proximity to establish personal contact with key people in the branches in Japan.

One more tack, three years later, and I arrived. Total time elapsed: five of the most fruitful, productive, and enjoyable years of my life, made that way because during each tack I concentrated on the job at hand and enjoyed the process of adding value rather than looking over my shoulder at the goal I'd temporarily put aside. What's more, the tacks I took (one voluntary, the other dictated by circumstance) have shown me a multitude of new career channels, some connected to Japan, some perhaps not, that lead to bigger and better career opportunities.

## CHOOSING JOBS THAT LEAD TO NEW CAREERS

**A**s I've mentioned, the international career network offers many more possibilities than the domestic market because it involves overlapping areas of expertise. In addition to the networks that you build through the industry sector you work in, you also create valuable contacts and opportunities in specialties that cut across industry lines. If you're knowledgable about a given country or geographic region—language, business practices, marketing channels, how to deal with host-country employees—or if you have specialized knowledge of an issue like intellectual property rights that affects a wide range of U.S. businesses overseas, you can move from one industry to another far more easily than you could in the United States.

One way to sort out the myriad possibilities is to divide them by job function. By approaching the matter in this way, you can do more to take advantage of generic expertise, even to the extent of offsetting possible weaknesses in industry-specific areas. *If you understand marketing in a given country or a class of countries such as Japan or Latin America or Socialist economies, you may have the jump on other marketing people, even though they may have more industry-specific experience than you do.* In manufacturing, if you know what it takes to attain consistently high quality in a specific newly industrialized country or lesser developed country (often no mean feat, as any experienced production manager will tell you), you have similar cross-industry value. And any in-depth capacity in language and business practices will serve you equally well.

Of course, this cross-industry approach has its limits. You should put the international network to best use by targeting jobs with the potential to lead directly to one or more different international careers that fit into your plan. Many careers and occupations have this potential, and of course some lines of work offer more possibilities than others. All this is for you to sort out in the light of your goals. Your assessment of the market will also depend on your own background, since for some jobs your domestic skills will be enough, while for others you'll need to acquire extra depth to meet specific international needs, be they an understanding of the Arabic legal system or a knowledge of the export bureaucracy in the PRC.

You'll probably find that the most promising jobs are in occupations, industries or professions that furnish essential services to other industries, because the work you do there will make you aware of opportunities and create professional contacts in those other industries. Banking, accounting, financial services, and law all offer good chances for intra-industry transfers. Other possibilities include transportation, communication, and leasing. All of these fields have both entry-level and management or executive openings, with most of the overseas positions in the latter categories.

Above all, try to get a feeling for the international career network, relationships on the production and distribution chain, contacts between service industries and their clients, openings generated by the activity of multipliers. This network touches every single job on the planet, including yours. Forget job descriptions — they're mainly for the personnel office files. Look at your work in terms of what you actually do, what you can do, and the settings in which you might do it.

**B**anking is one of the most practical and accessible channels through which to enter the international business world in either the private or the public sector. In the first place, banks will hire generalists and liberal arts majors. In the second place, just about everywhere has a bank or two. And because it has an aura of prestige and provides a solid, diversified business background, banking can lead to an astonishing variety of international careers.

If you have a fairly recent college degree, or if you're about to graduate from college, you can try to get into an international management training program at a major bank. Several internationally active U.S. banks have excellent entry-level programs designed to make international banking executives out of recent college grads. The competition is tough, but if you're willing to put in a full day at the office and study banking and financial theory at night, you can make it. However, don't go in with the expectation that you'll be in Tokyo or Paris after a couple of months of training. Bankers are businessmen, and they're hiring you to be a banker, not a tourist.

The program itself, which may last a year or more, will put you to work in different domestic divisions before you do any internationally oriented work. On completion, you'll most likely be assigned to an international desk in a major U.S. office for a couple of years before going overseas. And even then you may find yourself looking at service in some pretty grueling places before you get into the geographic region that you prefer. Keep in mind, however, that you're not in this to be a tourist either. You're looking for career value, not an endless session on the career ladder, and you're on this tack because it leads to many different channels. Banking is interesting, it provides good contacts, and it gives you a great background. It's also bureaucratic, slow-moving, and limiting in many respects. Do a good job, serve the best interests of your clients and the business community, keep an eye on your Big Picture, and tack again when the time is ripe.

Even while you're still in college (or if you haven't gone to college), you can get started on your international banking career by— you guessed it—getting a job at a local bank. If one or more banks in your area have extensive international operations or large international departments, try to get hired straight into the international department, even though the position you get may not seem directly related to international work. And don't be too proud to take a lower entry-level spot if it offers either international value or general business value.

If you aren't able to get a job in a bank's international department, or if there's no internationally active bank in your community, don't despair. If you're just starting out, your initial goal is to get business experience — any business experience — that will help you later on. If you get a position dealing with business customers, through commercial loans, business accounts, or whatever, you can make your job do double duty by learning about the customers' businesses, always on the lookout for international implications.

Your first choice, of course, shouldn't be just any bank. Find out which banks in your community are active in the international business world (the most basic requirement is that the bank have some sort of international department) and which ones have branches or other operations overseas. You also should try to get a fix on which banks have customers with international business. If you're involved with a local international trade association or other multiplier, you can do this in two ways: by talking to banker members about their clients, and by talking to internationally oriented business members about their banks. Target these banks for your most intensive efforts.

Once you're in, your next step (as always) is to learn as much as you can about all aspects of the business you're in. It's absolutely amazing what you can do with a little disciplined curiosity. If you take a constructive interest in your own future, you can easily learn whatever you need by asking questions and requesting assignments in related job areas. Take the initiative. Make it clear to your employers that you want to learn as much as possible about the business. If your bank is active internationally, learn about the types of lending they do, and find out what areas of the world they're most active in. Get and read their annual report. At the same time, learn as much as possible about local commercial clients and accounts with international business or international business potential.

Meanwhile, continue research on the competition (in this case, other banks). Investigate what competing banks are doing overseas; you may find their activities more suited to your career goals. For example, if your bank's international activity is pretty much limited to handling letters of credit and your ambition is to be involved in large-scale international commercial lending, at some point you'll want to make the move to another bank. Or if your bank is very active in Latin America and you believe (as many experienced internationalists do) that the real future of international business is in the Orient, there's likely to be a change of institutions in your future. But for now, you goal is learn, learn, learn.

# CHANGING YOUR LIFESTYLE

**F**or the vast majority of people, who haven't majored in international business and who have no close relatives on the board of an international corporation, creating an international career involves making a sustained effort. Not only should you devote time and energy both to your job and to appropriate multipliers, you may have to create the time for two sets of related activities, education and building a professional foundation. This will be possible only if you start to treat time as your most valuable resource.

A successful entrepreneur once asked me how I'd found the time to learn the foreign languages that have played an important part in helping me create an international career. I answered his question with another question: How many hours a week did he spend watching television? After some thought, he figured his weekly TV time totalled close to twenty hours. That's about one thousand hours per year! With that much time, you can control a couple of languages and master the basics of a new business in two or three years. You don't need to put on a hair shirt, but if you're serious about your future, give some thought to restructuring your use of time.

If you're going to get involved in language study (and I hope by now you've realized that you probably should), buy a portable cassette recorder and earphones. Be sure to get a recorder that has a quick "cue and review" feature. Get language tapes through a bookstore or university language program. All the wasted time you've spent on airplanes, commuter trains and the like can now become learning time.

What this all adds up to is a hard-driving, no-nonsense personal campaign to put yourself firmly in control of your international career. This is the most interesting, exciting and important project of your life, and you'll get out of it exactly what you put into it. You're setting out on a real voyage of discovery, and you don't want to take the chance of slowing yourself down because of sloppy or half-hearted preparation. Once you've conquered your new world, you'll have plenty of time to sit back and enjoy the fruits of your labor.

# TIMING IS EVERYTHING

**A**lthough it's never too late (nor too early) to begin an international career, you need to be conscious of a couple of points about time and timing. When you're relatively young (under thirty), most employers tend to be fairly tolerant of a background featuring lightweight jobs or a high degree of job mobility. Right from the start, however, the better positions will be much more available to you if your career history indicates stability and a sense of purpose and direction. Of course, you will present the best side of your background — that's why you never send the same resume twice — but it's still advisable to keep the following points in mind.

*When considering a possible job, think of it relative to your age*, partly because other people will. A job that looks like a good stepping stone for a person of twenty-two may be viewed as a dead end if taken or held by someone who's over thirty. At the same time, however, if it fits your Big Picture, has value, and provides a key tack, you need the confidence to listen to yourself instead of public opinion. For example, if you have most of the components for a lucrative career in the international gem and jewelry business (knowledge of stones and their value, contacts in source or market areas) but need to pick up actual experience in retailing and learn more about the distribution chain, you could benefit from even a relatively low-level job with a major jeweler. But in general, a good test is this: if you have to tone down your resume to keep from appearing overqualified (why would a Ph.D. in geology want a job in a jewelry store?), you should think twice about going after the job.

From an employer's point of view, major career switches also look a lot better when you're younger. If a forty-year-old accountant decides to become an aerobic dance instructor in Europe, it tends to raise eyebrows. This leads to another general rule of thumb: *the more tacks you have behind you, the more discernible your course should be.* At the beginning of your career, a little trial-and-error can be a good thing, but later on you should show clear signs of knowing where you're going. Thanks to the cross-industry opportunities in the international marketplace, this doesn't mean staying in one industry, but it often does imply staying in the same type of department or division (marketing, sales, personnel, or what have you) in your new industry. Our forty-year-old accountant will be better off if he uses his proven financial expertise to become the finance VP for an internationally franchised chain of aerobic dance studios, or takes some other job, say, in management or business development, where his knowledge of finance has evident value.

*Make a general commitment to remaining at least one year on any job you take.* Of course, if someone makes you a wonderful offer, or your friendly and cooperative supervisor is replaced by Captain Bligh, a move may be in order. But there's quite a bit to be said for the merits of sticking it out for a year or more. For one thing, it usually takes at least that long to gain a good understanding of your job, where it fits into the company, the industry and the international business community, and what new tacks it can lead to. If you're overseas, it will take about the same length of time to start understanding business life in the host country. Finally, a series of one- and two-year-jobs (to say nothing of stints of less than one year) will make you look like either an opportunist or a flake. Neither of these traits is particularly attractive to potential employers.

*In any job, make regular evaluations of what skills and expertise you're acquiring, and compare them to what you need to make a move up or onward.* Normally, the lower the job level, the more interchangeable the skills, but for some international fields, even entry-level positions may require special knowledge like language or international experience. Generally, middle-level to upper-level management skills (the ability to organize and motivate groups of people for productive purposes) are also fairly interchangeable, while production and marketing require more sector-specific and product-specific knowledge. In international management, however, the highly specific ability to work with foreign staff is an important qualification.

Further along, you'll find that many upper-level international management and marketing jobs require from three to eight (or even ten) years experience in the same general line of work. So try to plan job moves in such a way that you remain in the same general field for at least three or four years, while increasing your responsibility (managing larger numbers of people, handling a larger budget and more resources, supervising more important projects, and so on). If this is impossible, it's advisable at least to stick to some sort of logical job progression. For example, a change from international real estate broker to international investment broker makes sense. However, going from restaurant manager to dealer in imported art and antiques may give people the impression that you lack direction.

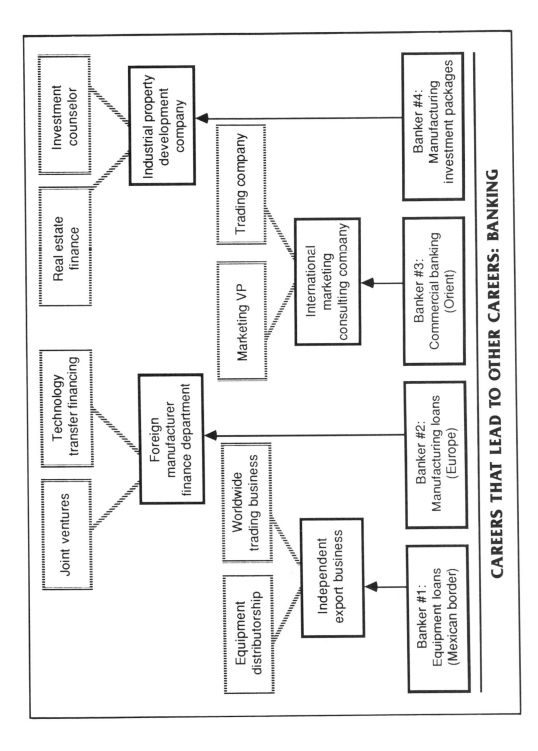

**CAREERS THAT LEAD TO OTHER CAREERS: BANKING**

Timing also can be important in the opposite sense. If you stay too long on certain types of jobs, particularly those with a fairly low level of responsibility, it can work against you. Although stability is a virtue, if you linger in a position that others view as a stepping stone you may create doubts about your own competence and drive. This can put your credibility at risk, and reduce your international career opportunities. One sign that people in the business community think you're working beneath your potential is when you begin to get questions like "What's you next move?" or "Where do you plan to go from here?"

Since every job is different, there's no single test of timing. The best guide is your own learning curve. If it's flattening out in spite of your best efforts to discover more about your job and its relationship with the international job and career network, it may be time to move on. But be sure to look at your job in the context of total value. If, for example, it makes you an ex officio member of a multiplier's governing board, or has you involved in a long-term project that you believe will generate major opportunities for you, it has value beyond the immediate nine to five experience.

## BE SELECTIVE

Occasionally, you may be tempted to take a job primarily because it's international, without considering the possible impact on your career. Although much of the time, even low-level international experience and exposure is better than none, there are some types of exposure that can be damaging to your career, at least on a short-term basis. There are several factors involved.

When considering a job overseas, it's important to understand how both a job and the industry as a whole are viewed in a given country. You also have to get away from American social perceptions to look at the different roles that each culture has defined as being acceptable for various social and ethnic groups, including women and men, the elderly, immigrants, and members of religious orders. When you do so, you often find that in the local context, an otherwise attractive job isn't worth the risk.

In the United States, public relations is an acceptable and lucrative occupation for anyone of any age, but in some parts of the world, people in PR are looked at as being more than a bit suspect. The same is true of entertainers, especially women. Real estate brokerage, which in the United States is often the domain of the dynamic and the upwardly mobile, is the preserve of the elderly in some other societies. In much of the Orient, Confucian tradition has conferred a great deal of status and political influence on farmers and academics, while denying it to merchants and businessmen — quite the opposite from common American patterns.

The point is simply this: to avoid running aground on the hidden reefs of foreign social and business practices, you need to consider any overseas opportunity in terms of the local ethos.

## STEERING CLEAR OF CAPTAIN HOOK

In addition to being selective about the type of job you go after, you should be selective abut the company, particularly when you're considering an overseas job with a foreign employer. Even if it's in the International Fortune 500, you don't have the same legal protection that you would in the United States. Reputable foreign companies can (and often do) slash salaries without warning or explanation, require horrendous amounts of forced overtime, and pay with products in lieu of salary when faced with slack markets. If you're employed by a lesser known, less honorable outfit, almost anything can happen, including your unwitting involvement in illegal activity. It's important to check with independent sources to verify all company promises and claims, and find out what sort of treatment the company is known for.

How can you get an idea of the business strength and reliability of prospective employers? Talk to multiplier organizations and, if you're overseas, the commercial sections of embassies or consulates, both American and foreign.

Although membership in a host-country chamber of commerce or trade association is no guarantee of reliability (especially since in many foreign countries, *all* businesses are required by law to belong to the chamber of commerce), most multiplier organizations encourage their members to adhere to sound, ethical business practices. Furthermore, by talking to members and staff, you often can get valuable background information on member businesses. AmCham chapters can often provide additional information, especially in blatant cases. Horror stories have a way of making the rounds. Don't become one of them. I've seen an awful lot of otherwise knowledgeable people taken in by high-flying hustlers and businesses that closed up shop almost overnight. And I've seen others damage their personal credibility by working for organizations that had a bad image or reputation. Working through local multiplier organizations, check out any potential employer before making a commitment.

■ CHAPTER ■

# 8

# THE HIDDEN TREASURE IN YOUR BACKGROUND

**I**f you're like most of us, you didn't get an early start in planning your international career. International business and related pursuits have only recently come to the fore in the United States, and very likely you prepared for some other career that was more in demand at the time. The greater part of a generation, for example, was brought up on science and technology. Others specialized in law, or trained to become teachers, or went after a Ph.D. because it was considered valuable in getting a job.

Naturally, some of these fields or specialties have, at different times, provided more opportunities than others within the confines of the U.S. career market, and it may be that right now your specialty is losing speed, or dead in the water. Or maybe you're just ready for a change, a challenge, and the allure of new horizons.

Whether you're aiming at an international career because the domestic job market doesn't look as promising as you might like, or primarily out of personal interest, you probably can go international with existing skills — the hidden treasure in your background.

One of the terrific things about the international career marketplace is its flexible practicality. I've mentioned the possibilities that result for generalists when overlapping areas of expertise like a knowledge of a foreign language plus a general background in a business, scientific, or other area create career opportunities that would be reserved for narrow specialists in the domestic market. Another great advantage is the business and technology gap that exists between the United States and many other countries of the world. These aren't just lesser developed countries or third world nations, either. Even in Europe and Japan, there are many areas where development has lagged or taken a different direction from the United States. In these areas, you have excellent chances of using existing skills to create a new career dimension.

The main lesson in all this is that your title or job description at work doesn't say much about your international career potential. Savvy international managers, directors and VP's know that what you can do is more important then what you call it. Show them your stuff, and you're on.

Sometimes, your opportunity will seem to come almost by accident, but it's really your eagerness to use your skills outside your normal role that makes things happen. A foreign firm is having trouble operating the sophisticated equipment your company sold them. The regular on-site training team is unavailable, or isn't geared for the kind of long-term, A to Z hand-holding that's clearly needed. Is there a qualified volunteer who's ready and willing to spend months overseas? This could be the first of many such assignments for you, as it has been for others. Each such assignment creates further new contacts and opportunities, in your company, in each client company, and elsewhere in the industry. Or perhaps your company wants to participate in an overseas trade show for the first time, as part of an industry pavilion. You've been tapped to put together the company exhibit, or to make sales at the show. The industry association, in which you've been active, needs a knowledgeable person to coordinate the entire pavilion. You wear two hats, and lay the foundation for a new international career as a trade event specialist.

Whether you're an aerospace engineer or an economist, or you're about to get a master's degree in sociology or chemistry or business, you can create an international career by using the skills and expertise you've spent so much time and effort to acquire. Sometimes, you'll be able to make a direct transfer or application from the domestic to the international sector. In other cases, you'll find the best opportunities require an innovative reworking and redirecting of skills you've used very differently in the domestic market. The point is that you have components with international value. The main ingredients you'll add are flexibility, creativity, initiative, and patience.

Because necessity is the mother of invention, people with less obvious international components in their inventory often create challenging and rewarding careers. Forced by circumstances to try harder, they tend to have more well-defined goals and to be more innovative in finding ways to attain their goals. Recognizing the limitations of simply following the tide, wind and currents, they develop new ways of rigging and handling their craft.

Regardless of your background, you can increase your creative career awareness and gain a tactical advantage with a simple technique that I call "marooned." First, you list the international jobs or careers that you're qualified to do. Then, imagine that all of them are permanently closed to you for reasons beyond anyone's control. Finally, get yourself off this career island and back in the current by coming up with alternatives.

The purpose of this exercise is to get you to dig for the international value in your background. The objectives are to open your mind to the fact that there are always new applications for existing skills, and that existing skills are often hidden in misleading titles and old job descriptions; find those applications, and fit them into your Big Picture.

Since it's a lot easier to tack when the hull under you is still in one piece, it's far better for you to practice "marooned" as an exercise instead of waiting until your ship is breaking up on a reef. If you wake up to the news that your division's been sold and you're out of a job, it's hard to think clearly, let alone develop new strategies. Even if your career is already foundering, however, you can still take to the lifeboats and come out a winner by using the exercise to redefine the way you intend to reach your objectives. John, a Ph.D. holder from a top private university, had earned a degree in Mexican studies, and had extensive international experience, all in Mexico. In addition to being a successful young assistant professor with a string of publications and innovative courses behind him, he'd spent a couple of years in Mexico on a consulting contract, and still did some occasional international consulting on the side. What could possibly go wrong with his international career?

Plenty. After four years as an assistant professor, John was informed that he would not get tenure. There was nothing wrong with his work, but economic difficulties were causing the university to cut back, and he was the junior nontenured professor in his department. He would have to look for another position.

At first, John was deeply disappointed, but not particularly worried. After all, he had an excellent track record, and his department chairman had promised him a strong recommendation. Besides, if need be he could develop his consulting activities. Unfortunately, however, his secure niche had caused him to lose touch with the current job market. Inflation, slack economic growth and an uncertain future had made not only universities, but government agencies and private companies cut back in all areas; international programs, with their high overhead and limited return, were among the first casualties. It didn't take John long to realize that his odds of finding another university teaching post (unless he was willing to cope with life in Lizard Flats, Arizona) were pretty close to zero, and less than that if he tried to maintain an international orientation. To top it all off, the worsening international economic situation was hitting Mexico, his area of special expertise, so hard that consulting opportunities were drying up. John had run aground.

After a lot of thought, John came to the conclusion that the international component of his career was more important than his specific occupation as a U.S. university professor. The problem was, he lacked the background to do much else outside of Mexico.

Since Mexico was a dead end, John looked to Europe. After a long period of researching and following up leads, he made a tack that put him in a modest position as an instructor teaching Spanish to English-speaking expats in Spain. The salary and status didn't match his previous job, but—as he'd surmised—the value was there. Within a few years he'd learned a lot about business, and made extenisve contacts in the European business world. With this background, he then moved into a purely business career. John was able to create his second international career by understanding the proper relative importance of price and value, and using existing career components—international business awareness, language, and teaching experience—to tack his way through a major career change.

Even if you don't have an internationally oriented university degree or international experience, there are many excellent international career opportunities open to you. It's up to you to be creative in identifying even seemingly far-fetched applications for your skills, and turning them into viable opportunities. Let's look at a specific example of a domestic profession with what we might call "typically unusual" international applications.

P erhaps you have (or are about to get) a law degree. If your odds of signing on with an international law firm in the United States don't look good, where might you turn? Simple reasoning can give you some ideas. For example, it's a widely publicized fact that lawyers are scarce in the

Orient. Due to a combination of tradition, philosophy, and political and social systems, countries like Japan, Korea, and China have very few lawyers in proportion to the size of their populations. In fact, some analysts believe that a lack of reliance on litigation allows countries like Japan to put more of their energies into productive activities, rather than wasting time and money on attorneys and courtroom proceedings.

This may be true, but now the countries of the Orient are awash in a rising tide of legal cases resulting from their increasing business and trade relations with the United States. What does this mean to aspiring international attorneys? Simply that there's a demand for people with their background and skills to help unravel the idiosyncracies of the American legal process, particularly as it relates to international trade and business. And who could better understand such inscrutable mysteries than a U.S.-trained lawyer?

The result of the bumpy legal interface between East and West is that enterprising young American lawyers can find steady work in places like Tokyo, Seoul and Hong Kong, helping smooth the rough edges that hinder the flow of business between two cultures. Although knowledge of one of the local languages is a tremendous help, you can begin without it. And if you're willing to take on this sort of international adventure, you can find ample rewards.

As is usual with international careers, there are several routes to follow. Perhaps the most obvious is to sign on with a U.S. law firm with correspondents or affiliates abroad, then transfer to an overseas assignment with one of them. A less direct course is to establish yourself in practice in the United States (either independently or with an existing law firm), and then create a relationship with a like-minded foreign attorney or firm. Every U.S. Embassy and Consultate (commercial, economic, or American services section) has a list of host-country attorneys that are active with American clients, and some of them will welcome the chance to create or expand a beachhead in the United States. After you gain some experience, you have the option of continuing as you are, or making arrangments to do a stint in the foreign country where you've developed contacts. Finally, you may work into an overseas assignment by doing international work for one or more U.S. clients and moving abroad to represent them on either a staff or consulting basis.

If you go after a law position overseas, be aware that in most foreign countries you technically won't be allowed to practice law or participate in court proceedings, but will be limited to serving as a "legal consultant" for a local firm (including correspondents and affiliates of stateside law offices). However, this arrangement will still give you plenty of action and exposure, because you'll be engaged in all the same noncourtroom activities that you would at home. Once again, it's what you do, not what it's called, that counts. Moreover, since the relatively scarce American attorney abroad is often the only lifeguard available or willing to rescue storm-tossed U.S. business people, you can form professional and personal relationships that will give you access to more than a proportional share of interesting business opportunities.

Since legal training and a law degree confer a high degree of credibility in the business community, many attorneys go outside the legal profession to develop and profit from international expertise. Rather than function purely as a lawyer, you may want to act as a stateside or foreign-based consultant, agent or provider of business services to firms and multipliers involved in trade, investment and other activities. Later, if you want to, you can transfer the contacts and skills you've acquired back to a full-time legal practice to make use of them there. You may find yourself doing so well that you decide to continue as you are.

Even if your life as an international attorney produces no immediate results beyond a series of run-of-the-mill business cases, the experience is invaluable, especially if you get it overseas. The long term result is the accumulation of a rare set of qualifications and expertise that will make you much more attractive to a wide variety of international firms. Not the least of these new assets is the language ability that you'll acquire if you make a commitment to studying the local language from the very first day that you land a position overseas or begin dealing with a specific country from your U.S. base.

If you go abroad, what happens when you come back to the United States? Your reentry job needn't be limited to a U.S. law firm. Your overseas experience (you should try for at least a year or two in one country or region) will make you attractive to many American businesses active in the overseas area where you've been working. And if you've been involved in the local AmCham chapter (one of the best overseas multipliers), you'll be well known to American overseas managers and executives of U.S. firms, who can give you recommendations when (and if) you decide to return to the United States.

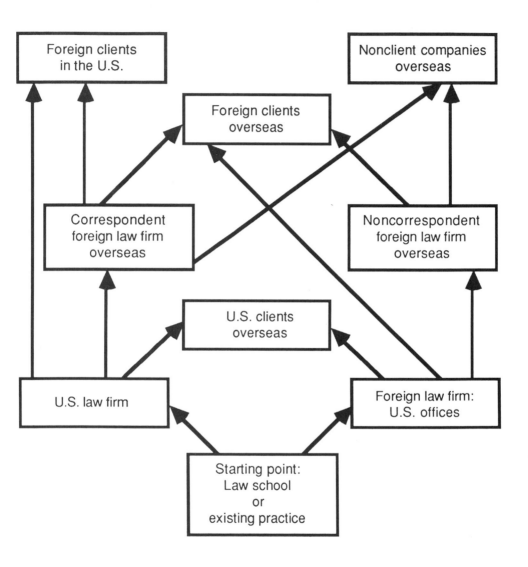

In many cases, you can be on two tacks at once: for example, working for a law firm overseas, and representing clients who are not clients of the law firm. Some American lawyers overseas provide representation for U.S. state trade development offices on a personal contract basis.

Foreign firms and governments operating in the United States also may play a major role in your future. More than one ambitious young law school grad has gone overseas, spent time learning the legal and business customs (and some of the language) of a foreign country, and gone on to be a lobbyist for foreign interests in Washington, D.C. or in a state capital.

A background in science, technology or medicine (including nursing) is another channel through which you can enter an international career. If your background is in high-technology electronics, medical equipment, computers, computer software, biotechnology, or similar fields, you can

## SCIENCE, TECHNOLOGY AND MEDICINE

develop especially good international career opportunities in marketing, or in technological transfer situations in which entire labs or manufacturing facilities are installed and set in operation for foreign companies. Because of the technological lead enjoyed by the United States in many product sectors, even without highly specialized or product-specific skills you often have good chances for direct, individual employment with foreign firms trying to develop their high-tech capabilities at home and their high-tech business worldwide.

Although a degree in medicine or nursing can have direct application in lower-ranked third world countries, virtually all developed countries, newly industrialized countries and lesser developed countries won't let you practice medicine or nursing without a degree from one of their medical or nursing schools. There are also extensive restrictions on research, especially where human subjects are involved. However, increasing numbers of U.S. medical personnel are discovering the advantages of applying their institutional or experimental expertise through joint ventures, licensing and technology transfer agreements. Many of these arrangements stress the business side of the medical industry, rather than the professional applications, although obviously professional expertise is involved. Business areas include geriatrics (still in its institutional infancy in most countries), home health care, and specialized treatment centers. New types of demand surface every day; America's first AIDS hospital (opened in Texas in 1986) is one example of a need that was recognized and responded to in advance of other countries.

If you have technical expertise or a medical, nursing or science degree (a B.S. is sufficient in many areas), you can also create opportunities in international marketing with companies that export technical and scientific equipment. Some of these companies, reasoning that sales and marketing experience is secondary to an understanding of the product, will gladly hire you on the basis of your medical, technical or scientific training. For example, a medical professional who's actually had to use the equipment, often can do a better job of selling blood-gas analyzers, sonic scanners and other medical equipment than a marketing specialist. In some cases, even a generalized knowledge of a scientific field will make it easier for you to relate to the scientific types that buy the equipment. Some employers may require some experience or education in sales or marketing but you can learn about marketing and sales far more readily than marketing and sales people can absorb large doses of scientific knowledge. In either case, the pragmatic flexibility of the international career market allows you to take full advantage of *all* your scientific skills and expertise, whether or not they fall within your formal specialty.

As is true in so many international career areas, you can discover new opportunities outside your nominal specialty in science, medicine and technology by looking at what you do rather than thinking in terms of your title. Let's look at how this might work if you were, say, a scientific researcher, maybe a chemist. Your Big Picture calls for escaping from the lab routine and getting into something more stimulating overseas, but your field of research lacks the broad market demand of sectors like state-of-the-art electronics and the pizzazz of high-flying areas like genetic engineering. You've got to identify another skill component that can get you started.

First, turn your thoughts to international trends that you see developing. You know that there's a lack of software design capability in newly industrialized countries that are trying to break into world computer markets. This means that expertise in computer program design and application is highly marketable in these countries, as they rush to develop indigenous software industries. Is there a connection with your own situation? Absolutely. Like many other scientific researchers, you make extensive use of computers in your daily work. This can be the link between your personal Big Picture and a new international career.

If you're in this position, or one somewhat like it, how do you proceed? Focus your ongoing study of major international trends on specific countries and industries that can use your expertise. Pay close attention to related articles in both news media and trade journals. Talk to friends and colleagues and work through major multipliers in the scientific community to identify foreign contacts in the computer software field. Based on what you learn, write up a solid background marketing summary that emphasizes your computer-related experience and ability. Of course, you'll tailor this summary to fit the context of each specific opportunity you discover.

If — as is probably the case — you haven't been active in any international multipliers, start getting involved. At meetings, talk to people whose international business includes your computer specialty. Find out what's going on overseas, and which U.S. businesses are active there. Since one of the major trends in computers and related fields is the widespread hiring of individual independent contractors or consultants for specific jobs (rather than using full-time employees), you have a good chance of identifying or creating a specialized niche in this role. If you have foreign language skills, concentrate on firms doing business in countries where you can use them. Your next track can be marketing for a U.S. or foreign company, or doing design, development, technical assistance or troubleshooting in a variety of settings in the U.S. and overseas.

$T$here are excellent international career opportunities, particularly in service businesses and international foundations and agencies, for people with humanities and social science backgrounds. As you discover new ways to apply the knowledge and skills acquired through your generalist or humanities training, you'll be amazed at the possibilities.

## HUMANITIES AND SOCIAL SCIENCES

International multipliers, consulting firms, specialized institutes and similar organizations often provide the greatest opportunities, especially if they're working in sectors where the United States has a developmental edge. In the settings they offer, you can develop organizational and managerial skills for later use in a move to a more specialized organization.

Worldwide demographic and economic changes mean that even countries that traditionally have used extended family structures and strong social traditions to deal with such issues as education, treatment of the aged, recreation, and overall personal and social well-being are now turning to professional methods and systems for further progress. In these areas, and in many others, America's pace-setting evolution to a service economy means there is a continual flow of service know-how to other countries in the world. As in the science and technology sector, the international development gap means more opportunities and more rapid advancement for qualified Americans at all levels. A skill level that would only qualify you as a staff member in a U.S. outfit might move you up to a managerial position overseas. Much of this flow is through the private sector, but an impressive amount is channeled through public agencies.

Both USAID, America's major foreign assistance agency, and private foundations with international programs use educators, specialists in library science, and humanities and social science generalists in a wide range of activities aimed at developing cultural infrastructure in lesser developed countries. If you have expertise in media or public relations, the U.S. Information Agency (USIA) offers attractive possibilities in its role as purveyor of the American image to virtually all countries of the world.

By contacting public agencies and private foundations for information on their international programs, you can kill two birds with one stone: you find out about possible applications for your skills within these agencies, and you also get a fix on demand and additional opportunities in specific countries. A USAID-backed education reform project in a Southeast Asian country means possible openings for educators, both inside and outside the project. A USIS seminar series on journalistic techniques in a specific country or region may reveal niches that a U.S. journalist could fill. A foundation's work with the aged overseas can spell opportunity in a growing industry for those with experience in this area. This is why it always pays to dig for information on the operations of any outfit you contact. Each one is like an island where you can find the buried treasure of a new international career.

There are vast possibilities in this area, and your only limit is your capacity to investigate and innovate. In addition to working through multipliers that serve specific disciplines (economics, sociology, education, and so on), start considering which U.S., U.N. and other agencies appear to be involved in areas that match your qualifications and interests. Since you're always looking for dual applications — both with the agency and in a wider context — you can use international agencies to do your homework for you. If the IMF is active in a certain area, for example, they've already done the research that shows you where the demand is and what the specific needs are. Your career efforts then should target both the IMF program, and the general area where they've shown that the demand exists. In the more centralized economies typical of many developing or newly industrialized countries, this demand will be both in the private sector and in planning departments, ministries of finance or education, and similar agencies where you can use your degree of experience in sociology, anthropology, economics and other humanities and social science fields. The U.S. Department of State, which has many positions (especially in the political and economic cones) for generalists, is another very promising place to begin (or diversify) your international career.

Many humanities majors have skills that can be marketed and applied in very different areas. What you have to do is *identify valuable components, repackage them in a well-targeted background summary, and market them to a target industry*. With this perspective, even the most esoteric, ivory-tower discipline can lead to an international career.

## JOURNALISM, PUBLISHING, AND MEDIA

Although U.S. standards in these areas are far higher than the world average, international opportunities are limited for a number of reasons. The most obvious problem is language: unless the periodical, radio or TV station, or other information medium is aimed at an English-speaking consumer population, your chances are almost nil. No matter what your level of managerial skill or editorial or journalistic expertise, it makes little sense to implant a foreign body (yours) into a non-English speaking business environment.

However, a large number of non-English speaking countries around the world have English-language media for the foreign business and tourist communities, and still others (like India) use English as a *lingua franca* in many situations. In these areas, most of the opportunities are designed to utilize your language skills (including writing and editing) more than other components in your professional inventory. Unless you're exceptionally creative and convincing, you'll have few shots at anything that smacks of management or executive decision-making. Instead, your activity will probably be confined to writing, translating (or correcting other people's translations), proofreading and editing—all subject to revision, including reinsertion of erroneous English, by local staff.

There are, however, opportunities with international publications and publishing companies, both in English-speaking and non-English-speaking countries. In the case of U.S.-based companies, hiring is usually done in the United States, and management positions often require experience in the company or in the industry.

The second restrictive factor is more difficult to overcome. Unlike the United States (which is one of a small minority of countries that believes in a free flow of information), most countries view information as a commodity at the service of the state. For this reason, not only information but those who deal with it are strictly controlled, and access to media careers, whether by consumers or professionals in the field, is restricted. Even in countries where the government isn't a problem, nationalistic unions can raise formidable barriers to entry by foreigners. In such environments, career opportunities are limited, so your first step in researching international publishing or media careers in any country should always be to determine the level of government control and restrictions on foreign participation.

So what do you do to make the leap, say, from a career in editing into the international marketplace? Look at what you do in your present work. Many editing jobs demand high levels of organizational skills, excellent computer and word-processing capabilities, a finely tuned eye toward marketing opportunities, and in the case of acquisitions editors, excellent contract negotiating and public relations capabilities. Now, as you can see, you have plenty of useful applications to bring to the international arena.

There are more direct applications, too. A big portion of the publishing business is now in subsidiary rights which includes sale of foreign rights and translation rights. Literary agencies handle these negotiations for independent, small publishers, while major publishing houses have separate divisions for this lucrative part of the business. Here is where what you know and who you know can come together to help you break into a fascinating international career. Most of the actual work will be done stateside, but there are important international book fairs held in Frankfurt, London, Bologna and Jerusalem yearly.

**SPORTS**

In a number of countries where U.S. sports like baseball are popular, American athletes willing to take their careers on an international tack have done quite well. Some Americans have even invaded exotic foreign sports like Japanese sumo wrestling! More importantly, transplanted U.S. athletes can combine their reputation (as foreigners, they often get extra media attention) with the language skills and international savvy they acquire to create international business careers as sporting goods marketing representatives or in-country managers or executives in charge of joint venture or license manufacturing of sporting goods equipment.

Of course, you don't have to be a professional jock to create an international career opportunity in sports. You can use any one of a number of sports-related specialties to make a position for yourself. Do you have special expertise in sports training or sports medicine? How about various aspects of sports business such as endorsements, contract negotiation and sports career management? Many countries lag far behind the United States in these and other specialties on the edge of the participatory sports world.

You may spot opportunities for yourself by looking at recent sports developments in America. The United States generates a wide range of new sports-related products and enterprises (from hula hoops to skateboard parks) that become commonplace in America while still relatively unknown overseas. This time lag can give you a definite advantage abroad, since often you can export business concepts into growing markets with relatively little competition. In the mid-1980s, for example, entrepreneurs in the U.K. sports industry announced their intention to create a professional league for American football. For any American with significant experience as a player, organizer, or supplier to the sport in the United States, this move by the British could generate a lot of opportunities.

There are also organizational activities related to youth sports, involving people ranging from professional managers, coaches and special tutors to organizers of noncompetitive sports-theme summer camps (tennis, wind-surfing and sailing, soccer and others) for children and adults from relatively wealthy families. Since many newly industrialized countries don't have enough experienced local nationals to satisfy the rapidly increasing demand for these specialized activities, your chances can be quite good, and the opening of a new market (like the U.K. football market) allows you to piggyback on the promotions and fanfare that the promoters put into developing their own market segment.

In some countries, specialized market demand has created unusual niches in certain sports-related occupations which can give you greater opportunities overseas than you could enjoy at home. In a number of countries, a growing expat population, expanding tourism, and increasing amounts of disposable income and leisure time are creating outstanding potential in the ski industry. In Korea, for example, the number of skiers is increasing exponentially, and the ski lift capacity has quadrupled in just a few years. In some Latin American countries, growth has been equally impressive in spite of local economic ups and downs. Even the People's Republic of China has embarked on a program to develop a ski resort industry. All this means opportunities in everything from ski lift machinery and resort design and engineering to rental equipment, clothing, and food service.

One way to tap this career market, and others like it, is to work in through the sporting goods industry in the United States, and transfer the experience to an international context. You might, for example, do as others have done and move from a position with a domestic wholesaler into an overseas slot supervising production or distribution by either an American or a foreign company in a foreign location.

Another method is to gain an entrée by using existing skills to aim at the tourist and expat niche. In the case of skiing, the common problem of too few English-speaking instructors to teach English-speaking beginners at host-country ski resorts means that you can put yourself near the center of the action simply by pointing out the increased revenues that resort operators can generate by offering English-language instruction for foreigners, and presenting yourself as the most likely candidate. Other tacks are public relations, foreign liaison (full- or part-time), and sales and rental agent for ski lodges and condominiums. Your objective, of course, isn't to be a ski bum or lodge lizard, but to spot other opportunities in the rapidly expanding ski equipment market and other ski industry segments which can generate new tacks for your international career. You might end up — as others have — representing U.S. or foreign equipment manufacturers, or becoming involved in spin-off industries on a ski theme (gift shops, Alpine-style restaurants and Bierstuben, and others). Any language and business skills you acquire can later be transferred to a different career environment.

# THE MILITARY

A military background can lead to a great variety of international careers. I've met many former military people in rewarding international positions, including the public relations director of an international consulting firm, an international trading company executive, an international marketing director, and many others. As in other areas, the key is to look at what you do, not what it's called (how many civilian businesspeople understand military designations, anyway?) and think about how it fits into the workd of international business. Do you have any special technical knowledge, particularly relating to defense industries? How about language skills, international personnel or management experience, or knowledge of a foreign area? All of these have value in the international career market.

As a military person, one of your great advantages is that you understand military needs from the user's point of view, and you can talk to the military in their own language. Even if your rank isn't high enough to be part of the military-industrial network, you have great credibility in marketing because you understand the equipment, how it's used, and what the military wants to know about it. If you're a specialist in radar, communications, security devices, nuclear or other technical specialties, you have knowledge and skills that are valuable in the international marketplace. If your background includes electronics, for example, you're valuable to U.S. defense electronics companies because they need people who understand military requirements, priorities, and thinking. Your value is even greater if you're familiar with the requirements — and thinking — of a foreign military.

Of course, you'll need more than a knowledge of the equipment to land a good job. To develop specific international career skills, consider taking courses in marketing and other business areas, and possibly language lessons. Talk to your education officer to find out what's available. To acquire in-country expertise and language skills, you may also want to do a tour in an area where economic and industrial growth or specialized military needs are creating good international career potential.

If you're overseas, you should talk to someone in the commercial section of the U.S. Embassy to find out what companies are marketing in the country, and get lists of U.S. exhibitors in local military electronics trade shows. Find out who the show sponsors are, and what American multipliers are involved. Find out how to get admitted to the show. If it's restricted, and many are, start working on getting a pass through the embassy commercial section, your unit, or the sponsoring organization. The hierarchy may make it tough, but it's worth the effort to try. You'll get a much better picture of what's going on in the industry, and you can talk to exhibitors' reps to get a feel for what types of jobs might be available to you.

At the show, get business cards. Find out as much as possible about the marketing structure of the companies and the industry, including marketing and export agents other than manufacturers. In many cases, it's easier to break in through an export management company or other international marketing company that represents smaller manufacturers of finished products or components. If you sense that you're getting a positive reaction, ask for names of people you can contact in the company.

Finally, contact a company decision-maker to present your qualifications and express your interest. In some cases, the best contact may be the overseas rep (who often will be a marketing director or VP) you've spoken to in person. As in other areas, you multiply your chances if you have something to offer. If you're overseas, try to identify a need in the U.S. forces or host-country military, and point it out when you contact potential employers. In countries with advanced industrial capabilities, you can also contact host-country manufacturers regarding products and components that they want to market in the United States.

I realize that for many military people, especially those who have spent several years in the service, it's hard to be this aggressive. However, nothing ventured, nothing gained. You can't get in by just hanging around outside the door; you have to knock loudly enough to be heard.

Of course, not everyone in the military has a background in a specialized technical area. A nontechnical military management background (especially one that includes liaison with host-country military personnel) and overseas experience are well suited to a career with a variety of international multiplier organizations and U.S. Government agencies, including the U.S. Department of Commerce (export controls), the U.S. Customs Service, the CIA, and others. There are also many civilian companies that sell to the military, both products for military use like uniforms and supplies, and items for PX or commissary sale. While you're in the military, you're in an ideal position to identify the suppliers and decide what opportunities they represent.

If you're overseas (or scheduled to go overseas), how about representing a nontechnical American firm in the country where you are (or will be) stationed? While overseas, you also can make arrangements to become a rep for a host-country company after you return to the United States. You can develop leads by using multipliers, the U.S. Department of Commerce, and the trade promotion office of the foreign country in question to find out what companies are in the market for new agents or reps.

# 9

INCREASING YOUR INTERNATIONAL I.Q.

ou may be able to parlay expertise and skills acquired in a domestic job directly into an international career. Often, however, you'll find that the best international positions require specific international skills and resources, or that being able to point to significant international background gives you much more control over the terms and conditions of your employment. On the whole, the more you have in the way of specifically international capabilities, the more marketable you are.

In many cases, potential employers have little or no international experience themselves, and they'll be counting on you (especially if you're to be based overseas) to be their eyes and ears. Whether stateside or abroad, you'll be like a pilot on the company ship, picking a safe passage through the tricky and sometimes treacherous waters of international trade and business. Based on your recommendations and evaluations, they'll make business decisions that will affect the future of the entire company. You need to have the right stuff in international terms.

Because success in the international business environment depends heavily on subjective intangibles like the ability to deal with foreign nationals or thrive in a foreign setting, a lot of your international expertise can be general, or even intuitive. You'll need a subjective understanding of how host-country people think and how they react to situations, a knowledge of host-country business practices, in-country contacts, and an ability to use the local language. I call this combination of specific knowledge and general awareness your international IQ, because it indicates your ability to tie different factors together and come up with results, rather than try to muddle through by applying someone else's textbook solutions to the unique problems and challenges that are part of all international operations. As a pilot who knows the international waters, it's not enough to know the location and depth of every reef and shoal. You have to be able to steer the ship safely among them, all the while responding to constantly shifting tides, winds, currents, and pieces of flotsam, or even an occasional iceberg—90 percent hidden beneath the surface. This is what international expertise— your international IQ—is all about.

When assessing your international IQ, be sure to give yourself credit for expertise acquired through unusual means. If you spent ten years in the United States doing volunteer work with Spanish-speaking aliens, or practicing judo with a predominantly Japanese team in an ethnic neighborhood, you know a lot about how Hispanics or Japanese think and act. Clearly, this knowledge has value in many business and professional situations; your job is to discover and define applications that raise your international value and enhance your credibility. Since most multipliers are always looking for appropriate essays and articles for their publications, a well-directed article or two ("Project Management in a Hispanic Environment;" "Japanese Resistance to Foreign Innovation") can establish the substance of your experience and add a lot of polish to your resume. You can also do as many international consultants do, and write a short piece (not a letter to the editor, but an article of 700 words or so) for an internationally respected business publication like the *Wall Street Journal*. It can help you acquire even greater name recognition and a reputation for knowledgeability. Of course, no single article or essay is going to get you a job, any more than a single exam or term paper got you through college. What counts is the cumulative effect of all your efforts. Each piece goes toward building up a track record.

If you think your career progress, either with your present employer or with other organizations, calls for a major increase in your international awareness, there are several ways to proceed. You may decide that course work, either in the United States or overseas, is in order. Or, if you have all the academic and theoretical background that you need, you can get country-specific experience in a foreign environment. Let's examine the possibilities.

## EDUCATION IN THE UNITED STATES

One simple way to raise your international I.Q. is through education. It's possible that your background could be much more marketable with the addition of a couple of courses in key areas. For example, if you're a humanities major with a good knowledge of one or more foreign languages, completing two or three courses in accounting, finance, and international economics and trade could well be enough to qualify you for a career with the international department of a bank, trading company, or other international service company. Similarly, as we've already seen, a few credits in sales and international business and marketing can make a science or technical background very attractive to companies that export medical, analytical and scientific equipment, computers, electronic production and test equipment, and related products. What you're looking for, as always, is added value in the form of a link that ties existing components into an internationally marketable whole.

If you've determined that you need additional education, first consider the possibility of getting it in your community, either on your own or through an organized course. There's certainly no point in quitting your present job and rushing off overseas if you can get what you need closer to home! Many universities have continuing education programs involving night or weekend classes or correspondence courses. You may decide that you can get the required knowledge independently, by studying key books and materials at home, or better yet, through involvement with a multiplier or other organization where you can make committee activities, volunteer service or an internship the basis for applied study, research and possibly publishable material to further your career. Many multipliers also offer periodic lectures, seminars and workshops on international matters; you may start out as an attendee and go on to become a featured speaker, another step in the right direction.

## EDUCATION OVERSEAS

Suppose you have career components that could be very valuable with the addition of some area-specific or country-specific course work that's not available through any local program. You could, of course, go elsewhere in the United States for training, but there's a good chance you can get what you need overseas at about the same cost, and with the added bonus of in-country experience, increased language capability, and new contacts.

If you find yourself in this situation while you're still in school, consider taking a year's leave to go to the area of your choice. By planning your overseas academic experience around your career Big Picture, including the next possible tack or two, you can do a lot to raise your international IQ, create contacts, and generate opportunities. Foreign universities around the world have courses in international economics, business, general area studies, language, and other humanities and social sciences, many of them designed for foreigners and taught in English. These will give you as much or more than what you can get in most U.S. schools. Many of these courses are given in cooperation with U.S. universities; in other cases your university will allow you to do course work overseas and get credit by examination or the completion of a project or paper upon your return. Of course, be sure to get a firm commitment for transfer or creation of credit before you go, and make sure that you can take courses, do research, and write papers that have direct application to the career you're planning.

As an alternative, American universities offer a wide variety of overseas programs, including overseas campuses, junior year abroad programs, and exchange programs with universities in a number of countries. The University of Pittsburgh even has a floating campus that provides full credit for international experience obtained on a study cruise around the world! This program is open to both degree and nondegree students, and I've seen some enterprising participants use it to establish some very interesting and potentially worthwhile contacts.

Check with local universities for details, and don't hesitate to write to major universities out of your area to find out what they offer. To finance your studies, apply for aid from organizations that offer scholarships for qualified students to spend a year studying, doing research, or working abroad. You can research the availability of grants and scholarships at your university library or financial aid office.

If it looks as though you'll need to go overseas for some of the education process, *try to take care of the U.S.-acquired part first.* There are at least two reasons for this: later you may find that you don't need the overseas education after all, and if you do go overseas, you want to be fully prepared (through your stateside training) to take advantage of any opportunity that comes up over there. Especially if you're involved with AmCham or other business multipliers abroad, it's not unusual to create a good career opportunity, which will be a lot easier to take advantage of if you have no loose ends—like a semester or two of course work—dangling in the United States.

If you decide on overseas education, allow plenty of lead time to arrange for both the educational program and any employment that you may need to survive. Remember that you'll probably need a work permit or work visa from the host-country government, which can be a time-consuming process. Even if you won't need work, you can't rush this type of project, since in some cases it may take you almost a year to get into an academic program.

If you're already living overseas, you may be able to get the courses you need through another type of U.S. university program. A number of universities have overseas programs (both degree and nondegree) designed primarily for American adults living abroad.

If you're overseas as a dependent, in the military, or some other capacity, and need additional training to attain your international career goals, this type of program could have what you're looking for. Check with the nearest American Embassy or Consulate. Ask for the "CLO" or Community Liaison Office; if there isn't one, ask for the American Services section. If you're near a U.S. military base, talk to the education officer. If it's difficult to get full information from these sources, try the Information Service (USIS). Or write directly to one of the U.S. universities that have this type of overseas program. (The University of Maryland, for example, has an extensive network.)

## OVERSEAS WORK PROGRAMS

**W**orking abroad not only can do incredible things for your international awareness, it can lead directly to new career opportunities. You can generate your own short-term jobs overseas, but you should check into programs that have created regular opportunities for students in business-related fields to go abroad for actual work experience in foreign firms. One of the major student organizations arranging this type of situation is called AIESEC (pronounced "eye-seck," Association Internationale des Etudiants en Sciences Economiques et Commerciales); others are AIPT (Association for International Practical Training) and USSTS (U.S. Student Travel Service). Check with your local university office of student organizations for details, or contact AIESEC, AIPT or USSTS directly (for this and other contact addresses and telephone numbers, see the directory in Appendix B). There's also an organization in Washington, DC called the National Association of Foreign Student Affairs (NAFSA). Although you might not guess it from the name, NAFSA has information on overseas employment, much of it related to English teaching.

To research overseas employment possibilities, including non-career and part-time positions, classified ads in English-language newspapers from foreign countries are a good starting point. Focus on opportunities that will build up your expertise in more than one critical area (for example, language plus marketing, or research experience plus management).

To do the most for your career, always look beneath the surface for hidden potential, especially future value. Does a short-term position have long-term possibilities? If there's no full-time position available, how about part-time, or even an unpaid position, that can become full-time? You can supplement your income through other activities like teaching, which is discussed below. Of course, be careful not to spread yourself too thin. At all stages in the research and contact process, review your needs and keep an eye on your Big Picture. If the overseas alternative doesn't look too promising, you may conclude that it's better to stay in the United States for a while.

## TEACHING OVERSEAS

**Y**ou can use teaching in a number of different ways to increase your international IQ, develop contacts, and create opportunities. One method is to take advantage of vacation travel to give lectures, workshops or seminars overseas to individual companies or to foreign or American multipliers like AmCham.

If you have a technical or scientific background, you have something to offer foreign companies, especially in areas where the United States has a technological lead. In textile producing nations, for example, companies that are squeezed by the ever-tightening international textile quota system are branching out into other labor-intensive manufacturing, including semiconductors. Since they often can't get as much information and advice as they need from local sources, there's a demand that you can help meet. To get practice, and create a track record, you can first give lectures to companies and multiplier groups in the United States, and then propose the same thing to foreign companies and groups, which you can identify through the U.S. Embassy and industry multipliers.

If you're in an area like leasing or financial services, which are more developed in the United States than in many foreign countries, you can do the same type of thing. The same approach is also useful if you have expertise in management, marketing, planning, real estate, or similar business-oriented specialties. You also can start making contacts and opening channels by using your overseas vacation travel to give a short course to a foreign management association, banker's association, or other appropriate multiplier. The contacts generated by this type of activity yield multiple returns by adding value to your background (potential U.S. employers are always looking for people with good overseas contacts and references) and by letting you show your stuff to potential employers in the foreign business community. They also can form the basis for an independent consulting practice.

Teaching can also be used as a source of income while overseas. Although I've met Americans of all ages abroad, who were teaching every conceivable type of course (including a yoga instructor in Bolivia and a fellow who was teaching karate in Japan, of all places), the mainstay around the globe is the one thing that every American presumably knows something about: the English language.

Even those countries that make it hard for foreigners to get a work permit (and believe me, in many countries the last thing you want is to get caught working without a permit) tend to encourage the teaching of English by foreigners. And you don't need a doctorate in English literature to qualify. In many cases, the fact that you're a native speaker is enough. Of course, if you have a degree in English or any professional background as a teacher, it's a point in your favor.

Although it's much more secure to have some sort of teaching job lined up before you head off across the water, many adventuresome types just hop on the plane and hope that something comes up before they run out of money. This approach seems to work best in the Orient, probably because the total number of foreigners is smaller, the educational systems tend to have very stiff English requirements, English is relatively harder to learn because it's so different from the local languages, and local teachers haven't had much chance to learn correct pronunciation. It also seems feasible in parts of Latin America. I'd recommend against it in Europe; the odds just don't seem to be there. In any case, before you make any major move, talk to someone who has been through it.

In some parts of the world a free-lance English (or other) teacher can make a decent living, but the continual search for students can be a tiring business. A much better arrangement is to work under contract, either for an English-teaching company, or as a direct hire, in-house instructor for a local company involved in international business. Examples are trading companies, businesses with large import or export divisions, and service businesses catering to foreigners, including airlines, hotels, and large restaurants. In many cases, these teaching jobs evolve into a wide variety of career opportunities in the company or industry in question.

In the latter categories, contact the offices of major hotel and restaurant chains with operations overseas to interest them in using your skills to improve the English abilty of their "foreign" (host-country) staff. First, go after those with operations in countries that are experiencing or anticipating a tourist boom. Prime candidates are countries that are within about two years of hosting a major international event such as the Olympics, which generates considerable demand for English skills in local service industries. You should also focus on countries and specific cities that host annual international conferences, such as the Frankfurt International Book Fair, held every autumn in Frankfurt, Germany. Events like this generate a constant demand for English-speaking host-country personnel, and for instructors to get them to the required level of fluency.

The actual hiring decision probably will be made on site, but you may be able to create an opportunity by making initial contacts in the United States. When trying to create an opening with a major international company (as opposed to a smaller, local firm), you'll need solid, verifiable qualifications, including a college degree or teaching experience.

If you're one of the millions who never intended to spend your life coated with chalk dust, you may be wondering why I'm discussing teaching. The reason is simple: at a minimum, it'll enable you to gain international experience and language skills. In addition, if you stay alert to other opportunities in the host country, you may well work yourself into a job with broader potential. In any case, you'll add to your international background. And English teaching isn't the only possibility; virtually all major cities in Europe and the Orient, and many in Latin America, have one or more private schools (attended mainly by the children of executives and diplomats from English-speaking countries) offering a complete curriculum, with all courses given in English.

To research teaching opportunities overseas, start with multiplier organizations, in this case, those dealing with the teaching profession. There are several multipliers that can provide information on overseas positions; the most frequently used are listed in the directory in Appendix B.

If you hold a valid teaching credential to teach subjects other than English, there may be a spot for you in a U.S. Department of Defense (DOD) school overseas. These schools are run by the U.S. Government for the dependents of military and DOD personnel serving overseas. U.S. Embassy people abroad also send their children to these schools, or to private schools. Check with the DOD.

Private schools are another possibility; they offer the additional advantages of a very cosmopolitan international clientele, less red tape, and more locations. Contact the multipliers listed in the directory to pinpoint opportunities. If you're interested in a particular geographic area, write to the nearest embassy Community Liaison Office or Information Service office, or to the AmCham office, to get the names and addresses of local international schools.

If you have other specialized skills (be they jazz piano, fly casting, or anything else that's teachable), give some thought to teaching them overseas, either through a school or business, or as a freelancer.

# LEARN THE BASICS OF INTERNATIONAL TRADE AND BUSINESS

**N**o matter what international career you end up in, trade and similar issues have become so important that every competent professional needs to understand the mechanics, issues and politics involved in trade. Luckily, you don't have to delay graduation, go back to school full time, or enroll in an advanced degree program to learn about international trade and business. Increasingly, these subjects are available through university extension or continuation courses. One big advantage of these programs is that often they're taught by seasoned professionals (rather than academicians) who can offer invaluable advice on international career possibilities and any additional preparation needed to qualify for them.

If you do decide that you need an advanced degree, you may want to consider a master's degree in international management. To my knowledge there's only one school in the United States that offers this degree: the American Graduate School of International Management (AGSIM), located in Glendale, Arizona. I have no connection with AGSIM, but during the course of my international career I've met so many of their graduates in good jobs around the world that I believe they must have a pretty good educational product and placement service. They have a high percentage of foreign students (more contacts) and they also have an exchange program (both students and faculty) with a graduate school of business (IIST) in Japan, which can add an interesting and valuable dimension to your experience and qualifications.

If you have considerable general business knowledge, expertise through exposure may be all you need, and additional formal education might be overkill. But even if you decide not to take extension classes or enroll in a full-time course of study, you should educate yourself about the basics of international trade and business. The principles generally are the same as those of domestic business, but some of the differences — such as totally different operating environments featuring nontransparent legal and administrative systems, lack of due process, currency controls, and other features not encountered in the United States — can be troublesome if you're not aware of them. If you do decide on formal education, it'll be much easier and more meaningful, once you've done some reading on your own.

There are many good handbooks and manuals on international trade and related issues. The quickest way to get a feel for business writing in your area of specialty is to check the reading list for international business courses at nearby universities. Just drop into the campus bookstore and browse the appropriate section; if you see something promising, buy it. You also can check the subject card catalogue of your local library, or the subject index of *Books in Print* at any bookstore, for books on doing business in geographic areas that you're interested in. Pick out a couple that seem to be most useful for your purposes, and read them.

## DEALING WITH FOREIGN LANGUAGES

**I**'ve mentioned foreign language skills already, but they're so important that they deserve extra attention. Although the realization has been slow in coming, people in the United States are beginning to understand that international capabilities are important, and that foreign language skills are the cornerstone of both a high international I.Q. and more specific international capabilities in any field. It's worth noting that the Japanese, who are currently knocking the stuffing out of the United States in international trade and business, and other Asians, who are right behind them, have (after a shaky and often comical start) learned this lesson well. In the rest of noncommunist Asia, too, (as in Europe) no one is seriously considered for an international career unless he or she has control of a foreign language.

Why is language so important? It's been said that language is culture, and there's no way you can interact adequately with people from another culture (whether for business, diplomacy, or other purposes), unless you have control of their language. Throughout my extensive experience in a dozen different countries on four continents, during which I've learned to use a half dozen different languages, this basic truth has been reconfirmed a hundred times.

*Without the local language, you can do no more than half the job you need to do,* even if the other party speaks English. Fortunately, many U.S. employers now realize this fact, which means that they'll tend to hire people with language skills over those who lack them. Keep in mind, however, that language skill is only part of your ability to do well in an international position, and remember that because America's collective international consciousness is still fairly low, you shouldn't expect prospective employers to be fully aware of the importance of language.

Since other job-specific abilities will be the main concern of any employer, you don't want to come across as a language and culture expert who's interested in a job. Instead, present yourself as a capable professional who happens to be fluent in one or more languages. You can and should make the prospective employer aware of your special language skills or knowledge of a foreign culture *as they relate to the position in question*, but you need to emphasize abilities that are more job-specific, and treat the language and culture as an added feature that increases your ability to get results.

How can you acquire practical language skills? Unfortunately, most academic language courses aren't career-oriented, and commercial programs can be very expensive. In addition, many courses take more time than you may have available, and short courses tend to be incomplete — as one frustrated businessman put it, "the first hundred hours of a thousand-hour course."

Let me give you a summary of what to look for in a language course, and, even better, explain how you can create your own practical language program tailored to your needs and interests.

## TAILOR-MADE LANGUAGE COURSES

The best language courses rely to a considerable extent on a direct method of teaching, in which words are learned through direct association with reality instead of through translation from (or to) English. For example, a top quality language teacher won't teach the Spanish word *puerta* by telling you that it means door. Instead, he or she will get you to understand the word directly by indicating the door and repeating the Spanish word, having you repeat the word, and having you say the word when the teacher or a classmate points to the door. In addition, the word (like other words and expressions that you learn) will be discussed in the context of your own reality, "Is this door open, or closed?" "How many doors does your house have?" "Please open the door."

Whether you take a language class or study on your own, you can use this direct method to speed your progress. At home and in your car, put tags or labels in the target language on everything you can, and repeat them to yourself every time you go near them or use them. For example, your refrigerator might bear the words "refrigerator," "food," "eat," "cold," "not hot," "ice," "open - close" and so on. A light switch might say "light - dark," "on - off." A stairway could say "up - down," "right - left," "wide - narrow." This would be written only in the target language, not English.

If you read and actually say the target words to yourself each time you go to the fridge, turn on the light, or use the stairs, you'll learn the words almost without effort in a very short time. Once you've learned them, you can increase your skill by replacing them with phrases or complete sentences ("I'm going upstairs," "There's no ice in the refrigerator") to repeat to yourself.

You may have noticed that I've used the expression "control a foreign language." This doesn't mean the acquisition of countless useless words and expressions that have no application in your personal or professional life. It's much easier and more sensible than that.

What you're aiming at is complete familiarity with a core of practical, commonplace words that can cover up to 95 percent of what you'll need to say on an average day in a foreign country. This is much easier than it sounds, since the average person uses only a couple of hundred words in any given day. You'll also need less than two dozen types of sentences that will allow you to express virtually any type of situation or idea. To this, add a few dozen words and phrases that are especially important to your particular line of work. *Voila!* You now have control of the language. This means that you can use it to understand others, to express your own ideas, and to make things happen. What's more, you understand how it works and how to increase your language skill in whatever area you choose.

Your core list of words should concentrate on words of opposite meaning (big-small, good-bad, hot-cold, go-come). There are two main reasons for this. First, your mind tends to make this kind of association very easily, so you can learn twice as many words with only a little extra effort. Second, if you can't remember a word, you can use its opposite (for example, you can say "not hot" for "cold") and still get your point across, instead of having to give up in mid-sentence because you have no way to say what you mean.

Should you take a class, or study on your own? Even if you have a good teacher, a typical classroom situation isn't very efficient because each person in the class gets so little time to practice using the language. For instance, in a fifty-minute class of twenty-five people, there's a maximum of two minutes available for each person to actually say something in the foreign language. Since a good part of the fifty minutes is used for giving assignments, asking questions, and hearing explanations by the teacher, in an average class you'll be lucky to have *one minute* of actual speaking practice per class period. Since this isn't a very effective way to spend your time, which is always in short supply, you often can do better on your own by using the method I've discussed.

At first, unless you have some prior exposure or a very good ear, you'll probably want someone to help you with pronunciation and with some of the special uses of words and patterns. You'll often find that skilled non-native speakers can help you the most, since they've been through the learning process themselves. To locate a tutor, call the foreign language department of the nearest major university, or visit the school yourself and look for announcements (usually posted in the language department or language laboratory) put up by students offering their services. Find out if you can use the language laboratory; many universities have excellent collections of tapes that nonstudents can use for a fee.

Control of at least one foreign language is a major asset in launching and developing an international career. When competing for a choice job, it's often the deciding factor if you're evenly matched with other candidates in other areas. And for an entry-level job, or one that you create simply as a first move in getting your international career under way, language skills often can get you on board regardless of shortfalls in other job-specific areas.

# 10

## MAKING AN INTERNATIONAL MATCH

**A**fter you've created and refined your Big Picture, analyzed your inventory of skills, and taken steps to acquire more expertise in vital areas, you still have one major job to do. To take advantage of the international career possibilities you've discovered, you still have to fit yourself into whatever channel you've selected for your next tack. No room for sloppy seamanship here—at this critical point you've got to read the water and the weather right. This means knowing what you can do, and understanding exactly where, when and how to fit it into the right place in the international career environment.

It's not enough to meet a job description, nor is it enough to be able to do the work, although as we've seen, the international career market puts more stress on the latter. While doing both of these things, you must be sure that you're making a good match in other ways, too. In addition to being a logical extension of previous work, and providing added value for your next move, any new position should be compatible with *all parts*, both personal and professional, of your Big Picture. Your functional style, which is your approach to your job and the people (including colleagues, subordinates, supervisors, and clients) involved in it, must fit the culture of the organization and also of the international environment where you'll be working and making contacts. This point is vital for your future.

# CHARTING YOUR COURSE

**A**fter each tack, you've got to remain alert if you want to be in position to take the next tack. To reach new career channels, you have to constantly adjust your heading, and maintain a clear, current chart of the steps you've taken, so that anyone—especially a potantial employer—can track your movement and see the relationship between your course, your current location, and the career channel you're trying to enter.

*Where you're going is always a function of where you've been.* No matter how attractive a specific job opportunity may appear, there's no way you can move directly into it if your previous tacks haven't left you in the right position. Of course, if you think there's even an outside chance of moving directly into a promising new international career, you should go for it. Even if you don't make it on this go-around, you'll get valuable practice in maneuvering. Meanwhile, you can do a much better job of picking winning tacks if you understand exactly what options your present course—and all the moves that led up to it—have created for you.

The first step is to inventory your career components. By doing so, you give yourself a look at your own future by tracking your progress up to now and projecting it, via the new job opportunities you'll target, onto possible tacks that you might make later on. The technique for plotting your trajectory is simple and interesting, and the results are sure to teach you something new about how your background relates to future opportunities. In addition, you can use the same method to create and evaluate the summaries you'll use to market your background to prospective employers.

# CREATING YOUR BACKGROUND MARKETING SUMMARY

**F**irst, you should summarize in writing your background and experience, beginning with the most recent position. If you're going after your first job, write down background items (career components) acquired through education, travel, volunteer work and other activities.

The next step is to write the stated job requirements for the target position at the top of your summary, *just as if the target position were part of your background.* If you don't know exactly what the position requires, try to find out. Fill in gaps by making educated guesses.

Now comes the evaluation. Starting from the bottom item on the summary and working up, read what you've written. *Do the description and requirements of the target position form the last step of a logical progression?* In other words, is the target position believable as part of your career path? To answer this question, compare the components you've acquired at each stage of your career with those needed for the target job. If success in the target job would require more than one or two major new components, you may not be able to enter this specific channel without making another tack to pick up additional components.

If it looks like you have the necessary components, you should rework and edit the material in your summary, section by section, until you've matched your background to the job. Don't leave anything to chance; examine every move you've made and everything you've done for new angles that can help you get into the desired channel. Almost every experience has value in more than one area, and it's up to you to identify and define that value by correlating to different sectors all the expertise you've gained from your job and life experience.

Of course, no amount of creative interpretation can turn a kayak into a luxury liner, or let a tiny sloop mount a challenge for the America's Cup. If you find you have to stretch your background too far, you may need to redefine your goals and target different sorts of opportunities until you've acquired additional career components in the target area. Conversely, *if the target job won't add marketable career components to your inventory, it may be below your level.*

Once you've given yourself a clear picture of where you've been, where you are, and where you can reasonably expect to go next, you have to communicate that picture to each prospective employer. It's not enough to send out a mass-produced inventory of career components, listing

## MATCHING YOUR BACKGROUND TO THE JOB

every tack you've ever taken. After all, if they want you to navigate the waters of the South Pacific, your credentials as a pilot in the Caribbean have only limited value. You need a targeted marketing document that shows how *you* can do the job *they* want done.

"Employment History: List all jobs held during the last ten years, beginning with your most recent employment". Ever seen this deadly line on a job application form? The fatal word here is "list," as though the market value of your experience and career components could be appraised adequately from a simple job chronology. And yet, this is the way most people still write their resumes.

It's been said — and with good reason — that one should never write or send a resume. All too often a typical resume is a brittle, fossilized record of educational and employment history. Like a prehistoric swamp from which the waters have long since evaporated, it contains a vertical cross section of the job seeker's past, laid down over the years layer by layer, and subject to change only on the surface, through the addition of new deposits of sediment. This is a far cry from what you need to qualify for the blue-water voyage of an international career!

Rather than damage your chances by giving such a lifeless museum piece to prospective international employers, you should keep one simple fact in mind. Each job you go after is different from every other job, just as you're different from anyone else who may be under consideration for the job. Therefore, it's counterproductive to provide identical information for different jobs. Instead, *present your experience in such a way that it matches the job you're going after. This is a big part of putting yourself in the context of the opportunity.* The appropriate vehicle for this is not a fossilized resume, but something more dynamic. You can call it anything you like, but for this discussion let's give it a descriptive name: "background marketing summary."

When you go after a career opportunity, you're involved in a highly important marketing activity. You're not just an applicant, but a supplier of services, and your prospective employer is also a prospective client or customer. Your task is to help the client (employer) understand how your background and experience will contribute to his/her business efforts. To do this, present your skills and

# ASSESSING CAREER COMPONENTS

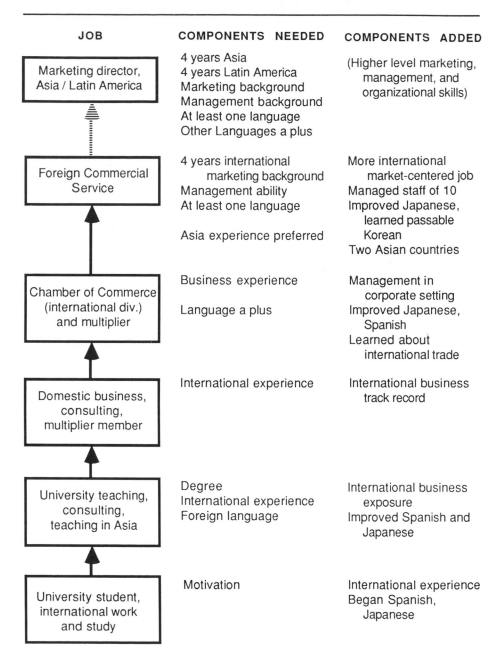

| JOB | COMPONENTS NEEDED | COMPONENTS ADDED |
|---|---|---|
| Marketing director, Asia / Latin America | 4 years Asia<br>4 years Latin America<br>Marketing background<br>Management background<br>At least one language<br>Other Languages a plus | (Higher level marketing, management, and organizational skills) |
| Foreign Commercial Service | 4 years international marketing background<br>Management ability<br>At least one language<br><br>Asia experience preferred | More international market-centered job<br>Managed staff of 10<br>Improved Japanese, learned passable Korean<br>Two Asian countries |
| Chamber of Commerce (international div.) and multiplier | Business experience<br><br>Language a plus | Management in corporate setting<br>Improved Japanese, Spanish<br>Learned about international trade |
| Domestic business, consulting, multiplier member | International experience | International business track record |
| University teaching, consulting, teaching in Asia | Degree<br>International experience<br>Foreign language | International business exposure<br>Improved Spanish and Japanese |
| University student, international work and study | Motivation | International experience<br>Began Spanish, Japanese |

This career component chart illustrates the type of logical progression that career builders should aim at when preparing a background marketing summary.

your potential in terms of the target job, using a background marketing summary that controls both the format and the content of the information you provide. The better you control the information and adapt it to the target job, the easier it'll be for a prospective employer to see exactly how you can fit into the organization's activities and plans.

Let me emphasize that I'm not suggesting that you lie at any point during the job seeking process, any more than your employer would suggest that you lie when promoting his/her company's products or services. Rather, your objective is to help your prospective employer understand how your background relates to the work he/she wants done.

To do this, you have to reach beyond the facade of job titles and descriptions and get a grip on what you've actually done and what expertise and skills it added to your inventory of international career components. For each background marketing summary, you'll work in two directions at once: cataloguing what you have to offer, and identifying the skills and capabilities that are needed for each specific position. The completed background marketing summary will show not only that you know yourself, but that you understand the needs of the organization. In other words, it identifies a problem and offers you — and your expertise — as the solution.

When selecting and organizing the components to highlight in your background marketing summary, keep in mind that the position you're seeking is part of a larger context: the organization. To help the employer see how he/she can use the components you're offering, you need to understand not only the target position but also its place in the organization. Therefore, *it is imperative that you learn something about the structure, present business and future plans of each outfit that you target.* If it's a local firm, you often can learn a lot through your multiplier contacts; if not, the annual report will give you much good information.

How can you tell if you've organized and presented your experience in an appropriate way? One quick test is to give your background marketing summary to someone who doesn't know anything about the position you're seeking. If you've created an effective, explanatory summary, any person reading it should be able to tell what sort of international position you're aiming at. The more closely the reader is able to identify the type of job you want, the more effective your background marketing summary is likely to be with the prospective employer. If you develop your summary by establishing a clear progression of steadily increasing value and added career components from one job tack to the next, your next tack — the job you're aiming at — should be obvious.

Get out your own resume. Simply by reading it, would a prospective employer know what type of position you're going after? If you answer yes because you've included a brief statement of your objective (you know, the one-liner that says something like: "Objective: a marketing position involving public opinion research"), you're missing the point. Although it may be a good idea to use such a statement *if you know for sure that it describes a specific open position in the target organization*, you should design your background marketing summary to tell a prospective employer exactly what you're ready, willing and able to do, by showing him/her what you've done up to now.

Take a look at an abbreviated version of a typical resume, drafted by Bill Doe. See if you can determine what general type of job and what specific position Bill's going after. Is this resume (as opposed to a background marketing summary) an effective marketing tool? What changes would you make to improve it by converting into a job-specific background marketing summary?

---

# BILL DOE

---

■ **Professional Background**
Administrative Assistant, Valley Growers Association (1984–present). Office work, research, extensive dealing with Spanish-speaking workers and union representatives. Administrative Officer, Picmor Farms (1982–1984). Supervise workers. Deal with labor contractors.

■ **Related Experience**
Administrative Assistant, Picmor Farms (part time, 1980–1982). Office administration and management.

■ **Educational Background**
B.A., Valley State University (1982). Teaching major. Spanish minor.

■ **Other interests**
4-H Club.

---

Although this resume (shown in abbreviated form) does list the bare facts about Bill's background, it says nothing about the variety of experiences he's had, nor does it give any idea of what he's aiming at or his potential value to employers. As a result, it's utterly incapable of opening up the many opportunities that might be available to him.

What if Bill decides to include more information? His resume (still abbreviated) than might look something like this:

---

# BILL DOE

---

■ **Professional Background**
Administrative Assistant, Valley Growers Association (1984–present). Office work, market research, public relations. Extensive dealing with Spanish-speaking workers and union representatives. Participated in labor-management negotiations. Gave talks to student groups and 4-H Clubs.
Administrative Manager, Picmor Farms (1982–1984). Supervise workers. Deal with labor contractors.

■ **Related Experience**
Administrative Assistant, Picmor Farms (part time, 1980–1982). Office administration and management. Worked on marketing plans and labor contracts.

■ **Educational Background**
B.A., Valley State University (1982). Teaching major. Spanish minor. Took courses in international relations. Some business courses.

■ **Foreign Languages**
Spanish: fluent.

■ **Other Interests**
4-H Club.

---

Does this longer resume make Bill's international career goal — and his ability to reach it — more evident? From the fact that he majored in education and minored in Spanish, you (or a prospective employer) might guess that his original career plan was to be a Spanish teacher. But what's he aiming at now? He's included more information about his job history, but because he's tried to create a single resume to send to any and all prospective employers, there's no sense of organization or focus. Instead, the employers see a random collection of items that may well cause Bill's international career plans to go the way of the dinosaur and the dodo.

As I've noted earlier, a good background marketing summary, by matching your background to the job, will *make it clear what sort of position you're going after*. Unfortunately for Bill, the resume he created makes him look like a would-be Spanish teacher who got agribusiness jobs because they were there. Although Bill has excellent qualifications for any number of very different careers, he doesn't appear particularly interested (nor qualified) in any specific field.

For example, let's suppose Bill has decided to go after a position with a labor-related organization, or in the labor relations section of a private firm. His background marketing summary should highlight and detail his considerable labor relations experience. Were there any major labor disputes while he was at Picmor Farms or with the Growers' Association? If so, what was his role? Did he participate in negotiations? Did he make use of his Spanish language ability? Did he come up with any suggestions that may have contributed to the resolution of any labor problems? How were his relations with labor? The answers to these and similar questions should be provided by Bill's background marketing summary, so that *both his objective and his value will be evident to potential employers.* The result might use many different formats, but it should provide this type of information:

# BILL DOE

## ■ Professional Background
Administrative Assistant, Valley Growers Association
(1984–present). Full responsibility for dealing with
Spanish-speaking workers and union representatives.
Special assistant to the president in labor-management
negotiations. Made extensive use of Spanish.
Formulated over half of final settlement package that
ended 90-day strike. As intermediary between labor
and management, defused potentially violent confrontation by
helping workers define their grievances, and arranging initial
bargaining session. Created special 4-H Club unit for workers'
children (only one of its kind in the state).
Also general office management, market research,
public relations. Administrative Manager, Picmor Farms
(1982–1984). Supervise workers. Deal with labor contractors.
Gained confidence of workers through use of Spanish.

## ■ Related Experience
Administrative Assistant, Picmor Farms (part time,
1980–1982). Office administration and management.
Wrote preliminary marketing plans and labor contracts.
Interpreted for president in labor negotiations.

## ■ Educational Background
B.A., Valley State University (1982). Teaching major. Spanish minor. Took all available business courses relating to management-labor issues. Also international relations.

## ■ Foreign Languages
Spanish: fluent; extensive interpreting and negotiating experience in labor relations setting.

## ■ Other Interests
4-H Club. Have given numerous talks to student groups and 4-H Clubs, and extensive guidance to special 4-H Club for workers' children.

---

What a difference! Simply by adjusting the focus to pinpoint and highlight his labor-related activities, Bill has shown his true value in terms of the specific career sector that he's aiming at. Suddenly, he has something to offer. He's converted a ho-hum, colorless list into a marketing document that should arouse the interest of any potential employer in the labor field, including international labor relations. He's not only emphasized key components, he's presented them in a way that clearly shows a logical progression from one job to the next, including increasing responsibility and initiative. He's also made clear the relevance of a special international skill — Spanish — that was left hanging in his previous resumes.

By using this approach to provide details on his extensive labor relations and negotiating experience, including the key role he played in helping settle a potentially destructive agricultural workers' strike, he gives himself an excellent shot at a position with an international labor union, the International Labor Organization, the U.S. Department of Labor, or a major international (U.S. or foreign) company that needs his expertise.

Bill also mentioned marketing. He may believe that he has sufficient background to create a career in international marketing. If he goes after a marketing position, this aspect of his experience should come to the fore. What major marketing campaigns has he been involved in? What did he contribute? Did he provide research, concepts, detailed plans? What were the results? Any notable success stories ("as a result, exports of avocados doubled in 18 months")? His background marketing summary should bring out these facts, and *his entire background should be presented in the context of the opportunity* he's aiming at.

Getting away from the resume concept and creating specific, informative background marketing summaries that make your goals and qualifications clear is one of the most important parts of the international career-building process.

# ADAPTING TO CULTURE

**U**nderstanding the value of your background and adapting it to fit a job may get you the job, but that's only half the battle. International career success also requires that you make an extra effort, more than is needed in domestic careers, to adapt your thinking and behavior to new psychological, social, and business environments.

One of the unique challenges of the international career environment is being alert and adaptable enough to deal with the widely different national and corporate cultures that are of vital importance to your career building efforts. The hidden tides and currents of these cultures can help move you along, or they can sweep you far from your goal before you realize what's happening. Like the water that buoys up a boat, they're the medium in which all your efforts take place, and regardless of the strength of your background, the value of your career components, or your ability to deliver what's needed, *failure to adapt to national and corporate culture can quickly nullify all your other efforts.* Quite often, the success of your career (in both objective and subjective terms) will be determined in large measure by your success in matching not only your background to the job, but also your professional style and abilities to the national and corporate culture surrounding you.

## FOREIGN CULTURE SHOCK

**U**nlesss your entire career is of the stateside-international variety, you'll have to confront the problem of culture shock. In general, culture shock is a nonadaptive reaction to a new cultural environment. Although not everyone experiences it, it affects a significant percentage of people who move to a different country. (Interestingly, it appears that men often are more susceptible than women, and macho types may have more difficulty than other men.) There are many signs of culture shock, including depression, reluctance to interact with the foreign environment, extreme irritation or even violent hostility toward local people, and constant criticism of local methods and conditions. Sometimes, there's a reaction in the opposite direction, and the transplanted manager or executive tries to overcompensate by going native. Either response can be devastating to your performace and your career.

Paradoxically, culture shock can hit you the hardest when you're the most satisfied, particularly if your decision to take an overseas position was based on unrealistic expectations of glamour, excitement, exoticism, or intrigue. When your expectations run afoul of reality—pollution, poverty, overcrowding, traffic jams, consumer shortages, high prices, the ineffectiveness of your favorite U.S. management techniques—culture shock rears its ugly head.

At first, you may feel very high about your new position, fairly bursting with enthusiasm. Within a few months, however, the glow fades. In its place comes a perception of the new culture and perhaps your job as less interesting, challenging, or promising than you had expected. You may find yourself becoming openly critical of the new environment, or making unfavorable comparisons with your old situation. Luckily, within a few more months, you'll acquire a more realistic viewpoint, neither rose-colored nor negative.

To a great extent, you can avoid culture shock by doing your homework on the country and approaching the assignment with the totally open mind of an explorer: no expectations, just interest and curiosity. But even a good match may go through a rocky adjustment period. Furthermore, the problem is two-sided: you may be genuinely satisfied with your new position, but people in the country, including host-country employees, may take some time to adjust to your presence and style.

The best treatment for culture shock is a combination of time and awareness. If you feel euphoric about your situation, realize that you may be in for a mood reversal before too long. Conversely, if you begin to have unreasonably negative feelings about your new situation (as opposed to an objective sense of possible imperfections), you can deal with them much better by recognizing their cause and reminding yourself that they'll disappear with time.

Examine your present position, and any international opportunities you're considering, for the possibility of a future let-down. If you're brimming with missionary zeal or feel that you've finally found the yellow brick road, look out!

If, on the other hand, you're extremely dissatisfied with your present situation, including your job, ask yourself to what extent your feelings may be the result of culture shock, rather than basic defects in the organization or in your particular position. How can you tell? Look for signs like across-the-board negativism ("nothing ever goes right around here") or highly emotional dislike of associates at work, perhaps coupled with either unbridled admiration or distaste for everything in the host country. If you find yourself complaining a lot in rather general terms, it may be a sign of culture shock.

To clarify your situation, write down a list of the problems you see, including management problems stemming from local nationals and attitude and communication gaps with the home office. Be sure they're clearly stated. How serious are they? Can you live with them for another six months to a year? What constructive action can you take to correct them? By letting some time pass, you can give yourself a chance to see whether things (and your perception of them) improve. Meanwhile, keep your conversations and your attitude as positive as you can.

## CORPORATE CULTURE SHOCK: THE INTERNATIONAL TWIST

An international career also entails a special set of corporate cultural challenges, including some subtle and potentially troublesome variations of corporate culture shock. In general, corporate culture is the whole package of values, beliefs, attitudes and resulting behavior that defines the character of any organization. There's nothing startling about this, but in the international arena, there are some twists that make your adaptation more critical and more complicated.

In the first place, the predominant corporate culture of your company, or of the entire industrial sector, is probably quite different from the subculture of the international division. The different functional style developed by international managers and executives in response to the more complicated demands of international business often ends up permeating the entire section or division. As a result, attitudes, behavior and performance that might win kudos from the international division may fall flat in other parts of the company, and vice versa.

The implications for your career are obvious. After breaking into the international division of your company—perhaps as a reward for outstanding performance in a domestic division—you start to feel that you're no longer appreciated. Suddenly, your best efforts (the same ones that earned you recognition and bonuses before) don't seem good enough. Unless you're alert to differences in the corporate subculture you've entered, you'll compound the problem. You'll frantically try to get back into your accustomed role by working even harder in the same vein, when what you need to do is change your approaches and methods to fit the new situation.

If you feel that this is or may be happening to you, drop back and analyze the situation. Look for differences in the objectives, strategy and tactics of the international division. If domestic management has always been product and profit oriented (as it often is), the international group may be trying to build up the company's profile and market share overseas, which will create different priorities and attitudes. Experienced international managers and executives will probably have learned to listen to the market, rather than dictating to it as many U.S. domestic managers do. These strategic and tactical orientations, based on the realities of the international marketplace, gradually create attitudes that become part of the international corporate subculture. Since you have to function in that subculture, it's imperative that you adapt to it. Luckily, in most cases the adaptation isn't as profound and forbidding as it sounds. It's probable that a relatively minor adjustment — often simply "thinking international" — will get you moving again. If you've been active in international multipliers, you'll be more in tune with the international business community in general, which should enable you to minimize the adjustment needed in a specific company.

Secondly, there may be an even bigger difference between the individual functional styles of U.S.-based managers and those based abroad. The overseas people are living in a different world, they've had their eyes opened to different realities, and they've developed different ways of dealing with the business environment. Working overseas can create serious problems of communication and perception between you and the home office in the United States. *Many expat managers and executives report that the biggest single problem they face is the home office.*

Many in-house, corporate culture discrepancies come directly from national social and business cultures. U.S. business culture tends to be informal, individualistic, openly competitive, top-down, and characterized by confrontational executive and management styles and labor-management relations. The corporate culture of any American company you work for will have most of these elements in varying degrees. To function successfully overseas, the expat manager may have to abandon this culture and adapt to one that is formal or ritualistic, collective, passive, participatory, and deferential. To carry this off — and still communicate with the home office in terms that they can understand — means sailing a narrow channel between success and schizophrenia. If you have the misfortune to work overseas for or with managers who have gone native (thus becoming totally blind to home office requirements) or who insist on doing things "the American way" (making it impossible to motivate local staff), your problems are multiplied.

As if this weren't enough, while negotiating this narrow channel you have to pay close attention to the expectations of host-country nationals, from your staff to customers, clients and competitors, who may have very definite ideas about the proper personal and business style of a specific industry. In this regard, you've circumnavigated the career environment, for even 15,000 miles from home, you have to deal with a domestic business mentality which, in this case, is that of your host-country.

The situation gets especially difficult if you're an overseas manager from an industry, say, sporting goods and recreation equipment, whose culture is more relaxed and informal than the host-country culture. Although their expectations are in the realm of superficial style, catering to these expectations is very definitely a matter of substance. After all, a bad image is bad business. So you'll have to observe and follow the host-country standards on this one.

The bottom line of all this is a conflict between various functional styles, with your home office on one end of the spectrum, and you and many host-country firms on the other. To further your career, you have to pay attention to the former, but to produce results, you have to concentrate on the latter. You've got to humor the home office, of course, but don't let their corporate culture dictate your culture overseas. You must fit into the context of the local ethos and the image of your business if you're going to get results.

Since visiting home-office firemen may attempt to impose U.S. values, you'll find yourself going through a charade. It's like rearranging the house when in-laws come over: you display your mother-in-law's picture in the living room, put your favorite chair in the garage, and try to act as expected by your guests. Of course, the local staff has to go along with the act, but since they've probably been doing this to you (whether you know it or not) they're more adaptable than you'd believe possible. In the same way, you often must change your style on visits to the home office, and be ready to adapt to the differing subcultures in other overseas branches.

Because culture shock may be triggered or intensified by the additional adjustment of joining a new organization, many international companies don't like to send new people overseas right away. Two new cultures at once (corporate and foreign) can overwhelm you. You're probably well-advised to keep this in mind, and refrain from pushing for an assignment offshore until you've had time to adjust to a new (to you) organization in the United States. Once you know what they expect, you're ready to take on the additional expectations of the foreign and expat cultures you'll encounter. When you come home after even a short stint out of the country, be aware that you may experience cultural readjustment (both corporate and general) as part of your reentry.

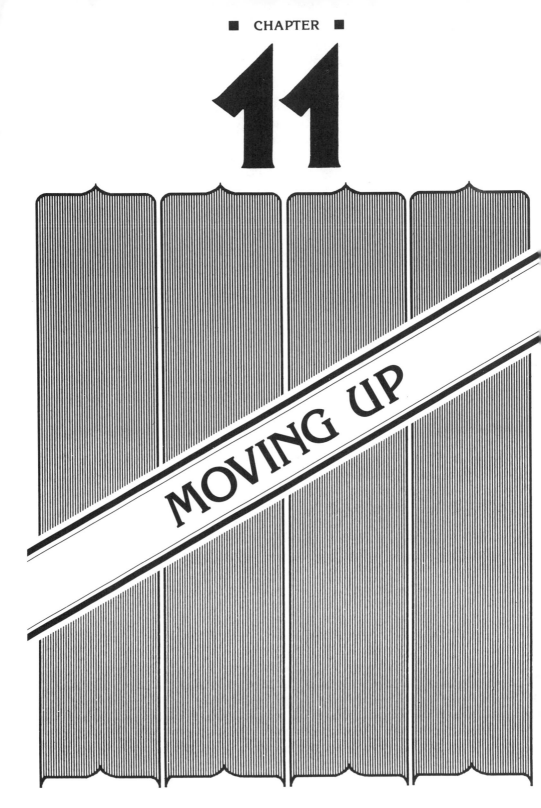

# 11

## MOVING UP

**B**ecause the international career marketplace offers many routes to the top, you're likely to make far more rapid progress in advancing to higher levels of responsibility, salary, and further opportunities than you could in the domestic field. In the first place, you're facing fewer qualified competitors; secondly, even in industry sectors or geographic areas with a higher percentage of expertise, the existence of many channels means fewer bottlenecks.

*Every reward implies some sort of risk*, however. If you have a secure, substantial job now, it's all too easy to get complacent, and use the risk inherent in major changes as an excuse for inaction. In fact, this may be one of the biggest pitfalls in the international career environment. Especially if you're an expat manager or executive, you can pretty much run your own shop. Few people in the domestic side of the business understand what you're doing, and often they don't really care, as long as your reports show that you're alive and not in the red. If it's a small part of your company's total business, your entire operation may be virtually overlooked unless there's some unusual activity. Like an absentee landlord, the home office will keep maintaining your operation automatically, without stopping to question whether or not your territory should be producing greater revenues.

Under these circumstances, it's all too easy for you to slip into a relaxing routine of periodic reporting, occasional meetings with customers, suppliers and distributors, and a courtesy call on the home office once or twice a year. As one regional marketing manager put it, "The trick is to do just enough to justify your existence." The best way out of this Sargasso Sea is to hang onto your Big Picture. If this doesn't work, sooner or later the home office will put you on another tack whether you're ready or not. Far better to take the initiative yourself.

Even if you're out there setting the world on fire, you'll find that distance and the relatively small size of your operation may keep the home office from noticing the glow you've generated. Luckily, your fellow expat managers will notice, and when they move on — say, from country manager to regional manager, or from regional manager to international manager or VP — they'll often let their home office know that you'd be a perfect candidate for their company. For this reason, activity in multipliers overseas is even more important than in the United States: it lays the groundwork for the tacking that compensates for expats' lack of contacts with the home office.

Regardless of your international or home office network, *you often can move up by transferring knowledge acquired on your present job to a higher level in another company*, especially if you're giving that knowledge a new twist or applying it in a new way. If you're working on some aspect of licensing, for example, you can parlay your expertise into a new and better position by proposing a new international licensing program to a company with high international visibility and marketable names or images. Although you could make such a move successfully within your own company, the odds are that your idea would merely serve to promote one of your superiors.

In fact, your list of prospects in this licensing example shouldn't be limited to companies in the same product or service sector you work in, but should include any sort of company with broad appeal and an image that might successfully be associated with a wide variety of products. Possibilities include real and fictitious characters and personalities, theme parks, lines of consumer goods, and regular international fairs, festivals and other events.

As in the example I've just given, the best way to make this kind of move is usually to locate somewhere else along the transaction chain in a specific field. Often, this will involve either a bigger piece of a smaller pie—as when you go from regional marketing manager for a big company to VP international for a smaller firm—or a relatively smaller piece of a bigger pie, as would be the case if you tacked from president of a small importer or distributor of foreign products to VP of a large foreign supplier's U.S. operation. In either case, you should end up with both higher price and higher value.

Of course, you can make this type of tack at any level of employment. For example, if your position has made you an expert on trade negotiations, could you give your career a boost by becoming a negotiator? Or if you're the manager in charge of your company's participation in trade shows, could you get a significantly better position—say, VP for sales—with one of the organizations that puts on the shows? If your job has made you an expert on export documentation and procedures, you might head up an export department in another company, or become a consultant to small firms that are too small to have complete export departments of their own. Or you may parlay a position in an ad agency into a slot as VP for public relations for a foreign manufacturer in the United States. If you're an attorney or accountant who works on business or financial plans for companies offering international investment services, you might use your knowledge of how these entities function to become part of one yourself, not as a hired hand, but as a corporate officer or working partner. In each of these examples, a move would yield not only higher price (salary, position and perks), but also the increased value of an extended circle of higher-level contacts among clients and competitors.

## TACKING YOUR WAY TO THE GOLD

**W**hen you make a move up by transferring to another company, you obviously want to come in at the highest possible level of salary, fringe benefits and responsibility. Often it's hard to get what you're worth because your new employers aren't sufficiently aware of the differences in living costs and salaries in different parts of the world. If they look only at raw numbers, they may get an erroneous impression.

At any given level, a manager might make twice as much in Honolulu or Tokyo as in Tuscaloosa or La Paz, simply because the cost of living (and therefore the average salary scale) is far higher. Clearly, you're at a disadvantage if you're hired out of a low-cost area, and vice versa.

If you're going to build your salary through international tacking, your earnings background (including all fringe benefits) should first be adjusted to give you the best possible starting point. If you're coming into a stateside position from a relatively low-cost, low-salary region or low-paying industry, your first move has to be to get at least on a par with the rest of the United States, and preferably with the higher-priced region or industry you're entering. This is both fair and logical, but don't be content merely to point this out in salary negotiations. It's up to you to convincingly translate your previous salary level into higher numbers that are fair and realistic for the position you're seeking.

If you're coming from employment with a multiplier or government agency into the private sector, you should figure at least 20 percent more for comparable work; only above that will you actually be negotiating an increase in terms of the private-sector price structure. If you're coming from a low-cost area, or a country where exchange rate fluctuations or other factors have made your price look lower than it is, you should make a similar conversion. If you present adjusted figures, be sure to indicate clearly that you're doing so. You don't want to appear dishonest. Come up with concrete figures, and be prepared to prove your point with cost of living and salary data obtained from the local chamber of commerce (AmCham, if you're overseas) or the U.S. Government. Major international accounting firms also have available cost of living data on various countries and cities around the world.

Regardless of your starting point, you can use the salary and fringe gap to pump up your salary in a series of tacks from U.S.-based to overseas jobs. Say you work in the United States at a base salary of $60,000, plus the usual fringe benefits that go with it. If your company sends you overseas, you should be able to get an additional $5,000 to $10,000 annual incentive pay, plus up to 20 percent in the case of a hardship (i.e., unpleasant) assignment, and/or whatever it takes (say, 10 percent) to cover additional cost of living expenses in countries where exchange rates or the internal price structure make life significantly more pricey than in the United States. Throw in the car, house, and utilities that can also be part of the deal, and your $60,000 salary has just about doubled.

If you go back to the United States with the same company, of course, they'll take away all these goodies when you return. If a significantly higher salary is a major part of your Big Picture, it may be time to tack from overseas directly to another outfit in the United States, using the total compensation figure of about $120,000 as your starting point for negotiations.

Even if you're dealing with a company that knows about all the extra benefits that go with an overseas assignment, psychologically, the reality of the high package you received while abroad gives you a tremendous bargaining advantage. The result can be a salary increase far in excess of what you could obtain by doing a tack while remaining within either the United States or the overseas market. Instead of going into a new company with a salary, say, 20 percent higher than your former base salary, an increase of 50 percent is totally within reason. After all, it represents 25 percent less than what you were getting overseas.

After establishing yourself in the United States, making new contacts, and perhaps negotiating a raise or two, you may want to engineer another hefty increase by doing another stint abroad. This time, you're adding all the overseas incentives and other allowances to a base salary that may be nearly twice as high as what you made just a few years earlier, thus laying the groundwork for consolidating these gains (which, after all, are theoretically only temporary when you're overseas) through another tack into yet another company in the United States. Clearly, there's a limit to how far you can take this procedure, but it will get you a lot farther financially than staying exclusively in either the domestic or the stateside-international market, and it sure beats the career ladder.

# GO WITH THE FLOW— TO A POINT

**A**t all stages of your career-building process (a process that will continue throughout your professional life), you'll need to keep yourself aware of career possibilities. Do research to find new channels, adapt your background to fit them, and plan new international career tacks to take full advantage of them. In the meantime, stay flexible enough to react to unexpected opportunities, but don't let yourself get sidetracked by jobs that can't add significant value to your background. The idea is to stay pointed in the right direction while you develop your international potential. Then, when you uncover or create a major career opportunity, you'll be ready to take advantage of it.

By using your own initiative, you have the power to create a rewarding international career. Unfortunately, it may seem easier to slack off and let nature take its course. Resist the temptation! Long term (or even over a period of two or three years), you'll see that it's well worth the effort to *stay on top of your career so that you can control events instead of letting them control you.* Of course, if you have enough to offer, you may end up somewhere near your goals by merely drifting along in the current, but you'll spend a lot more time than you need to, and you may suffer the frustration of seeing great opportunities floating just out of reach, or have the unpleasant experience of getting swept into heavy surf.

Equally as dangerous is the common tendency to go after targets of opportunity without regard for their relation to your goals. In every area of business, there are opportunities so enticing that at the sight of them, your goals begin to fade from mind. Again, you've got to keep an eye on the compass. On the surface, almost any attractive offer might not seem like a bad move. After all, no matter what business you get involved in, there's a demand for it all over the world, right? Not so, and even in those sectors that aren't culturally or linguistically demanding, dominated by a few large firms, or characterized by heavy or prohibitive restrictions on foreigners, a big part of the value in any job is its relevance to your goals. *It's no good to make a move that advances you a long way in the wrong direction.*

To keep your career in the best international channels and out of false bays and stagnant backwaters, you should occasionally take a moment to question your direction. Will it lead to greater international opportunities? List them. How about international career components and value—what's your present situation adding to your background? If you can't discover anything, you've either been on your present tack too long, or perhaps made the wrong move altogether.

If you've made this common mistake, don't give up. Start looking for ways to give international value to the experience you're getting. Look for international applications for your skills, and try to find an international twist in your work.

The same tactics will work for you if you haven't yet made international career plans or created your Big Picture. You may be entering or reentering the job market. Maybe—like hundreds of thousands of other Americans in domestic industry—your present job is being eliminated. Instead of plodding mechanically to the nearest domestic career ladder, make this your chance to go international. Analyze your skills in the light of their international potential, and rather than taking just any domestic job, pick a product, service or industrial sector with international potential. Come in as high as you can on the production and distribution chain, at the mouth of an international channel, if possible. Learn more about the business and get closer to international possibilities. If you work for a wholesaler, for example, identify suppliers with international business or international potential. Your contacts with them can lead to an international marketing or management slot.

With informed planning, you can avoid the uncertainties, dead ends and unnecessary detours that even talented, hardworking people are bound to encounter in an unguided search for an international career. In particular, by sticking to the basic concepts of tacking and the Big Picture, you'll be far more successful—and satisfied—with your international career.

International careers bring incredible rewards. Besides the financial benefits, you can gain an interesting life, the chance to utilize all your abilities, far more flexibility and freedom to change your job, your residence, your outlook on life. Beyond yourself, there's the satisfaction of contributing to the goals of an international trade association, AmCham chapter or other multiplier, and the sense of pride that comes from helping a company evolve from an inward-looking domestic operation to an increasingly aggressive exporter.

There are a lot of opportunities out there—start sketching out your Big Picture, plot a course, and go after them.

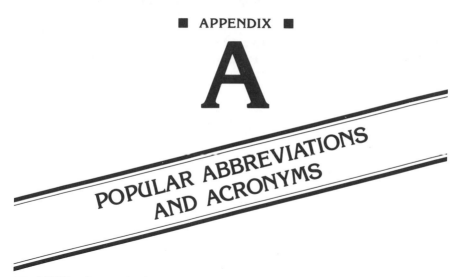

# A

## POPULAR ABBREVIATIONS AND ACRONYMS

**AIPT: Association for International Practical Training.** A good source of information about overseas work programs.

**AISEC: Association Internationale des Etudiants en Sciences Economiques et Commerciales.** An international student organization dedicated to placing international business students in temporary jobs in foreign countries.

**AIT: American Institute in Taiwan.** A supposedly private organization that has taken over many of the functions of the former U.S. Embassy since the United States recognized the People's Republic of China — and withdrew recognition from Taiwan — in 1979.

**AmCham: American Chamber of Commerce.** U.S. businesses overseas usually form AmCham chapters or branches in cities where significant numbers of U.S. companies have offices. However, communist countries tend to discourage this practice. In many countries, foreign companies (sometimes even host-country companies) may join AmCham.

**B & F: Budget and Fiscal.** The accounting section of a U.S. Embassy.

**CLO: Community Liaison Office/Officer.** Responsible for helping U.S. Embassy personnel participate more fully in the life of the foreign community (host country) in which they live. Often staffed by the spouse of a Foreign Service Officer.

**COCUSA: Chamber of Commerce of the United States.** The parent organization for chambers of commerce throughout the United States and American Chambers of Commerce overseas.

**CODEL: Congressional Delegation.** U.S. Government jargon.

■ **DCM: Deputy Chief of Mission.** At a U.S. Embassy, the ambassador's right-hand man and executive officer. Takes over ambassadorial duties in the ambassador's absence. Usually a career Foreign Service Officer from the political "cone" of the State Department.

■ **DEA: Drug Enforcement Administration.** Responsible for stemming the illegal use of drugs.

■ **DITI: Department of International Trade and Industry.** In the early 1980s, many practical people in Washington, DC favored the formation of such a department, which would absorb, among others, the functions of the Foreign Commercial Service (now under the Commerce Department) and the U.S. Trade Representative (now under the State Department). Unfortunately, this idea foundered beneath bureaucratic infighting. (See MITI.)

■ **EEC: European Economic Community.** Often referred to as the "Common Market". Those countries in Europe that have agreed on fairly united trade policies, including the reduction or elimination of trade barriers among themselves. Founding members (1958) were Belgium, France, the Federal Republic of Germany, Italy, Luxembourg, and the Netherlands. In 1973, Denmark, Ireland and the United Kingdom joined. Spain and Portugal joined in 1986. The EEC is often at odds with the United States over trade policy with the Soviet Union and Japan.

■ **EMC: Export Management Company.** A company, generally based in the United States, which for a fee will handle some or all of the export promotion and paperwork for a U.S. manufacturer or distributor.

■ **FAM: Foreign Affairs Manual.** The operating manual of the State Department, containing all the rules and regulations governing foreign service work and personnel issues. Other federal government civilian agencies overseas tend to adhere to the FAM, but are not necessarily required to do so.

■ **FAS: Foreign Agricultural Service.** The overseas arm of the U.S. Department of Agriculture.

■ **FCS: Foreign Commercial Service.** The overseas arm of the U.S. Department of Commerce.

■ **FCSO: Foreign Commercial Service Officer.** A commerce department officer, usually serving in a U.S. Embassy or Consulate overseas. Most FCSOs overseas have diplomatic status.

■ **FSN: Foreign Service National.** A foreign citizen, usually a citizen of the host country, working at a U.S. Embassy or Consulate.

**FSO: Foreign Service Officer.** A state department officer, usually serving in a U.S. Embassy or Consulate overseas. FSOs have diplomatic status overseas.

**FTZ: (1) Foreign Trade Zone.** A designated area in which goods from abroad may be introduced duty-free for the purposes of storage, repacking, assembly, and processing. No duty is paid on the goods unless and until they leave the FTZ for import into the customs territory of the United States or other host country in which the FTZ is located. The main advantage to the importer or processor is deferred payment of customs duties; cities and other areas near an FTZ may use an FTZ to attract industry.

**(2) Free Trade Zone.** A designated duty-free area, in which items may be bought duty-free for use in the customs territory of the United States or other host country. Functions much like the duty-free shops in airports, but on a larger scale. The main direct beneficiaries of a Free Trade Zone are consumers and the retail community.

**FX: Foreign Exchange.**

**IIST: International Institute for Studies and Training.** The English-language name of Boeki Kenshu Senta (Commerce Training Center), a graduate business school supported by the Japanese government.

**IMF: International Monetary Fund.** Arranges loans to countries for various purposes.

**ITA: International Trade Administration.** The division of the U.S. Department of Commerce responsible for international trade. The Foreign Commerical Service (FCS) is a part of the ITA.

**JETRO: The Japan External Trade Organization.** Under MITI, promotes the export of Japanese products. In the mid-1980s, with Japan facing increasing international pressure to rectify a huge annual trade surplus, JETRO adopted a posture of helping foreign companies penetrate the Japanese market.

**LDC: Lesser Developed Country.** Generally, a country with little industry, relying mostly on primary products or tourism to generate foreign exchange. Most countries in the so-called Third World fall into this category.

**MITI: The Japanese Ministry of Trade and Industry.** Many foreign countries have a similar ministry. (See DITI.)

**NAFSA: National Association of Foreign Student Affairs.** Information on overseas employment, much of it related to English teaching.

■ **NIC: Newly Industrialized Country.** A country that has created a solid industrial infrastructure and become competitive in some areas of manufacturing.

■ **NTE: New To Export.** Commerce Department terminology for a U.S. company that is exporting (or attempting to export) for the first time.

■ **NTM: New To Market.** Commerce Department terminology for a U.S. company that has exported before, but is trying to enter a given overseas market for the first time.

■ **PRC: The People's Republic of China.**

■ **R & D: Research and Development.**

■ **ROC: The Republic of China.** Taiwan. The United States no longer recognizes the Chinese government on Taiwan, but maintains close unofficial relations through the American Institute in Taiwan (AIT).

■ **ROK: The Republic of Korea.** "South Korea." (North Korea calls itself the Democratic People's Republic of Korea.)

■ **USAID: United States Agency for International Development.** This is the agency responsible for administering most of America's foreign aid program.

■ **USCS: United States Customs Service.**

■ **USDOC: United States Department of Commerce.**

■ **USIA: United States Information Agency.**

■ **USIS: United States Information Service.** The overseas name of USIA. USIS runs American Centers—which include small, high-quality libraries and American cultural programs—in many foreign cities.

■ **USSTS: United States Student Travel Service.**

■ **USTC: United States Trade Center.** An overseas trade promotion center, often located in or near a U.S. Embassy, that puts on trade shows and provides services to U.S. exporters. Staffed by Commerce Department employees, who may or may not be members of the FCS.

■ **USTR: The United States Trade Representative.** Under the Department of State. The chief negotiator and spokesman of U.S. positions on foreign trade matters.

■ **USTTA: United States Travel and Tourism Administration.** Part of the Commerce Department. Responsible for encouraging and promoting foreign tourism in the United States.

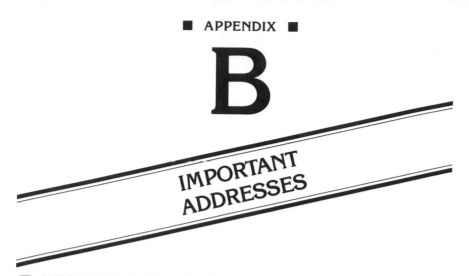

# B

IMPORTANT ADDRESSES

■ **AIESEC-US,** 14 West 23rd Street, New York, NY 10010. Telephone: (212) 206-1888. AIESEC stands for Association Internationale des Etudiants en Sciences Economiques et Commericiales; the organization runs an international employment exchange program for students in business-related fields.

---

## SCHOOLS, TEACHING, EDUCATION, OVERSEAS JOBS

---

■ **American Graduate School of International Management (AGSIM),** Glendale, AZ 85306. Telephone: (602) 978-7250.

■ **Association for International Practical Training (AIPT),** American City Building, Suite 217, Columbia, MD 21044. Telephone: (301) 997-2200. Helps arrange on the job practical training overseas for sophomores through graduate students. This international exchange is mainly for students specializing in engineering, architecture, mathematics, sciences, and agriculture.

■ **Association of Teachers of English as a Second Language (ATESL),** 1860 19th Street N.W., Washington, DC 20009. Telephone: (202) 462-4811. ATESL is a section of NAFSA. See also TESOL, a competing organization.

■ **Institute of International Education (IIE),** 809 United Nations Plaza, New York, NY 10017. Telephone: (212) 883-8200. IEE runs a computer referral service for U.S. scholars and post-secondary teachers, and provides information and advice on higher education in the U.S. and abroad.

■ **International Institute for Studies and Training (IIST),** 15-3 Kamiide, Fujinomiya-shi, Shizuoka-ken, Japan. The Japanese-language name for this school, Japan's only graduate school of business, is "Bôeki Kenshû Sentâ," or "Trade Research Study Center." IIST has a student and faculty exchange with AGSIM in Arizona.

■ **International Schools Association (ISA),** CIC Case 20, CH-1211 Geneva 20, Switzerland. This outfit helps supply teachers for schools that are located in outlying areas, far from major recruiting centers.

■ **International Schools Services (ISS),** P.O. Box 5910, 126 Alexander Street, Princeton, NJ 08540. Telephone: (609) 921-9110. ISS, which provides various educational services for American and international schools overseas, operates a school placement and information bank for teachers. ISS also operates schools for U.S. industry abroad, and recruits and recommends personnel.

■ **Modern Language Association (MLA),** 62 5th Avenue, New York, NY 10011. Telephone: (212) 741-5588.

■ **National Association for Foreign Student Affairs (NAFSA),** 1860 19th Street N.W., Washington, DC 20009. Telephone: (202) 462-4811. ATESL is part of this organization.

■ **Overseas Education Association,** 1201 16th Street N.W., Washington, DC 20036. Telephone: (202) 822-7850. A membership organization for teachers employed by the DOD overseas. Affiliated with the National Education Association.

■ **Teachers of English to Speakers of Other Languages (TESOL),** 202 DC Transit Building, Georgetown University, Washington, DC 20057. Telephone: (202) 625-4569. See also ATESL, a competing organization.

■ **U.S. Student Travel Service (USSTS),** 801 2nd Avenue, New York, NY 10017. Telephone: (212) 867-8770. USSTC offers complete international student services, including summer employment exchange programs and homestays.

## OTHER AGENCIES AND MULTIPLIERS

■ **Chamber of Commerce of the United States,** 1615 H Street N.W., Washington, DC 20006-4902. Telephone: (202) 659-6000.

■ **National Association of Foreign Trade Zones (NAFTZ),** Commerce Tower, Suite 1020, 911 Main Street, Kansas City, MO 64105. Telephone: (816) 221-0707.

■ **Sister Cities International (SCI),** 1625 Eye Street N.W., Suite 424-426, Washington, DC 20006. Telephone: (202) 293-5504.

■ **United Nations General Information,** First Avenue & 46th Street, New York, NY 10017-0000. Telephone: (212) 754-7113.

■ **U.S. Department of Agriculture,** 14th Street & Independence Avenue S.W., Washington, DC 20250-0000. Telephone: (202) 447-2791.

**U.S. Customs Service,** 1301 Constitution Avenue N.W., Washington, DC 20002-6419. Telephone: (202) 566-5286. In the U.S., USCS operations are divided into nine regions. For information on the headquarters of each region, contact USCS in Washington, or inquire at the nearest Federal Information Center.

**Foreign Agricultural Service (FAS),** Agriculture Building, Washington, DC 20250-0002. Telephone: (202) 447-7115.

**U.S. Department of Commerce (USDOC),** 14th & E Streets N.W., Washington, DC 20230-0000. Telephone: (202) 377-3263.

**International Trade Administration (ITA),** Commerce Department Building, Washington, DC 20230-0002. Telephone: (202) 377-5087.

**Foreign Commerical Service (FCS),** Commerce Department Building, Washington, DC 20230. Telephone: (202) 377-3133. (NOTE: This is the number for personnel. There is no number for general information about the organization.)

**U.S. Department of Defense (DOD),** The Pentagon, Washington, DC 20301-0999. Telephone: (202) 545-6700. For information on DOD schools, you'll also want to check with the Overseas Education Association.

**U.S. Department of State,** Bureau of Economic and Business Affairs, Office of Business and Export Affairs, 2201 C Street N.W., Washington, DC 20520-0000. Telephone: (202) 632-0354. This is the office to call for information on the Foreign Service overseas.

**U.S. Immigration and Naturalization Service (INS),** 425 Eye Street N.W., Washington, DC 20001-2542. Telephone: (202) 633-5231.

**United States Information Agency (USIA),** 301 4th Street S.W., Washington, DC 20547. Telephone: (202) 485-8597.

**World Trade Centers Association (WTCA),** One World Trade Center, 63W, New York, NY 10048. Telephone: (212) 775-1370.

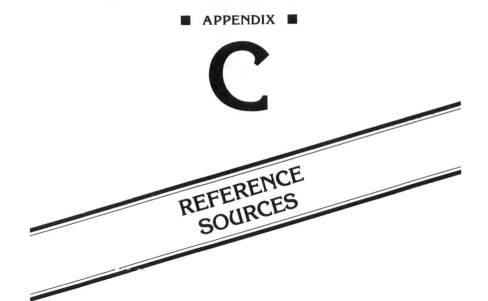

**C**

**REFERENCE SOURCES**

■ **Business International Corporation.** Annual survey of executive business costs. Business International Corporation, 1 Dag Hammarskjold Plaza, New York, NY 10017. Telephone: (212) 750-3600. This survey, compiled each year in January and released in April, compares living costs in major cities in the U.S. and around the world. It's a prime source of information when negotiating salary and adjusting your salary history.

■ **Directory of American Firms Operating in Foreign Countries.** World Trade Academy Press, published by Uniworld Business Publications, Inc., 50 East 42nd Street, New York, NY 10017. The Directory lists alphabetically by company (telling you all the countries each firm operates in) and also by country (so that you can target a country and find out what U.S. companies are operating there). Treat this publication for what it is: a starting point only. It's not complete by any means, and some very important players are missing.

■ **Encyclopedia of Associations.** Gale Research Company, Book Tower, Detroit, MI 48226. This is a great source for locating multipliers, including American Chamber of Commerce chapters overseas, manufacturers' associations, and many others.

■ **Key Officers of Foreign Service Posts (Guide for Business Representatives).** This little brochure, available at USDOC District Offices or from the Superintendent of Documents, U.S. Government Printing Office, Washington, DC 20420, lists all U.S. Embassies and Consulates, as well as the various sections at each. In addition, it gives the address and phone number of all the USDOC District Offices in the United States. It's updated every 6 months (in May and November).

■ **The National Directory of Addresses and Telephone Numbers.** Concord Reference Books, Inc., 850 3rd Avenue, New York, NY 10022-6203. Telephone: (212) 223-5100. This directory, smaller than many city phone books, is an absolute gold mine of information, including leading U.S. corporations, multipliers, chambers of commerce, government offices, Federal Information Centers, and many others.

■ **Statistical Abstract of the United States.** Published yearly by the U.S. Department of Commerce, Bureau of the Census. This is another source to use when adjusting your stateside salary history and negotiating with new or present employers. The three sections of greatest interest to you are Section 13 (Labor Force, Employment and Earnings), Section 14 (Income, Expenditures, and Wealth) and Section 15 (Prices). You can use the statistics in this book, for example, to show that you previously earned less than another new hire because the prevailing wage rate (and cost of living) is lower in the area where you held your previous job. You can get the Statistical Abstract at any U.S. Department of Commerce District Office, or by ordering from the Superintendent of Documents, U.S. Government Printing Office, Washington, DC 20402. Telephone: (202) 783-8238. You may find it easier to look at the Statistical Abstract at the nearest public or university library and copy the information you want.

# MORE GOOD BOOKS FROM
# 🏵 WILLIAMSON PUBLISHING

## AFTER COLLEGE
### The Business of Getting Jobs

by Jack Falvey

Wise and wonderful . . . don't leave college without it. Filled with un-orthodox suggestions (avoid campus recruiters at all costs!), hands-on tools (put your money in stationery, not in resumes), wise observations (grad school? - why pay to learn what others are paid to learn better). You've al-ready spent a fortune on textbooks. Now for only $10 you can have the most valuable book of all.

192 pages, 6 x 9
Quality paperback, $9.95

## WHAT'S NEXT?
### Career Strategies After 35

by Jack Falvey

Falvey explodes myths right and left and sets you on a straight course to a satisfying and successful mid-life career. Bring an open mind to his book and you'll be on your way. A liberating book to help us all get happily back into work.

192 pages, 6 x 9
Quality paperback, $9.95

## HOW TO IMPORT A EUROPEAN CAR
### The Gray Market Guide

by Jean Dugay

Here's everything you need to know to purchase a car in Europe, drive it on your vacation, and ship it legally into the United States. You can save up to 25% on foreign car purchases — at the very least pay for your whole trip in savings! Names, addresses for reliable European dealers, best U.S. conversion centers, shippers. Covers DOT, EPA, cus-toms, financing, bonding. Cost comparison for 200 models. Authoritative.

192 pages, 8½ x 11, illustrated, tables.
Quality paperback, $13.95

## CAREER DIRECTORY SERIES

**Advertising**              **Public Relations**

**Book Publishing**          **Newspaper Publishing**

**Magazine Publishing**      **Marketing**

Each directory contains many, many informative, eye-opening articles written specifically for these directories by the top CEO's in each field from the big name companies. Complete breakdown of job specialization in each career field. List of company policies, personnel procedures, key contacts, internships. Excellent. Does all the leg-work for you and tells how to get a foot in the door.

375–400 pages, 8½ x 11
Quality paperback, $17.95

## THE CAMPER'S COMPANION TO NORTHERN EUROPE
### A Campground & Roadside Travel Guide

## THE CAMPER'S COMPANION TO SOUTHERN EUROPE
### A Campground & Roadside Travel Guide

by Dennis & Tina Jaffe

More than just campground directories, these travel guides share the best of each country off-the-beaten path. The Jaffes rate over 700 campgrounds covering all of Northern Europe in one. volume, Southern and Eastern Europe and Northern Africa in the other volume. Country-by-country campgrounds.

300 pages, 6 x 9, maps, tables.
Quality paperback, $13.95

---

# TO ORDER

At your bookstore or order directly from Williamson Publishing. Send check or money order to Williamson Publishing Co., Church Hill Road, P.O. Box 185, Charlotte, Vermont 05445. Please add $1.50 for postage and handling. Satisfaction guaranteed or full refund without questions or quibbles.